Managing H̶u̶̶̶̶̶̶̶̶̶̶̶̶̶̶̶̶̶̶ s in North America

This unique new text covers the key issues in North American human resources today. Providing an overview of new and emerging issues in North American human resource management (HRM), the chapters are divided into three parts. The first part examines how changes in the business environment have affected HRM; the second part looks at topics that have escalated in importance over the last few years; and the third part analyzes topics that have recently emerged as concerns.

Each chapter is authored by a leading figure in the field and features case vignettes to provide practical illustrations of the points in hand. The chapters also conclude with guidelines to help HR professionals deal with the issues raised.

A companion website featuring online lecturer and student resources is available for this text and can be visited at www.routledge.com/textbooks/0415396867.

Managing Human Resources in North America is intended as a core text for current issues in HRM courses in North America and as a supplementary text for students studying international HRM in other countries. It will be invaluable reading for all those studying HRM in North America or currently working in the field.

Steve Werner is Associate Professor of Management at the University of Houston. He has published over three dozen academic and practitioner papers on HRM and international business. Professor Werner serves on the editorial board of the *Human Resource Management Journal* and *Human Resource Management Review*.

Routledge Global Human Resource Management Series

Edited by Randall S. Schuler, Susan E. Jackson, Paul Sparrow and Michael Poole

Routledge Global Human Resource Management is an important new series that examines human resources in its global context. The series is organized into three strands: Content and issues in global human resource management (HRM); Specific HR functions in a global context; and Comparative HRM. Authored by some of the world's leading authorities on HRM, each book in the series aims to give readers comprehensive, in-depth and accessible texts that combine essential theory and best practice. Topics covered include cross-border alliances, global leadership, global legal systems, HRM in Asia, Africa and the Americas, industrial relations, and global staffing.

Managing Human Resources in Cross-Border Alliances
Randall S. Schuler, Susan E. Jackson and Yadong Luo

Managing Human Resources in Africa
Edited by Ken N. Kamoche, Yaw A. Debrah, Frank M. Horwitz and Gerry Nkombo Muuka

Globalizing Human Resource Management
Paul Sparrow, Chris Brewster and Hilary Harris

Managing Human Resources in Asia-Pacific
Edited by Pawan S. Budhwar

International Human Resource Management 2nd edition
Policy and practice for the global enterprise
Dennis R. Briscoe and Randall S. Schuler

Managing Human Resources in Latin America
An agenda for international leaders
Edited by Marta M. Elvira and Anabella Davila

Global Staffing
Edited by Hugh Scullion and David G. Collings

Managing Human Resources in Europe
A thematic approach
Edited by Henrik Holt Larsen and Wolfgang Mayrhofer

Managing Human Resources in the Middle-East
Edited by Pawan S. Budhwar and Kamel Mellahi

Managing Global Legal Systems
International employment regulation and competitive advantage
Gary W. Florkowski

Global Industrial Relations
Edited by Michael J. Morley, Patrick Gunnigle and David G. Collings

Managing Human Resources in North America
Current issues and perspectives
Edited by Steve Werner

Managing Human Resources in North America

Current issues and perspectives

Edited by Steve Werner

Routledge
Taylor & Francis Group

LONDON AND NEW YORK

First published 2007
by Routledge
2 Park Square, Milton Park, Abingdon, Oxon OX14 4RN

Simultaneously published in the USA and Canada
by Routledge
270 Madison Ave, New York, NY 10016

Routledge is an imprint of the Taylor & Francis Group, an informa business

Typeset in Times New Roman and Franklin Gothic by
RefineCatch Limited, Bungay, Suffolk
Printed and bound in Great Britain by
MPG Books Ltd, Bodmin

British Library Cataloguing in Publication Data
A catalogue record for this book is available from the British Library

Library of Congress Cataloging in Publication Data
Managing human resources in North America: current issues and perspectives /
edited by Steve Werner.
    p. cm.
  Includes bibliographical references and index.
  ISBN 0–415–39685–9 (hard cover)—ISBN 0–415–39686–7 (soft cover)
1. Personnel management—North America. I. Werner, Steve, 1964–
  HF5549.2.N7M36 2007
  658.3—dc22   2006025540

ISBN10: 0–415–39685–9 (hbk)
ISBN10: 0–415–39686–7 (pbk)

ISBN13: 978–0–415–39685–1 (hbk)
ISBN13: 978–0–415–39686–8 (pbk)

Contents

Illustrations

Figures

Tables

Contributors

Bradford S. Bell is an Assistant Professor at the School of Industrial and Labor Relations, Cornell University. His research interests include technology-based training and the development of training systems.

Teri J. Elkins is an Associate Professor at the C.T. Bauer College of Business, University of Houston. Her research interests include discrimination, gender issues, and organizational justice.

Gerald R. Ferris is the Francis Eppes Professor of Management and Professor of Psychology at Florida State University. He has published well over one hundred articles on various aspects of social influence processes in organizations.

Michael T. Ford is a doctoral student in the Psychology Department at George Mason University. His research interests include individual decision-making processes in potentially hazardous situations, organizational influences on safety-related behavior, and quality of life issues.

Luis R. Gomez-Mejia is a Council of 100 Distinguished Scholar and Professor of Management at the W.P. Carey School of Business, Arizona State University. He has published over one hundred articles and written or edited a dozen management books in such areas as CEO pay, compensation strategy, and HRM in small firms.

Wayne A. Hochwarter is an Associate Professor in the Department of Management at Florida State University. He has published more than fifty articles in such areas as social influence in organizations, motivation, workplace cynicism, job stress, and measurement.

Hannah L. Jackson is a doctoral student in the Department of Psychology at the University of Minnesota. Her research interests include group differences in personality and situational judgment tests.

K. Michele Kacmar ("Micki") is the Durr-Fillauer Chair of Business Ethics and Professor of Management at the University of Alabama. She has published over sixty articles in such areas as ethics, impression management, and organizational politics.

Brian S. Klaas is Professor of Management at the Moore School of Business, University of South Carolina. He has published dozens of articles in such areas as HR outsourcing, compensation, workplace dispute resolution, and employee relations.

Steve W.J. Kozlowski is a Professor in the Department of Psychology at Michigan State University. He has published over fifty articles on learning processes and other related issues.

Marianna Makri is Assistant Professor of Management at the University of Miami. Her research interests include chief executive officer (CEO) pay, learning alliances, and other aspects of business strategy.

Joseph J. Martocchio is a Professor in the Institute of Labor and Industrial Relations at the University of Illinois at Champaign. He is the author of numerous articles and two books on such human resource management issues as compensation, benefits, employee training, and absenteeism.

Timothy A. Matherly is an Associate Professor in the Department of Management at Florida State University. His research interests include strategic management, business ethics, and organizational behavior.

Deniz S. Ones is the Hellervik Professor of Industrial Psychology at the University of Minnesota. She has published more than one hundred articles in such areas as personnel selection and personality, integrity, and cognitive ability measurement in staffing.

Pamela L. Perrewé is Distinguished Research Professor and the Jim Moran Professor of Management at Florida State University. She has published over seventy articles in such areas as job stress, coping, organizational politics, and personality.

Randall S. Schuler is Professor of Human Resource Strategy at Rutgers University and a Research Fellow at GSBA Zurich. He has published over a hundred articles and thirty books in various areas of human resource management.

Jason D. Shaw is an Associate Professor at the Carlson School of Management, University of Minnesota. He has published dozens of papers in such areas as strategic human resource management, compensation systems, and personality–environment congruence issues.

Ibraiz Tarique is Associate Professor of Management at the Lubin School of Business, Pace University. His research interests include international human resources management, HRM in international alliances, training and development, and global leadership development.

Lois E. Tetrick is a Professor and Director of the Industrial and Organizational Psychology Program at George Mason University. Her research interests include safety, occupational stress, the work–family interface, and psychological contracts.

Steve Werner is Associate Professor of Management at the C.T. Bauer College of Business, University of Houston. He has published dozens of articles in such areas as compensation, human resource management, and international management.

Foreword

Global Human Resource Management is a series of books edited and authored by some of the best and most well-known researchers in the field of human resource management. This series is aimed at offering students and practitioners accessible, coordinated and comprehensive books in global HRM. To be used individually or together, these books cover the main bases of comparative and international HRM. Taking an expert look at an increasingly important and complex area of global business, this is a groundbreaking new series that answers a real need for serious textbooks on global HRM.

Several books in this series, **Global Human Resource Management**, are devoted to human resource management policies and practices in multinational enterprises. For example, some books focus on specific areas of global HRM policies and practices, such as global leadership development, global staffing and global labour relations. Other books address special topics that arise in multinational enterprises across the globe, such as managing HR in cross-border alliances, developing strategies and structures, and managing legal systems for multinational enterprises. In addition to books on various HRM topics in multinational enterprises, several other books in the series adopt a comparative, and within region, approach to understanding global human resource management. These books on comparative human resource management can adopt two major approaches. One approach is to describe the HRM policies and practices found at the local level in selected countries in several regions of the world. This approach utilizes a common framework that makes it easier for the reader to systematically understand the rationale for the existence of various human resource management activities in different countries and easier to compare these activities across countries within a region. The second approach is to describe the HRM issues and topics that are most relevant to the companies in the countries of the region.

This book, *Managing Human Resources in North America: Current Issues and Perspectives*, edited by Steve Werner, takes the second approach, describing the HRM issues and topics that are most relevant to the companies in North America. Steve has done an excellent job in identifying twelve HRM issues and topics that are important to companies in North America today. He has also done an outstanding job in gathering all the relevant experts to share their insights and perspectives. The issues and topics include staffing and developing the multinational workforce, advances in technology-based training, the challenges of the legal environment, the role of the family, ethics, safety and health, competitive advantage through HRM, counter-productive leader behaviour, outsourcing, employee benefits, executive compensation, and HRM after 9/11 and Katrina. Steve offers a final chapter that contains his concluding thoughts on the HRM issues and topics presented in detail by all the authors.

This Routledge series, **Global Human Resource Management**, is intended to serve the growing market of global scholars and professionals who are seeking a deeper and broader understanding of the role and importance of human resource management in companies as they operate throughout the world. With this in mind, all books in the series provide a thorough review of existing research and numerous examples of companies around the world. Mini-company stories and examples are found throughout the chapters. In addition, many of the books in the series include at least one detailed case description that serves as convenient practical illustrations of topics discussed in the book.

Because a significant number of scholars and professionals throughout the world are involved in researching and practising the topics examined in this series of books, the authorship of the books and the experiences of companies cited in the books reflect a vast global representation. The authors in the series bring with them exceptional knowledge of the human resource management topics they address, and in many cases the authors have been the pioneers for their topics. So we feel fortunate to have the involvement of such a distinguished group of academics in this series.

The publisher and editor also have played a major role in making this series possible. Routledge has provided its global production, marketing and reputation to make this series feasible and affordable to academics and practitioners throughout the world. In addition, Routledge has provided its own highly qualified professionals to make this series a reality. In particular we want to indicate our deep appreciation for the work of our series editor, Francesca Heslop. She has been very supportive of the series from the very beginning and has been invaluable in providing the needed support and encouragement to us and to the many authors in the series. She, along with her staff including Emma Joyes, Victoria Lincoln, Jacqueline Curthoys, Lindsie Court, and Jonathan Jones, has helped make the process of completing this series an enjoyable one. For everything they have done, we thank them all.

Randall S. Schuler, *Rutgers University and GSBA Zurich*

Susan E. Jackson, *Rutgers University and GSBA Zurich*

Paul Sparrow, *Manchester University*

Michael Poole, *Cardiff University*

Preface

This book is part of Routledge's **Global Human Resource Management** series edited by Randall S. Schuler, Susan E. Jackson, Paul Sparrow, and Michael Poole. As the title suggests, the book focuses on current issues in North American HR. North America is generally considered to cover the land area north of the Isthmus of Panama, including the Central American countries, Mexico, the islands of the Caribbean Sea, the United States, Canada, Greenland, and the Arctic Archipelago. However, North America often refers to the United States and Canada only, with Central America referring to Mexico and the countries south until one reaches South America. Since this book covers current HR issues in the United States and Canada only, we use this latter definition.

The purpose of the book

Most HR books cover the basics of conventional HR functions such as compensation, training, performance appraisal, etc. Rather than look at the HR functions, this book covers the topics that are currently the most important issues in North American HR today. The chapter authors are world renowned in their field and are top authors in HR today. This book can serve several purposes. First, because it covers current important topics in greater depth, it can serve as a useful supplement to an introductory HRM text. Second, the book can stand alone as a text for a current issues in HRM course. Finally, the book can also be useful to HR practitioners for coverage of and solutions to current HR problems.

How the topics were generated

In order to be sure that I included all the most important current issues, topics were generated from three sources. First, I used various reports from the Society of Human Resource Management. The Society of Human Resource Management (SHRM) is the premier HRM professional association, and was founded in 1948.

Reports from SHRM included their *2004–2005 The Workplace Forecast: A Strategic Outlook*, the *SHRM Special Expertise Panels 2005 Trend Report*, and the *SHRM Special Expertise Panels 2006 Trends Update*. The workplace forecast report is based on a survey of HR professionals, while the trend reports and update are created by special expertise panels comprised of between five and fifteen SHRM professional members for each of twelve different HR areas. Second, we used *The Hot HR Issues of the Next 2 Years*, a report by the Conference Board of Canada (2004), to include the Canadian perspective. Since both of these sources are based on the opinions of HR practitioners, I also wanted input from HR experts in academia. Thus, I queried Academy of Management HR Division members about their views of the most important current issues in HR. Based on these three sources, a list of topics was generated that are, I believe, the most important issues in North American HR today.

Acknowledgments

I would like to thank the chapter authors for their valuable contributions and their professionalism throughout the process. I would like to thank the series editors, Randall S. Schuler, Susan E. Jackson, Paul Sparrow, and Michael Poole; for their help and guidance. I would also like to thank Moira Praxedes for her help in the preparation of this book.

1 Introduction to managing HR in North America

STEVE WERNER

Human resource management (HRM) matters. A large and growing number of studies has shown that human resource management dramatically affects the firm. Numerous HRM practices have been shown to affect different plant and business performance measures including financial performance, turnover, and productivity (Huselid and Becker, 2000). HRM effectiveness has been shown to be positively related to corporate performance indicators including market value, cash flow, and productivity (Huselid *et al.*, 1997) as well as perceived firm performance (Delaney and Huselid, 1996). An effective HRM department will help firms attract and hire the right people, train them properly, pay them fairly, evaluate their performance accurately, motivate them, and it will achieve this within the current legal constraints and appropriate ethical boundaries. However, the business environment is constantly changing, raising many challenges for HRM. This book looks at those challenges, how they can affect the firm and human resources (HR), and how HRM can address them.

The structure of the book

The book is structured as follows. The topics are organized into three parts. The first part is "Major changes in environmental factors and HRM." In this part, the chapters look at how changes in the business environment have affected HRM. The second part is "Areas of increased importance." In this part, the chapters explore HRM topics that have increased in importance over the last several years. The third part is "Emerging trends and new issues." In this part, the chapters analyze topics that have recently emerged as concerns to HRM. Each chapter concludes with guidelines to help HR professionals deal with the current issue. The book concludes with a summary chapter that looks at the major environmental changes and points out some common themes across the chapters.

The topics

Here is a brief overview of each chapter in Part I, "Major changes in environmental factors and HRM."

Chapter 2, by Ibraiz Tarique and Randall S. Schuler, is titled "Staffing and developing the multinational workforce." This chapter looks at the recent research on expatriates, locals, and third country nationals. It also covers new issues in staffing and developing employees in multinational enterprises.

Chapter 3, by Bradford S. Bell and Steve W.J. Kozlowski, is titled "Advances in technology-based training." This chapter looks at how environmental factors have influenced training. The chapter also looks at the benefits, costs, and challenges of training technology, and how training content, technological capabilities, and trainee characteristics affect the effectiveness of technology-based training.

Chapter 4, by Teri J. Elkins, is titled "New HR challenges in the dynamic environment of legal compliance." This chapter looks at current trends in personnel law. Specifically, the chapter looks at new laws and new court rulings and how they affect the HR function. Topics include sexual harassment, age discrimination, alternative dispute resolution, and corporate reform.

Chapter 5, by Pamela L. Perrewé, is titled "The changing family and HRM." The chapter looks at the changing demographics of the workforce and how they affect employers and HRM. Topics include dual-career families, the changing shape of families, the aging workforce, and diversity and how organizations are responding to these changes.

Here is a brief overview of each chapter in Part II, "Areas of increased importance."

Chapter 6, by K. Michele Kacmar, is titled "Ethics and HRM." This chapter provides a brief overview of ethics and how current trends have raised ethical concerns. It looks at how HR can be used to instill ethics in the workplace and the costs and benefits of such programs.

Chapter 7, by Lois E. Tetrick and Michael T. Ford, is titled "Health, safety and HRM." This chapter looks at some current issues involving health, safety, employees, and the HR department. Issues covered include the Americans with Disabilities Act, the Family and Medical Leave Act, rising health care insurance costs, and general workforce trends. The chapter looks at how organizations can address these issues with safety management, employee assistance programs, health promotion, and work–life balance initiatives.

Chapter 8, by Jason D. Shaw, is titled "Competitive advantage through HRM." This chapter looks at how firms can strategically respond to environmental changes. Topics include commitment-enhancing practices, leveraging HR practices strategically, HRM investment, and enhancing the flexibility and agility of the HRM system.

Chapter 9, by Hannah L. Jackson and Deniz S. Ones, is titled "Counterproductive leader behavior." This chapter looks at the current issue of counterproductive leader behaviors. Topics include recent research on counterproductive behaviors, antecedents and rationalizations of counterproductive behaviors, how environmental factors and individual differences are related to counterproductive behaviors, and how HR can deal with them.

Here is a brief overview of each chapter in Part III, "Emerging trends and new issues."

Chapter 10, by Brian S. Klaas, is titled "Outsourcing and HRM." This chapter looks at the current trends in outsourcing HRM and other functions. It provides an overview of the trend, and introduces factors that may be responsible. The chapter discusses how firms can improve outcomes when outsourcing and what factors can influence the outsourcing arrangement.

Chapter 11, by Joseph J. Martocchio, is titled "The costs of employee benefits." This chapter looks at the trend of rising costs of employee benefits, why it has come about, and what HR departments are doing about it. The chapter focuses on health care and looks at the implications as well as the costs and benefits of different solutions.

Chapter 12, by Marianna Makri and Luis R. Gomez-Mejia, is titled "Executive compensation: something old, something new." This chapter looks at new issues in executive compensation. Topics covered include CEO overpayment, the role of risk in CEO contracts, shareholder activism, the Sarbanes–Oxley Act, Securities and Exchange Commission (SEC) disclosure rules, and CEO pay in high-technology firms and family firms.

Chapter 13, by Gerald R. Ferris, Wayne A. Hochwarter and Timothy A. Matherly, is titled "HRM after 9/11 and Katrina." This chapter looks at how 9/11 and Katrina have changed HR. The chapter looks at how firms can prepare for catastrophes, including the role of HR before and after the disaster.

The book ends with my "Concluding thoughts" chapter that looks at some common themes across the chapters using the organizing framework as a reference point.

The organizing framework

To help organize the chapters, each author used a similar framework (see Figure 1.1). The framework begins by looking at the changes in the internal and external environmental factors that have led to the current issues. These environmental changes lead to HR and firm responses. These responses will result in outcomes that can affect the company and all its stakeholders, including the HR department, management, other employees, company owners, and even society as a whole. The model also includes moderating factors, which can change the effects of the responses. Finally, the model includes guidelines that should help firms increase the

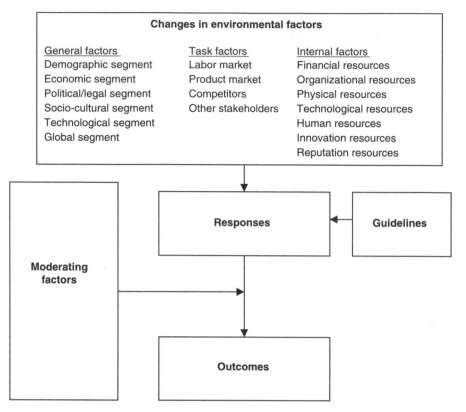

Figure 1.1 The organizing framework

probabilities of positive outcomes and reduce the possibilities of negative outcomes to stakeholders.

Changes in the environment

The business environment is comprised of the general environment, the task environment, and the firm's internal environment (Anthony *et al.*, 2006). Each of these environmental components shapes what the firm can and should do.

The general environment

The general environment is comprised of factors in broader society that affect a firm and its industry indirectly, usually through the task environment. The factors include the demographic segment, the economic segment, the political/legal segment, the socio-cultural segment, the technological segment, and the global segment (Hitt *et al.*, 2007). The demographic segment is defined by the characteristics of the people who are external stakeholders in the firm. It includes the size and geographic distribution of the relevant population and their age structure, income distribution, and ethnic mix. The relevant population can represent a firm's pool of possible employees (labor market), consumers, and surrounding community. Thus, changes in the demographic segment can affect a firm on many levels.

The economic segment is comprised of the economic and financial condition of the firm's environment. It includes relevant inflation, interest, unemployment, and savings (business and personal) rates. It also includes other economic indicators such as gross domestic product (GDP), change in GDP, and level of trade and budget deficits. These economic variables can affect a firm's labor market, sales potential, material costs, labor costs, suppliers, market value, and cost of capital. Thus, changes in the economic segment can also affect a firm on many levels.

The political/legal segment is comprised of the laws and dominating political climate that impact the firm. It includes all laws affecting the firm, such as tax laws, antitrust laws, employment laws, training laws, consumer protection laws, and environmental regulations. The political segment also includes aspects affected by the current political climate such as deregulation philosophies, educational philosophies, and political agendas, which can all affect the regulatory environment. Clearly, this segment affects all aspects of the firm from the rights of employees to how the firm can dispose of its waste.

The socio-cultural segment is defined by the values held by the firm's external stakeholders. It includes the attitudes and cultural values of society. Examples include attitudes about the quality of work life, work and career preferences, product and service preferences, and environmental concerns. The values may affect aspects of the demographic segment such as workforce diversity.

The technological segment is defined by the technology available to the firm. It includes available product technologies, communication technologies, applications of knowledge, data management technologies, and applicable software. The technologies can affect everything the firm does from manufacturing to training employees.

The global segment is comprised of the non-domestic factors that could impact the firm and its industry. It includes world political events, global product markets, global material availability, global labor markets, and the values and culture of other countries. These may overlap some of the other segments.

Task environment

The task environment is comprised of factors that directly affect the firm and its industry. The factors are likely to be influenced by the general environment. The task environment includes the labor market, the product market, competitors, and other stakeholders (Anthony *et al.*, 2006). The labor market is the labor pool from which the firm can choose its employees. The product market is the nature of the firm's customers and clients. Competitors are other firms against which the firm is competing. Other stakeholders include the government, special interest groups, and the immediate community.

Internal environment

One way to look at a firm's internal environment is to consider its resources (Barney, 1991; Dess *et al.*, 2006). The firm's resources can be categorized as tangible or intangible. The tangible resources include financial resources, organizational resources, physical resources, and technological resources, while the intangibles include human resources, innovation resources, and reputational resources. Financial resources are the firm's current financial position and its capability to change that position. This would include its current cash holdings, borrowing capacity, and ability to generate funds. The organizational resources are the current management structures of the firm and its capabilities to change them. These resources include the policies and procedures, the organizational structure, and the current management systems in place. The physical resources are the actual materials, land, and buildings that a firm owns or has access to. The technological resources are the processes the firm uses to make its product and manage the company.

Of the intangible resources, human resources are the employees and managers of the firm. They are resources based on their knowledge, trust, capabilities, skills, experience, and flexibility. The innovation resources are the firm's current abilities to innovate. They include the capacity of the employees to innovate and create, and their technical and scientific skills, as well as the firm's innovation culture. The reputational resources are the firm's reputation with different stakeholders. These intangible resources can be at the firm, brand, or product level as perceived by customers, suppliers, and society as a whole. These intangible resources may be influenced by the general or task environment. They are important because they can determine not only how the organization responds to environmental changes, but also the outcomes of those responses.

Responses

Changes in the general environment usually will lead to changes in the task environment. These task environmental changes can lead to HR and firm responses. Of course, there are usually numerous different responses available. Responses may entail: changing selection, training, compensation, or other HR procedures; introducing new policies; investing in new HR programs; gathering information; communicating information to employees; or even doing nothing. The amount of effort, resources, and commitment needed for each response can, of course, vary. For example, a new law covering the hiring of employees could require a complete retooling of the selection process, a simple change in procedure, a one-time employee notification, or no changes if the firm is already in compliance. As the response can vary, so can the outcome.

Outcomes

Responses will result in outcomes that can affect the company and all its stakeholders, including the HR department, management, employees, company owners, and even society as a whole (Jackson and Schuler, 2006). Ideally, these outcomes will be positive for all stakeholders, but they may also be positive for some stakeholders and negative for others. For example, layoffs tend to increase stock prices in the short term, benefiting shareholders (Wyans and Werner, 2001), but are detrimental to the employees losing their jobs and the cities hit hard by plant or office closures. Because the same responses by different firms in different situations may lead to different outcomes, the model also considers moderating factors.

Moderating factors

Moderating factors can change the effects of responses. That is, the same responses may lead to different outcomes depending on a number of factors. These factors include the firm's internal environment and the context of the response. For example, changing the firm's pension benefit may lead to very negative publicity if it is done during a time when "big business's mistreatment of employees" is a currently popular political topic. Relatedly, changing pension benefits may also lead to great employee dissatisfaction if the workforce is largely older and they are negatively affected. Firms need to consider moderating factors when determining responses.

Guidelines

Finally, based on the outcomes of the responses and moderating factors, guidelines are introduced to help firms increase the probabilities of positive outcomes and reduce the possibilities of negative outcomes to stakeholders. For example, the guidelines might suggest that certain types of firms have a different response, or that firms in certain industries respond differently. The guidelines also address the possible outcomes to different stakeholders.

Conclusion

Rather than looking at specific HR functions, this book looks at the "hot" HR issues in the United States and Canada today. The topics are organized within the categories of major changes in environmental factors and HRM, areas of increased importance, and emerging trends and new issues. Each chapter uses a framework to help organize the material. The framework includes the changes in the internal and external environmental factors that have led to the current issues, the HR and firm responses to these changes, the resulting outcomes that can affect the company and all its stakeholders, including the HR department, management, employees, company owners, and even society as a whole. The model also includes moderating factors, which can change the effects of the responses and guidelines that should help decision makers in their responses.

References

Anthony, W.P., Kacmar, K.M. and Perrewé, P.L. (2006) *Human Resource Management: A Strategic Approach*. Mason, OH: Thomson Custom Solutions.

Barney, J.B. (1991) Firm resources and sustained competitive advantage. *Journal of Management*, 17: 99–120.

Delaney, J.T. and Huselid, M.A. (1996) The impact of human resource management practices on perceptions of organizational performance. *Academy of Management Journal*, 39(4): 949–969.

Dess, G.G., Lumpkin, G.T. and Eisner, A. (2006) *Strategic Management: Creating Competitive Advantages*, 3rd edn. Boston, MA: McGraw-Hill Higher Education.

Hitt, M.A., Ireland, R.D. and Hoskisson, R.E. (2007) *Strategic Management: Competitiveness and Globalization*. Mason, OH: Thomson South-Western.

Huselid, M.A. and Becker, B.E. (2000) Comment on "Measurement error in research on human resources and firm performance: How much error is there and how does it influence effect size estimates?" *Personnel Psychology*, 53: 835–854.

Huselid, M.A., Jackson, S.E. and Schuler, R.S. (1997) Technical and strategic human resource management effectiveness as determinants of firm performance. *Academy of Management Journal*, 40(1): 171–188.

Jackson, S.E. and Schuler, R.S. (2006) *Managing Human Resources through Strategic Partnerships*, 9th edn. Mason, OH: Thomson South-Western.

Schramm, J. (2004) *2004–2005 The Workplace Forecast: A Strategic Outlook*. Alexandria, VA: Society of Human Resource Management.

Wyans, V.B. and Werner, S. (2001) The impact of workforce reductions on financial performance: A longitudinal perspective. *Journal of Management*, 26(2): 341–363.

Part I

Major changes in environmental factors and HRM

2 Staffing and developing the multinational workforce

IBRAIZ TARIQUE AND RANDALL S. SCHULER

The rapid development of the international economy is an important environmental change for North American firms. Multinational enterprises (MNEs) in North America are growing in size and number at a faster rate than ever before due to this change (Schuler and Jackson, 2005). These MNEs are spread all over the world encompassing dozens or hundreds of locations, languages, and cultures (Briscoe and Schuler, 2004). In the next section we discuss the several types of employees that form a multinational workforce (MWF). In the subsequent sections we describe major issues and challenges that have emerged in recent years regarding how MNEs staff and develop the MWF. These issues and challenges are based on the MNEs' concerns for cultural competencies, costs, skills for the job, company knowledge and loyalty, flexibility, control/coordination, learning and sharing knowledge, standardization/ localization and managing complexity.

The multinational workforce

MNEs recognize that human resources play an important role in developing and sustaining a competitive advantage in today's highly competitive global business environment (Schuler and Tarique, 2007). The task of international human resource management (IHRM) professionals in MNEs is to build a competent, high-performing workforce that gains and sustains a competitive advantage throughout the global marketplace (Briscoe and Schuler, 2004). To operate successfully today, MNEs need employees who have qualities such as: cultural competency, job skills, knowledge about the company, flexibility, a willingness to learn and share knowledge, and an ability and willingness to deal with ever growing amounts of complexity (Evans *et al.*, 2002). The employees of MNEs are typically described as being of three different "generic" types: *parent country nationals* (PCNs), *host country nationals* (HCNs), and *third country nationals* (TCNs).

Parent country nationals

PCNs are defined as employees of the MNE who are citizens of the country where the MNE's corporate headquarters is located. Prior research (e.g., Harzing, 2004) has characterized PCNs as having three fundamental competencies: familiarity with the MNE's corporate culture; ability to effectively communicate with headquarters; and ability to maintain control over the subsidiary's operations. In general, the presence of PCNs in a subsidiary provides some assurance that the subsidiary will comply with the organization's strategic objectives, policies, and goals (Tarique *et al.*, 2006).

PCNs have received considerable recent attention from professionals and academics in IHRM. When PCNs are posted or assigned to another country for more than one year, they are generally referred to as *expatriates* (Briscoe and Schuler, 2004). An expatriate could be any employee temporarily or permanently residing in a country other than that of their legal residence. In the IHRM literature, however, the term expatriate is synonymous with PCN (Harzing, 2004).

IHRM researchers have suggested that there are many different categories of expatriates, some numbering them as high as twenty (Briscoe and Schuler, 2004). In 1974, Hays proposed four types of expatriates: (1) the structure reproducer (one that builds, in the foreign subsidiary, a structure similar to a structure that exists elsewhere in the company); (2) the troubleshooter (one that analyzes and solves a specific operational problem); (3) the operational element (one that performs as an acting element in an existing operational structure); and (4) the chief executive officer (one that oversees and directs the entire foreign operation). Three years later, Edström and Galbraith (1977) argued that assignments can be differentiated on the basis of their primary purpose: to fill positions, to develop managers, and to develop organizations. Harzing (2001a) suggested that expatriates can be classified based on the type of personal control they exercise: spiders (control through informal communication), bumble bees (control through socialization and shared values), and bears (direct personal control). Finally, Caligiuri (2006) offered a typology based on the performance goals for expatriate assignments: (1) technical; (2) functional/tactical; (3) developmental/high potential; and (4) strategic/executive. It is important to note that IHRM practices such as selection, training, and repatriation programs will differ for each category of expatriates (Tarique *et al.*, 2001).

Host country nationals

HCNs are employees of the MNE who work in a foreign subsidiary and are citizens of the country where the foreign subsidiary is located. HCNs are generally recognized as having two core competencies: familiarity with the cultural, economic, political, and legal environment of the host country, and ability to respond effectively to the host country's requirements for localization of the subsidiary's operations. HCNs, however, lack familiarity with the parent country culture; this deficiency can be addressed through socializing HCNs at the parent country headquarters.

Socialization is the process by which HCNs learn about the corporate culture and become acquainted with the values and behaviors expected of them. HCNs can be socialized in a variety of ways such as training, mentoring, coaching, and observing other employees. HCNs can further be categorized into two subgroups: HCN_p and HCN_H. HCN_p refers to HCNs who have been socialized at the parent country headquarters and HCN_H refers to HCNs who have been socialized at the host country subsidiary (Tarique *et al.*, 2006). Socialization at the MNE headquarters allows HCNs to develop knowledge of the company that is similar to that developed by PCNs.

In contrast to the literature on PCNs and expatriates, there is much less published literature on HCNs (Briscoe and Schuler, 2004). Nonetheless, research suggests that the high costs of managing and supporting PCNs on foreign assignments have made these assignments less attractive for MNEs, and as a result, MNEs are more actively exploring ways to effectively utilize HCNs to satisfy international subsidiary staffing needs (Scullion and Collings, 2006).

Third country nationals

TCNs are neither the citizens of the country where the MNE is headquartered nor citizens of the country where the foreign subsidiary is located. TCNs are generally viewed as a compromise between PCNs and HCNs. TCNs are less expensive to maintain than PCNs, but lack familiarity with the host country's culture and the MNE's corporate culture. Like HCNs, TCNs can be socialized at the parent country headquarters to develop familiarity with the MNE's corporate culture and can also be socialized at the host country subsidiary to develop familiarity with the cultural, economic, political, and legal environment of the host country. In addition, TCNs can be socialized at the regional headquarters (if any) to develop familiarity with cultural norms of specific geographic regions. Therefore, TCNs are further classified into three subgroups: TCN_P, TCN_H, and TCN_{RH}. TCN_P refers to TCNs who have been socialized at the parent country headquarters, TCN_H refers to TCNs who have been socialized at the host country subsidiary, and TCN_{RH} refers to TCNs who have been socialized at the regional headquarters (Tarique *et al.*, 2006).

As with HCNs, there is little published research on TCNs. Reynolds (1997) examined how companies in various stages of globalization and headquartered in different countries and regions utilize TCNs to explore their strengths and weaknesses relative to other groups of employees. Selmer (2002) examined the cross-cultural effectiveness of TCNs. His findings suggest that Asian TCNs neither adjust better socio-culturally when compared to Western TCNs, nor do they adjust better with respect to Western PCNs.

MNE concerns for its MWF

As the above discussion suggests, MNEs have a variety of employees whom they can use to form their MWF. In their attempts to gain and retain a competitive advantage and to be effective, MNEs in North America increasingly realize that a competent MWF is critical. Competence in their MWFs fulfills the concerns that MNEs have. These concerns include cultural competencies, costs, skills for the job, company knowledge and loyalty, flexibility, control/coordination, learning and knowledge sharing, standardization/localization, and the ability and will to manage complexity.

As suggested by Schuler *et al.* (2002), there are many IHRM policies and practices that can address these concerns. For example:

- Human resource planning can ensure that the MNE has the appropriate people in place around the world at the right time.
- Staffing policies can be designed to recruit and select PCNs, TCNs, and HCNs with the required competencies and skills.
- Performance appraisals can help ensure that employees are doing the right job correctly and offer improvement plans.
- Compensation policies can help motivate employees and minimize total compensation costs.
- Development initiatives can prepare individuals to operate effectively in their overseas locations and to cooperate with other MNE units.

While these are several IHRM policies and practices that can be helpful in serving an MNE's concerns for its MWF, we will focus here on some of the major issues and challenges that have emerged in recent years regarding staffing and development. Such issues and challenges in MNEs today are based on the concerns mentioned earlier. It is important to point out that although we do not discuss other IHRM activities such as human resource planning, performance appraisal, compensation and labor relations, these activities should be part of a comprehensive IHRM system for managing an MWF. We would suggest, however, that they should also be based on the concerns listed above, for these are the ones that MNEs see as linked to their success in gaining and retaining competitive advantage and in being effective.

Staffing a multinational workforce

Global staffing refers to the process of acquiring, deploying, and retaining a global workforce in organizations with operations in different countries (Scullion and Collings, 2006). Much of what we know about global staffing comes from the research on MNE subsidiaries. Some studies have focused on determinants of global staffing (e.g., Harzing 2001b). Others have analyzed issues related to expatriate management such as expatriate selection (e.g., Caligiuri, 2000a), alternatives to expatriation (e.g., Evans *et al.*, 2002), willingness to relocate internationally/to assume a global assignment (e.g., Konopaske *et al.*, 2005), and expatriation of women managers (e.g., Harvey and Buckley, 1998). In this section, we discuss issues related to recruiting and selecting an MWF in MNEs.

Recruitment from the MNE's perspective

Research suggests that recruiting top talent is a major concern for MNEs (e.g., Sparrow *et al.*, 2004). One aspect of this concern is learning how to attract the best applicants. *Organizational attractiveness* has received considerable theoretical and empirical attention during the last few years. Prior studies have shown that potential candidates for jobs vary in the extent to which they are attracted by organizational attributes such as geographic dispersion (e.g., Turban and Keon, 1993), type of ownership (Turban *et al.*, 2001), and level of internationalization (e.g., Lievens *et al.*, 2003). Despite their important contributions to a better understanding of applicant attraction and job choice processes, the majority of organizational attractiveness studies have been conducted in the domestic context. There is ample scope for future research in this area. A cross-cultural approach to the study of organizational attractiveness will not only extend insights developed by the domestic studies, but also make a useful contribution to the IHRM literature in general and to the global staffing literature specifically.

Tarique (2006) attempted to examine what draws people (or does not) to MNEs. Based on data from sixty-one potential job-seekers, Tarique (2006) described how recruits differentially seek out job opportunities in MNEs. The study found that individuals' *global job pursuit intentions* (intentions to pursue a job in an MNE) and *attraction to an MNE* (overall evaluation of the attractiveness of the MNE) are affected by their early international life experiences and their personal characteristics (e.g., extroversion and openness to experience). These results suggest that companies should consider recruiting early career individuals with the propensity for later international career growth. For example, IHRM professionals should attract applicants who have strong inclinations toward the individual characteristics examined in this study.

Recruitment from the individual's perspective

Another issue of concern to the MNEs is an *individual's willingness to accept a foreign assignment*. Velde *et al.* (2005) examined gender differences and differences in willingness to accept international assignments, or to follow partners on international assignments. These authors found that male assignees were more willing to accept a foreign assignment and more willing to follow their partners than female ones. In another study Konopaske *et al.* (2005) attempted to address an important problem that is associated with dual career couples: potential assignees' unwillingness to take global assignments due to spouse refusal to accompany them. The study found strong support for the importance of certain individual, family, and organizational variables as antecedents of spouse willingness to relocate internationally. The results showed that: a spouse's job involvement negatively influenced his/her willingness to relocate internationally for periods of less than one year, a spouse's adventurousness was positively related to spouse willingness to relocate overseas for short and long periods of time, and a spouse's willingness to relocate overseas for short and long periods of time was positively related to the employee's short- and long-term global assignment willingness. Overall, research in this area has shown that individuals are more receptive to global assignments in locations culturally similar to their own; disruption, displacement, and uncertainty seem to be higher in culturally dissimilar locations (Aryee *et al.*, 1996).

Selection

The selection decision needs to receive full management attention and support (Schuler *et al.*, 2002). Errors in the selection process can have major negative impact on the success of overseas operations (Briscoe and Schuler, 2004). The specific criteria an MNE uses to select a global assignee have a lot to do with his/her future success of living and working in a new culture (Caligiuri and Tarique, 2005). Research suggests that the selection process is based on the identification of *critical job dimensions* (e.g., maintaining business contacts, technical competence, working with others, communicating/persuading, and initiative/effort) and the *cross-cultural competencies* (e.g., knowledge of foreign language, adjustment to living abroad, and adjustment to foreign business practices) required to effectively manage a wide diversity of people (e.g., co-workers, host government, local clients, customers, business partners, and the company's headquarters). Assessing to what extent applicants are likely to have these dimensions is important regardless of where the applicants are found (Briscoe and Schuler, 2004).

Research suggests that an individual's ability to adjust to a foreign country (*cross-cultural adjustment*) is at least as important to the successful completion of an overseas assignment as is the individual's technical ability. Individuals who are not prepared to confront the challenges (i.e., to cope with the culture shock) of living and working in a foreign country find it difficult to adjust and hence incur, and impose on others, costly implications (Tarique and Caligiuri, 2004). For example, individuals who are unable to adjust are more likely to perform poorly. Poor performance on a global assignment has costly implications for the individual (such as low self-esteem, low self-confidence, and loss of prestige among co-workers), for the parent firm (such as lost business opportunities), and for the host company (such as damaged company image) (Aycan, 1997).

Studies have shown that well-adjusted individuals tend to share certain personality traits (for more details see Caligiuri and Tarique, 2005). An important personality trait, as it relates to an individual's success in a foreign country, is *openness to experience* (Caligiuri, 2000b). Individuals high on openness to experience have less rigid views of right and wrong, appropriate and inappropriate, etc. and are more likely to be accepting of the new culture (Caligiuri, 2000b). In addition to openness to experience, another useful trait, as it relates to international assignee success, is *prior international experience* (e.g., Selmer, 2002). Expatriate management research has demonstrated that prior international work experience can facilitate an individual's ability to function and work in a foreign country. An example is the study by Takeuchi *et al.* (2005), which examined, among other things, the effects of expatriates' current assignment experience and past international experiences on cross-cultural adjustment. Based on the study of 243 expatriates and their supervisors, the authors found support for the unique moderating effects of past international experiences on the relationship between current assignment tenure and general and work adjustment.

Developing a multinational workforce

The term *developing the multinational workforce* refers to a wide variety of international training activities and international development activities used by MNEs to develop the competency base of their employees (Caligiuri *et al.*, 2005). The goals and objectives of both international training activities and international development activities are to foster learning among the organizational members and develop enriched and more capable workers who, in turn, can enhance organizational competitiveness and effectiveness internationally (Caligiuri and Tarique, 2005). It is important to point out that an activity can be used for both training and developmental purposes (Tarique, 2005). For example, in the expatriate management literature, *cross-cultural training* has been used for training purposes (e.g., Earley, 1987) and for developmental purposes (e.g., Lievens *et al.*, 2003).

Cultural competencies

In addition to staffing programs, success in international assignments may be facilitated through the training and development of *cultural competencies* or cultural intelligence (Earley and Ang, 2003; Earley and Peterson, 2004). Organizations recognize the importance of international training and development activities and increasingly use them to prepare individuals for the challenges and opportunities associated with living and working in new cultural environments, with diverse teams and across national borders. It appears that having more cultural competencies enables individuals to be more effective in these situations, and that these competencies can be developed (Earley and Mosakowski, 2004).

Cross-cultural training

Cross-cultural training is defined as "any planned intervention designed to increase the knowledge and skills of expatriates to live and work effectively and achieve general life satisfaction in an unfamiliar host culture" (Kealey and Protheroe, 1996: 145) and has become a major form of training used by organizations (Tarique and Caligiuri, 2004). There are many reasons why organizations use cross-cultural training. The most common reasons cited in the literature include improving cultural sensitivity by increasing knowledge and appreciation about a new country and its culture, increasing awareness of the norms and behaviors needed to be successful in a new culture (Black and Mendenhall, 1990), and improving cross-cultural skills by increasing communication skills, transition skills, negotiation skills, leadership skills, and management skills (Kealey and Protheroe, 1996).

An important aspect of any cross-cultural training initiative involves determining how cross-cultural training effectively enhances employees' cross-cultural competencies, facilitates their adjustment to the new cultural environments, and improves their performance. The cross-cultural training literature suggests that it is important to follow a systematic approach to designing cross-cultural training programs (see Tarique and Caligiuri, 2004 for a thorough description of the entire systematic approach). Based on Tarique and Caligiuri's (2004) five-phase systematic approach to designing cross-cultural training initiatives, a well-designed cross-cultural training initiative would involve:

● identifying the type of employee
● determining the specific cross-cultural competency need, such as knowledge-based competencies (e.g., cultural general knowledge), skills-based competencies (e.g., interpersonal skills), and ability-based competencies (e.g., learning ability)
● establishing short-term and long-term learning goals and measures for determining short-term and long-term cross-cultural training effectiveness
● developing and delivering instructional content
● evaluating whether the cross-cultural training program was effective.

As mentioned earlier, there are different types of expatriates and IHRM practices such as selection, training, and repatriation programs will differ for each category of expatriates. With respect to cross-cultural training, the cross-cultural skills and knowledge required for the successful completion of each assignment will vary depending on the type of assignment. Using Caligiuri's (2006) typology as an example, the type of cross-cultural training that should be offered to expatriates before and during global assignments will vary depending on the type of assignment. Training methods which improve cross-cultural knowledge and behavioral skills can be visualized on a continuum ranging from practical information training (knowledge about a country) to intercultural effectiveness skills training (awareness of appropriate norms and behaviors in the host country) (Kealey and Protheroe, 1996). Thus, training for expatriates on a technical assignment, which does not require significant interactions with host nationals, needs to be centered on providing practical information training (e.g., information on the shopping and transportation systems of the host country). In contrast, the training for expatriates on developmental/high potential assignments and strategic/executive assignments, which both require significant interactions with host nationals for successful completion of assignments, must focus more on intercultural effectiveness skills training. Somewhere in between, functional/tactical assignees who are sent to fill technical positions but who interact with host nationals on a daily basis may need training which extends beyond practical information training but which is not as extensive as the intercultural effectiveness skills training.

Organizations expect specific performance improvements from cross-cultural training. However, in the realm of academic research, studies that have examined the likely success of cross-cultural training have shown that cross-cultural training programs have failed to meet those performance improvement needs (Kealey and Protheroe, 1996; Mendenhall *et al.*, 2005). For example, Kealey and Protheroe (1996) reviewed empirical studies used to assess cross-cultural training effectiveness and found that while cross-cultural training seems to be effective in achieving immediate learning results, its impact on individual performance is not clear. Similarly, the literature review by Mendenhall *et al.* (2005: 19) found that "cross-cultural training seems to be effective in enhancing knowledge and trainee satisfaction, but seems to be less effective in changing behaviors and attitudes, or in improving adjustment and performance." These findings can be viewed as the classical *transfer of training problem* which is defined as the failure of the trainee to effectively and continually apply the knowledge and skills gained in training to his/her job (Broad and Newstrom, 1992). The domestic training literature has shown that training content often does not transfer to the actual work setting (Saks and Belcourt, 2002). For this reason, research examining the ways to facilitate or improve transfer has received much attention in the recent past (e.g., Ford and Weissbein, 1997). Meanwhile, to date no research has examined the transfer problem within a cross-cultural training context (Caligiuri and Tarique, 2005).

Global leadership development

An important area within the training and development field is *global leadership development*. Several studies have examined issues related to global leadership development (for reviews see Morrison, 2000; Suutari, 2002). A few studies have described trends and cross-country differences in development (e.g., Dickson *et al.*, 2003). Others have directly analyzed issues related to the development of global leaders. Substantive issues include early identification of executive potential (e.g., Spreitzer *et al.*, 1997), competencies needed to work effectively in a global environment (e.g., Gupta and Govindarajan, 2002) and competency models and methods for developing transnational competencies (e.g., Black and Gregersen, 2000). A few studies have proposed competency frameworks and models (e.g.,

Morrison, 2000) that identify and describe transnational competencies associated with successful global leaders.

Morrison (2000) conducted one of the first literature reviews of twelve studies published before 2000 that had been undertaken to examine issues related to global leadership development. The findings showed that most of the existing research was limited to descriptive essays, was based on small-scale samples of convenience, and was based on the author's consulting experience or work in one or two countries. In addition, Morrison concluded that for researchers much more work needs to done on essentially every aspect of global leadership. Similarly, in a related literature review, Suutari (2002) provided further support to Morrison's findings. Suutari found that research on global leadership development is still scarce and future research opportunities abound in a variety of areas including strategies for developing global leaders.

Caligiuri (2006) built on Morrison's and Suutari's suggestions by conducting a descriptive analysis of global leaders of one large multinational conglomerate headquartered in the United Kingdom. Based on an assessment of the firm's current leaders, the study examined the early developmental experiences, professional developmental experiences, and personality characteristics related to effective global leadership. In particular, the study attempted to better understand what is different about effective globally active leaders, compared to those who are less effective. The results showed that leaders who are the most globally active may have gravitated toward (or self-selected into) their global positions based on earlier interests and early life experiences (Caligiuri and Tarique, 2005). Compared to leaders who are less globally active, for example, globally active leaders were more likely to have studied international business, to have come from a culturally diverse family, and to have lived abroad as young adults. Of those who are highly globally active, the more effective leaders have greater family diversity and are somewhat more likely to be fluent in another language. With respect to personality characteristics, among those highly globally active leaders, the most effective leaders are significantly lower in neuroticism, and higher in conscientiousness, agreeableness, openness, and extroversion. Finally, the most effective globally active leaders in this firm believed developmental opportunities which were more experiential and had more cross-national contact helped develop their global leadership ability.

In a similar study, Tarique (2005) used social learning theory to propose a generalized model to explain how the extent of participation in international developmental activities (e.g., long-term, short-term, and expatriate assignments) influences two dimensions of a global leader's success (global work effectiveness and supervisory rated work performance). The findings, based on secondary analysis of data from 256 global leaders of one large multinational conglomerate headquartered in the United Kingdom, suggested that the extent of participation in international developmental activities is positively related to global work effectiveness. Furthermore, the personality traits of openness to experience and extroversion moderated this relationship. Specifically, the relationship between the extent of participation in international developmental activities and global work effectiveness was stronger for global leaders high on openness to experience or extroversion. The finding that greater participation in international developmental activities was associated with higher levels of global work effectiveness has important implications for designing effective developmental programs. For example, IHRM professionals should encourage global leaders to participate in multiple programs to experience the consequences of using learned behavior or skills and to learn new skills and behaviors (Tarique, 2005).

Global careers

Another important area related to international development is *global careers* (Thomas *et al.*, 2005). Global careers is an emerging area of research that has the potential to lead to greater understanding of how training and development activities (e.g., mentoring, coaching) can be used to meet the challenges related to career development. For instance, Lazarova and Tarique (2006) proposed a conceptual framework describing important conditions under which expatriate assignments result in successful "reverse" knowledge transfer. It is well known that expatriation provides the opportunity to acquire overseas knowledge, and repatriation creates the opportunity to transfer and apply this knowledge in the organization (Kamoche, 1997). Lazarova and Tarique (2006: 362) note that "successfully capturing knowledge upon repatriation is not automatic. First, not all knowledge is equally easy to capture. Second, individuals and organizations do not necessarily have coinciding goals with respect to using knowledge as a basis for developing a competitive advantage." The authors argue that knowledge transfer upon repatriation can be maximized if a fit is achieved between *organizational receptivity* to repatriates' knowledge and repatriates' *readiness to transfer* knowledge. They propose that such a fit is possible only if MNEs consider the correspondence between the type of knowledge gained during an assignment and the transfer mechanisms (e.g., training activities) they employ to capture that knowledge.

Conclusion and guidelines

This chapter provided a broad discussion of issues and challenges related to staffing and developing an MWF in North American MNEs. We discussed the several types of employees that form an MWF: parent country nationals (PCNs), host country nationals (HCNs), and third country nationals (TCNs).

We described major issues and challenges that have emerged in recent years regarding how MNEs staff and develop the MWF. The discussion of staffing included applicant attraction to MNEs and job choice processes, willingness to accept a foreign assignment, and criteria an MNE uses to select its international employees.

Table 2.1 Guidelines for staffing and developing the multinational workforce

1 Recruit early career individuals with the propensity for later international career growth by recruiting applicants who have had early international life experiences and who score high in characteristics such as Openness to Experience and Extroversion.
2 Start employees on international assignments in locations culturally similar to their own.
3 Increase foreign assignment success by selecting employees with prior international experience and who score high on openness to experience.
4 Select employees who have cross-cultural competencies as well as critical job competencies.
5 Adapt the type of cross-cultural training to the type of expatriate.
6 Focus on the transfer of training, because it is particularly important in the success of cross-cultural training.
7 Use multiple assignments and more cross-national contacts as developmental opportunities to help employees develop their global leadership ability.

The discussion of development included designing effective cross-cultural training programs, developing global leaders, and current trends in global careers. Our discussion provides a number of guidelines that organizations can follow to improve the selection and development of the MWF. Table 2.1 lists some specific guidelines mentioned in the chapter. Our discussion also suggests many avenues for future empirical and theoretical work in staffing and developing an MWF. As noted by Schuler and Tarique (2007), with the greater need for coordination and control through people across a wide variety of countries and cultures, MNEs are trying to create global mindsets (Evans *et al.*, 2002). Future research might investigate effective ways of doing this and the specific staffing and development activities that can be used. Another area for future research would be to explore the impact on MNEs of using non-traditional forms of global employment such as offshoring and outsourcing (Schuler and Tarique, 2007). Finally, future research can investigate whether or not North American MNEs can embrace the reality of the MWF or at least regional workforces (RWFs), and develop staffing and developmental activities that are identical for all (Schuler and Tarique, 2007).

References

Aryee, S., Chay, Y. and Chew, J. (1996) An investigation of the willingness of managerial employees to accept an expatriate assignment. *Journal of Organizational Behavior*, 17(3): 267–283.
Aycan, Z. (1997) Expatriate adjustment as a multifaceted phenomenon: Individual and organizational level predictors. *International Journal of Human Resource Management*, 8(4): 434–456.

Black, J. and Mendenhall, M. (1990) Cross-cultural training effectiveness: A review and theoretical framework. *Academy of Management Review*, 15: 113–136.

Black, J.S. and Gregersen, H.B. (2000) High impact training: Forging leaders for the global frontier. *Human Resource Management*, 39(2–3): 173–184.

Briscoe, D. and Schuler, R. (2004) *International Human Resource Management: Policies and Practices for the Global Enterprise*, 2nd edn. London: Routledge.

Broad, M. and Newstrom, J. (1992) *Transfer of Training: Action Packed Strategies to Ensure High Payoff from Training Investments*. Boston, MA: Addison Wesley.

Caligiuri, P. (2000a) The big five personality characteristics as predictors of expatriate success. *Personnel Psychology*, 53: 67–88.

Caligiuri, P. (2000b) Selecting expatriates for personality characteristics: A moderating effect of personality on the relationship between host national contact and cross-cultural adjustment. *Management International Review*, 40: 61–80.

Caligiuri, P. (2006) Performance measurement in a cross-national context: Evaluating the success of global assignments. In W. Bennett, D. Woehr, and C. Lance (eds.), *Performance Measurement: Current Perspectives and Future Challenges* (pp. 227–243). Mahwah, NJ: Lawrence Erlbaum.

Caligiuri, P. and Tarique, I. (2005) International assignee selection and cross-cultural training and development. In I. Björkman and G. Stahl (eds.), *Handbook of Research in IHRM* (pp. 302–322). Northampton, MA: Edward Elgar.

Caligiuri, P., Tarique, I. and Lazarova, M. (2005) Training, learning, and development in multinational corporations. In H. Scullion and M. Linehan (eds.), *International Human Resource Management* (pp. 71–90). New York: Palgrave Macmillan.

Dickson, M., Hartog, D. and Mitchelson, J. (2003) Research on leadership in a cross-cultural context: Making progress, and raising new questions. *Leadership Quarterly*, 14: 729–768.

Earley, C. (1987) Intercultural training for managers: A comparison of documentary and interpersonal methods. *Academy of Management Journal*, 30(4): 685–698.

Earley, C. and Ang, S. (2003) *Cultural Intelligence: Individual Interactions across Cultures*. Stanford, CA: Stanford University Press.

Earley, C. and Mosakowski, E. (2004) Cultural intelligence. *Harvard Business Review*, March: 139–146.

Earley, C. and Peterson, R. (2004) The elusive cultural chameleon: Cultural intelligence as a new approach to intercultural training for the global manager. *Academy of Management Learning and Education*, 3: 100–115.

Edström, A. and Galbraith, J.R. (1977) Transfer of managers as a coordination and control strategy in multinational organizations. *Administrative Science Quarterly*, 22(2): 248.

Evans, P., Pucik, V. and Barsoux, J.L. (2002) *The Global Challenge: Frameworks for International Human Resource Management*. Boston, MA: McGraw-Hill.

Ford, J. and Weissbein, D. (1997) Transfer of training: An updated review and analysis. *Performance Improvement Quarterly*, 10: 22–41.

Gupta, A. and Govindarajan, V. (2002) Cultivating a global mindset. *Academy of Management Executive*, 16: 116–126.

Harvey, M.G. and Buckley, M.R. (1998) The process for developing an international program for dual-career couples. *Human Resource Management Review*, 8: 99–123.

Harzing, A.-W. (2001a) Of bears, bumble-bees, and spiders: The role of expatriates in controlling foreign subsidiaries. *Journal of World Business*, 36(4): 366–379.

Harzing, A.-W. (2001b) Who's in charge? An empirical study of executive staffing practices in foreign subsidiaries. *Human Resource Management*, 40(2): 139–158.

Harzing, A.-W. (2004) Composing an international staff. In A.-W. Harzing and J.V. Ruysseveldt (eds.), *International Human Resource Management* (pp. 251–282). Thousand Oaks, CA: Sage.

Hays, R.D. (1974) Expatriate selection: Insuring success and avoiding failure. *Journal of International Business Studies*, 5: 25–37.

Kamoche, K. (1997) Knowledge creation and learning in international HRM. *International Journal of Human Resource Management*, 8: 213–225.

Kealey, D. and Protheroe, D. (1996) The effectiveness of cross culture training for expatriates: an assessment of the literature on the issue. *International Journal of Intercultural Relations*, 20: 141–165.

Konopaske, R., Robie, C. and Ivancevich, J. (2005) A preliminary model of spouse influence on managerial global assignment willingness. *International Journal of Human Resource Management*, 16(3): 405.

Lazarova, M. and Tarique, I. (2006) Knowledge transfer upon repatriation. *Journal of World Business*, 40: 361–373.

Lievens, F., Decaesteker, C., Coetsier, P. and Geirnaert, J. (2003) Organizational attractiveness for prospective applicants: A person–organization fit perspective. *Applied Psychology: An International Review*, 50(1): 30–51.

Mendenhall, M., Stahl, G., Ehnert, I., Oddou, G., Osland, J. and Kühlmann, T. (2005) Evaluation studies of cross-cultural training programs: A review of the literature from 1988–2000. In D. Landis and J. Bennett (eds.), *The Handbook of Intercultural Training* (pp. 129–144). Thousand Oaks, CA: Sage.

Morrison, A. (2000) Developing a global leadership model. *Human Resource Management*, 39: 117–131.

Reynolds, C. (1997) Strategic employment of third country nationals. *Human Resource Planning*, 20: 33–43.

Saks, A. and Belcourt, M. (2002) So what is a good transfer of training estimate? A reply to Fitzpatrick. *The Industrial-Organizational Psychologist*, 39: 29–30.

Schuler, R. and Jackson, S. (2005) A quarter-century review of human resource management in the U.S.: The growth in importance of the international perspective. *Management Revue*, 16: 11–35.

Schuler, R. and Tarique, I. (2007) International human resource management: A thematic update and suggestions for future research. *International Journal of Human Resource Management* (forthcoming).

Schuler, R., Budhwar, P. and Florkowski, G. (2002) International human resource management: review and critique. *International Journal of Management Reviews*, 4: 41–70.

Scullion, H. and Collings, D. (2006) *Global Staffing*. London: Routledge.

Selmer, J. (2002) Practice makes perfect? International experience and expatriate adjustment. *Management International Review*, 42: 71–87.

Sparrow, P., Brewster, C. and Harris, H. (2004) *Globalizing Human Resource Management*. London: Routledge.

Spreitzer, G., McCall, M. and Mahoney, J. (1997) The early identification of international executive potential. *Journal of Applied Psychology*, 82: 6–29.

Suutari, V. (2002) Global leader development: An emerging research agenda. *Career Development International*, 7: 218–233.

Takeuchi, R., Tesluk, P., Yun, S. and Lepak, D. (2005) An integrative view of international experiences: An empirical examination. *Academy of Management Journal*, 48: 85–100.

Tarique, I. (2005) International executive development: The influence of international developmental activities, personality, and early international experience on success in global work activities. Unpublished dissertation, Rutgers University, New Brunswick, NJ.

Tarique, I. (2006) Predicting global job pursuit intentions and attraction to MNEs: The role of prior non-work international experience, openness to experience, and extroversion. Paper presented at the Sixty-sixth Annual Academy of Management Meeting, Atlanta, GA.

Tarique, I. and Caligiuri, P. (2004) Training and development of international staff. In A.W. Harzing and J. Van Ruysseveldt (eds.), *International Human Resource Management* (pp. 283–306). Thousand Oaks, CA: Sage.

Tarique, I., Caligiuri, P. and Lazarova, M. (2001) Strategic international human resource management from a training and development perspective. Paper presented at the Sixty-first Annual Academy of Management Meeting, Washington, DC.

Tarique, I., Schuler, R. and Gong, Y. (2006) A model of multinational enterprise subsidiary staffing composition. *International Journal of Human Resource Management*, 17: 207–224.

Thomas, D., Lazarova, M. and Inkson, K. (2005) Global careers: New phenomenon or new perspectives? *Journal of World Business*, 40: 340–347.

Turban, D. and Keon, T. (1993) Organizational attractiveness: An interactionist perspective. *Journal of Applied Psychology*, 78(2): 184–193.

Turban, B., Lau, C., Ngo, H., Chow, H. and Si, X. (2001) Organizational attractiveness of firms in the People's Republic of China: A person–organization fit perspective. *Journal of Applied Psychology*, 86: 194–206.

Velde, M., Bossink, C. and Jansen, P. (2005) Gender differences in the determinants of the willingness to accept an international assignment. *Journal of Vocational Behavior*, 66: 81.

THE NEW FACTORY

The management of Welltec, a large pharmaceutical company, has decided to open a new factory in the Czech Republic. This will be their second factory in that country. Their other factory in the Czech Republic has helped lower their production costs and provided an easy route to enter the Central and Eastern European markets. Unfortunately, it doesn't have enough capacity to meet the customer demands of the region and can't be expanded. Management is trying to decide who should run the new factory. Eva Petrova is the second in command at the other Czech factory. Jim Phelps is the second in command at the company's factory in Tennessee. Michael Nederlander is the second in command at the company's factory in Germany. Management believes that all three are now capable of being the top manager of a factory and that all are viable candidates for the job.

Related questions

1 What would be the advantages and disadvantages of each of the three candidates?
2 What other factors might influence the decision of whom to hire?
3 Whom would you hire?

3 Advances in technology-based training

BRADFORD S. BELL AND STEVE W.J. KOZLOWSKI

There is a growing utilization of technology-based training in the workplace. The *2005 State of the Industry Report* published by the American Society for Training and Development (ASTD) revealed that in the average organization, technology-based training accounted for 28.1 percent of all training hours in 2004 (Sugrue and Rivera, 2005). The report also revealed that the utilization of technology-based training has almost doubled since 2002 and is projected to further increase to 32.5 percent in 2005. In this chapter, we examine this trend and explore recent advances in technology-based training. We begin by discussing the environmental factors pushing companies to adopt technology-based training and examine the different technology-based training applications available in the marketplace. We then compare the costs and benefits of technology-based training and identify several factors that can influence its effectiveness. Finally, we conclude the chapter with a few guidelines on how companies can effectively use technology to deliver training and meet their human capital development needs.

Environmental factors influencing technology-based training

The proliferation of technology-based training has been caused by multiple environmental factors. Globalization, economic pressures, and work–life concerns have combined to create a business environment that demands innovative, flexible training solutions. However, technological advances have helped to position technology-based training applications as practical tools for addressing these demands. In the following sections we briefly discuss each of these factors and how they have influenced the growth of technology-based training.

Globalization

Observers have noted that a substantial portion of training costs – upwards of 80 percent – is devoted to simply getting trainees to the training site, maintaining them while there, and absorbing their lost productivity (Kozlowski *et al.*, 2001). For highly decentralized organizations with employees dispersed around the globe, these variable training costs can become prohibitively expensive. Even if an organization has a bottomless training budget, centralized, classroom training is not an efficient means of delivering timely training to a global workforce. Technology enables companies to deliver training to employees almost anywhere and at any time and to be more responsive in today's fast-paced business environment. For example, many large financial institutions that operate on a global scale, such as Citigroup and HSBC, rely heavily on technology to distribute compliance training (e.g., financial regulations, institutional policies and procedures) to their employees located in dozens of countries (Sussman, 2006). Technology-based delivery allows these and other companies with dispersed workforces to bypass many of the costs associated with classroom training (e.g., travel, lodging) and deliver just-in-time learning solutions to their employees.

Economic pressures

The growing importance of human capital to creating sustained competitive advantage means that, now more than ever, organizations must rely on workplace learning and continuous improvement to remain successful (Salas and Cannon-Bowers, 2001). At the same time, companies face tremendous economic pressures to cut costs and increase shareholder value. The result is that human resource professionals are being asked to do more with less. In the training field this translates into maintaining, or often increasing, a firm's employee development activities while at the same time reducing training expenditures. Technology-based training can help organizations respond to this dilemma. Although technology-based training incurs significant upfront costs (e.g., development, software/hardware), as noted above it also helps organizations reduce variable costs associated with the classroom. The US Army National Guard, for example, saved nearly $1.6 million, much of it in travel costs, by converting one of their officer training programs to a distance-learning course (Leonard, 1996). In the past, officers had to travel to Washington, DC for the training, but technology made it possible to transmit the course to a variety of remote sites. Technology-based training can also lead to cost savings in other areas, such as program updating and employees' time off the job. These issues surrounding cost will be discussed in more detail below, but the key point is that technology can be used to help companies lower variable training costs and, therefore, realize a greater return on their training investment.

Work–life issues

Research by the Society for Human Resource Management (SHRM) concluded that one of the employment trends anticipated to have the greatest impact on the workplace is the increased demand for flexible work schedules from employees (Schramm and Burke, 2004). Possible causes of this trend include generational differences and the growing number of employees who have childcare and/or elder care responsibilities. (See Chapter 5 for more on the changing family and HRM.) In addition to flexible schedules, many employees increasingly desire flexible work arrangements, such as telecommuting. At JetBlue Airways, for example, 80 percent of all phone reservationists work from their homes in the Salt Lake City area. This perk helps the company successfully recruit and retain individuals for what is a relatively low-wage and typically high turnover job. While flexible work arrangements help employees balance work and life issues, they also create logistical challenges when trying to bring employees together for training. One solution is to use technology-based training to distribute to remote workers so they can complete training off-site and on their own schedule (Burgess and Russell, 2003). For example, CIGNA has embraced technology-based training as an effective and efficient mechanism to deliver continuous education to its dispersed workforce of nurse consultants, many of whom work from home and are based in rural locations. An industry report conducted by *Training* magazine found that most (88 percent) technology-based training activities take place during employees' paid time (Galvin, 2002). However, this figure is likely to be highly variable across companies and we may see more technology-based training conducted on employees' personal time as companies continue to search for ways to maximize employee productivity. In the future this may create a new set of work–life issues for employees to manage.

Technological advances

While globalization, economic pressures, and work–life issues have forced companies to rethink traditional approaches to training and development, recent advances in computing power and connectivity have probably done the most to position technology-based training as a viable alternative to classroom-based instruction. For a number of years, learning technologies were limited to relatively basic computer-based text programs or video-based instruction. However, recent technological advances have expanded greatly the breadth and depth of training technologies (Salas *et al.*, 2002). Today's high-end technologies offer greater bandwidth, which means that the programs can transmit more information-rich content (e.g., multimedia) and immerse trainees in high fidelity, synthetic training worlds. In addition, advances in communication media (e.g., synchronous audio and video) create greater opportunity for trainer–trainee and trainee–trainee interactivity, opening the door to collaborative and team-based learning. An implication of these advances is that today's high-end technologies can increasingly approximate conventional, instructor-led classroom training. This capability, combined with the fact that the media (e.g., compressed video, personal computers, internet) that support these advanced technologies have become more cost-efficient, reliable, and accessible, has led organizations to increasingly utilize technology-based training to respond to their emerging employee development needs. In the next section we examine several of the training technologies currently available in the marketplace.

Training technologies

There is a wide array of technologies – ranging from more basic to advanced systems – that can be used to deliver training. At the more basic end of the technology continuum are CD-ROM, DVD, and interactive video systems, which offer the capability to integrate text, graphics, animation, audio, and video into a multimedia presentation. One advantage of CD-ROM, DVD, and interactive video over more traditional videotape or audiocassette programs is that the computer-based delivery makes it possible to create programs in which trainees interact with content using a keyboard, mouse, or joystick. Another widely used technology is web-based training. There is tremendous variability in web-based training programs; some simply represent computer-based delivery of text while others integrate multimedia, hyperlinks to references, communication systems, and assessment tools into a high-tech instructional experience.

Next in the level of sophistication are electronic performance support systems (EPSS) and intelligent tutoring systems. These systems are more advanced than the typical disk- and web-based programs because they have the capability to deliver highly individualized instruction. An artificial intelligence component analyzes trainee performance by comparing it to an expert model and provides tailored advice and coaching. Finally, at the high end of the technology continuum are distributed interactive simulation (DIS), game-based training environments, and distributed mission training (DMT). All of these systems use synthetic task environments to create "scaled worlds" that immerse trainees in realistic contexts (Schiflett *et al.*, 2004). Moreover, these systems typically offer the capability to conduct real-time, distributed training exercises with multiple participants or teams.

Each of the systems mentioned above is a configuration of technological features. Some of the most common technological features and tools include text, images, video, audio, interactive media, synchronous communication systems, chat, and bulletin boards. Different combinations and variants of these features create the potential for a vast number of unique applications. Thus, it is important to recognize that even within each of the categories mentioned above there is the potential for considerable variability in the configuration of specific systems. Web-based training, for example, can range from very simple, text-based HTML programs restricted to individual users to very advanced multimedia programs that allow for multiuser interactivity and collaboration.

Benefits of training technology

The growing adoption of technology-based training in organizations has been fueled largely by the potential practical benefits offered by these systems. However, it is important not to overlook the opportunity to use technology to create stimulating learning experiences. Below we discuss some of most frequently cited benefits of training technology.

Cost reduction

Most studies have found that technology-based training can deliver a training program for lower cost than more traditional methods. Wisher and Priest (1998), for example, found that using teletraining for an Army National Guard Unit Clerk Course, instead of the traditional classroom training, would lead to savings of $292,000 a year. Technology-based training reduces or eliminates many of the variable costs associated with the classroom, such as travel, lodging, meals, materials, and instructor salaries (Welsh *et al.*, 2003). In addition, cost savings can be achieved by using technology to automate many of the tasks involved in course administration, including registration, assessment, and certification. In large organizations, these cost savings multiply across programs and trainees, and can add up to millions of dollars annually. However, it should be noted that these savings can be realized only *after* the costs of the technology infrastructure are considered. The upfront costs associated with technology-based training (e.g., purchasing hardware/software, program development) are significant and are frequently discussed as one of the biggest drawbacks of using learning technologies (Welsh *et al.*, 2003).

Accordingly, cost savings are typically achieved only when a program is administered several times and/or to a significantly large number of students. That is, one needs to take advantage of the scalability of technology-based training to amortize the fixed, upfront costs across multiple administrations and a large number of trainees. An important implication is that technology-based training may not produce a positive return on investment for one-shot programs or those with relatively low enrollments.

Reduction in training time

Another factor that contributes to cost savings is the fact that technology-based training often leads to a reduction in the time that individuals spend in training. Research suggests that putting a training program online can reduce total training time by a quarter to a third. The result is less time off the job and greater employee productivity. The source of this time saving can be found in the ability of trainees to streamline their progression through the training material. That is, technology-based training gives trainees considerable control over many instructional design elements, including control over the content, sequence, pace, method of presentation, provision of optional content, and difficulty of instruction. Trainees can use this control to focus their attention on the material they need to learn, spend less time or skip over material they already know, and structure the training in a way that fits their learning style. As we will discuss in more detail below, however, there are some important drawbacks associated with learner control.

Pedagogical capabilities

While the practical benefits discussed above have been the key drivers of companies' decisions to adopt technology-based training, it is important to highlight the potentially powerful effect that technology can have on learning. Current training technologies offer new and exciting pedagogical strategies that have simply been impossible or impractical in traditional classroom environments. For example, technology can be used to provide trainees with a highly personalized learning experience. Intelligent tutors can be used to monitor trainees' progress and provide individualized instruction that is simply not feasible in the typical classroom environment. Competency assessments can be integrated into technology to provide trainees with personalized feedback that is frequent, immediate, and detailed. Training technology can also be used to immerse trainees in high-fidelity, dynamic simulations that give them an opportunity to practice using their skills and knowledge in realistic situations. A variety of multimedia components can be used to make training more engaging and deliver training through multiple modalities (e.g., visual, audio) to accommodate the preferred learning styles of different trainees. Finally, technology can be used to connect learners to subject matter experts, databases, other learning resources, and one another. Together these and other features of technology-based training can have a positive impact on overall training effectiveness.

Diversity and accessibility

A less frequently discussed, yet important, benefit involves issues of diversity and access. Some have argued that online learning can increase collaboration among individuals from diverse backgrounds by leveling social barriers. In online environments, the cues that underlie various stereotypes are often either absent or less salient, which may facilitate collaborative learning among individuals drawn from diverse ethnic, cultural, racial, gender, and socio-economic backgrounds. In addition, the flexibility offered by remote learning may provide increased access to individuals who otherwise may be unable to attend training or classes, such as individuals with disabilities (Salas *et al.*, 2002).

Other benefits

Although the benefits discussed above are the most frequently cited advantages of technology-based training, there are several other benefits that deserve mention. First, technology-based training makes it possible to deliver a consistent message companywide to all trainees or employees (Burgess and Russell, 2003). For example, when Dow Chemical discovered many of its locations were either not conducting its "Respect and Responsibility" class or delivering inconsistent messages in the training, it turned to technology-based training to provide a standardized, worldwide class (Welsh *et al.*, 2003). Second, technology-based training can help create an environment in which learners have more responsibility for their personal success. Learning technologies can help empower employees to address their skill gaps and manage their career development.

Costs and challenges of training technology

Despite the numerous benefits discussed above, there continue to be several costs and challenges associated with leveraging technology to deliver training. In this section we review several of these challenges.

Learner choices

As noted above, technology-based training provides learners with unprecedented control over their learning (DeRouin *et al.*, 2004). Not only can designers incorporate features, such as hyperlinks and menus, that make it possible for trainees to proceed through training in a nonlinear fashion, but also trainees no longer have access to the guidance and support of an instructor or trainer. The result is that trainees are left with complete control over how they approach the training, and research suggests they typically do not make good use of this control (Bell and Kozlowski, 2002a). More specifically, when given control over their learning, most trainees either will exit training before having mastered the subject matter or will practice well beyond the point at which concepts and skills have been learned. The result is that the training is either ineffective or inefficient, both of which are undesirable outcomes.

A related problem concerns trainees' willingness to begin and complete voluntary online courses. For example, a 2001 ASTD/Masie Center study reported that only 69 percent of employees choose to begin compulsory online courses and 32 percent start voluntary online courses (Rossett and Schafer, 2003). In addition, there have been reports from some companies of dropout or non-completion rates as high as 75 percent for their online, self-study courses. These figures stand in direct contrast to the prediction by proponents of technology-based learning that shifting control from the bureaucracy and instructor to the learner would increase trainees' enthusiasm and eagerness. Many companies have responded by requiring individuals to pass post-training assessments, tying completion to important rewards (e.g., salary, bonuses), or by employing other strategies designed to force compliance. However, this does not resolve issues surrounding trainee motivation and may lead to other problems. Brown (2005), for example, found that employees who volunteered for an online course spent more time in e-learning. Based on this finding, he concludes "e-learning programs should rely on invitations and marketing rather than forced compliance" (Brown, 2005: 476–477). Thus, the key challenge seems to be how to most effectively capture and sustain the interest of learners in technology-based learning environments.

Social environment and collaboration

Although some high-end learning technologies enable trainees to engage in very elaborate virtual social exchanges that approximate face-to-face interactions, most learning technologies possess only minimal interactivity and communication capabilities. The result is that in many technology-based training environments trainees may have little or no contact with one another. There is an emerging literature on collaborative learning that suggests that individuals can learn more and learn better by teaching one another. Other training strategies, such as behavior modeling, also rely heavily on social learning. Similarly, some observers have argued that group atmosphere, interactions among trainees and between trainees and trainers, and sense of community offered by traditional, face-to-face instruction are critical for learning (Webster and Hackley, 1997). A high level of interactivity is not necessary in all training programs, but when it is important for learning, the challenge is how to most effectively connect learners in remote environments using communication and group support tools.

A related issue concerns the fact that technology-based training does not provide employees with opportunities to socialize and network with their colleagues. For many employees, training is an opportunity to step away from their day-to-day activities and connect with their co-workers. Training can also provide employees with opportunities to network with management or subject matter experts in their field. It is important to evaluate whether remote learning is consistent with an organization's culture. In organizations that emphasize a "high touch" culture, employees may resist technology-based training because it is inconsistent with the companies' values. This occurred at Starbucks, a company known for its workplace environment and social climate, and caused the company to reassess its move toward using technology-based training.

Moderating factors of effectiveness

One may notice that we did not cite training effectiveness as either a benefit or a cost in the discussion above. This is because research that has directly compared technology-based and more traditional, classroom-based delivery of the same course has generally revealed either very small or non-significant differences in student satisfaction and learning outcomes (e.g., Allen *et al.*, 2002; Allen *et al.*, 2004; Russell, 2006). Some proponents have embraced this finding as evidence of the superiority of technology-based training, arguing that the benefit of technology-based training is that it can create the same level of learning as classroom-based instruction at a lower cost. However, we would argue that this finding may be obscuring two important considerations. First, if we are satisfied with the "no significant difference" finding, we are less likely to approach technology-based training as an opportunity to enhance trainees' learning. That is, we avoid fully tapping the unique pedagogical capabilities of learning technologies to create a more powerful and effective learning experience than what can be achieved in the classroom. Second, there is some evidence that the effectiveness of technology-based training is moderated by a number of factors, including the nature of the training content, the delivery technology utilized, and the characteristics of trainees. Thus, the "no significant difference" finding overlooks the fact that technology-based training tends to be a good fit for some training programs and learners, but not others. These more fine-grained results are often lost in comparisons of technology versus classroom instruction.

In the following sections we examine several factors that may influence the effectiveness of technology-based instruction. The better we understand these factors and their influence on the success of e-learning initiatives, the better equipped we are to make informed decisions about when learning technologies should and should not be used.

Training content

How does a company decide which of its training programs should be delivered via technology? Given the attractive practical and financial benefits of technology-based training, many organizations have rushed to put as much of their training as possible online. One result has been a practice known as "repurposing," wherein existing training content from classroom courses is simply mapped onto an existing technology, such as the web. Other companies have been a bit more selective in the courses they transfer online, often restricting technology-based training to courses very heavy in cognitive content (i.e. facts, rules), such as compliance training (e.g., laws, regulations). Still other organizations have focused on creating a specific blend (e.g., 60 percent technology, 40 percent traditional) of different kinds of courses across the company.

The first approach discussed above is clearly not very strategic. Repurposing overlooks the fact that not all training is going to be a good fit for technological delivery and it also gives little consideration to the type of technology that is best suited for delivering a particular course. For example, many observers have questioned whether technology-based training is an effective means of teaching soft skills, such as interpersonal skills (Welsh *et al.*, 2003). The second approach restricts technology-based training to courses that are heavy in content. This strategy is consistent with research showing that self-directed learning is an effective strategy for cognitive learning outcomes (e.g., knowledge). However, this approach may lead to the underutilization of technology-based training for other types of training (e.g., skill-based) where it might be an effective strategy. The final approach focuses on blending technology and traditional forms of delivery to administer a company's training programs. Recent research suggests there is considerable value in blending technology with traditional instruction not only across a company's training offerings but also within an individual program. Blended learning was rated as the most effective and efficient form of training in a survey of 150 US learning professionals (Anonymous, 2004). In essence, blended learning allows a company to draw on the strengths offered by both technology-based and instructor-led training to optimize training effectiveness.

British Petroleum (BP), for example, adopted a blended learning approach for its global health, safety, and environment (HSE) course. An e-learning course provides employees with the foundation of knowledge on HSE policies before they embark on a one-day, hands-on session on risk assessment and root cause analysis ("Global 'blended' learning at BP," 2003). Companies should avoid, however, trying to adhere to an arbitrary ratio of technology-based and traditional learning. How much or how little of its training a company puts online should be driven by the nature of the training content, the training technologies available, and the fit between the two.

Technological capabilities

A second factor that has been identified as potentially impacting the effectiveness of technology-based training involves characteristics of the technology. Research has found that the "quality" of the technology often exhibits a relationship with training effectiveness. For example, Webster and Hackley (1997) examined the effect of technological issues on students' reactions to twenty-nine technology-mediated (video) distance learning courses taught at six North American universities. They found that students who reported higher levels of technology reliability and quality had more positive attitudes toward the technology and had more positive attitudes toward distance learning as an educational medium. A second study by Horwath (1999) found that novice e-learners in a virtual classroom became anxious and distracted if the technology failed to respond within fifteen seconds. Although technology reliability remains an important issue, technological advances have greatly reduced unintended interruptions and have created more seamless learning experiences. The result is that reliability is not as much of a concern as it once was.

Trainee characteristics

Training practitioners are increasingly cognizant of the fact that trainees enter a program with a set of personal characteristics that influence how they approach, interpret, and respond to training. Trainees display different learning styles and preferences based on their past experiences, individual characteristics (e.g., age), and dispositions. The result is that instructional designers need to be careful to avoid a "one size fits all" approach to training and consider how to design training to accommodate the needs of different learners.

Some have argued that individual differences are likely to be especially critical in technology-based training environments. Brown (2001: 276), for example, states, "In computer-based training, the learner generally does not experience the external pressures of a live instructor and of peers completing the same activities. Thus, individual differences should be critical determinants of training effectiveness." Fortunately, technology-based training creates an opportunity to adapt instruction to the characteristics of learners to support their strong features and mitigate their weak ones. The challenge, however, is that technology-based training is still in its infancy and we do not yet have a strong grasp of which individual differences are critical in this environment and how best to accommodate them. Yet, based on prior research in other self-directed learning environments, we can identify several individual differences that are likely to influence the success of technology-based instruction.

One important facet is cognitive ability or intelligence. Prior research suggests that individuals high in cognitive ability tend to perform quite well in less structured environments that provide room for self-directed learning. High-ability individuals have the cognitive resources available for monitoring their learning progress and developing effective learning strategies. However, individuals low in cognitive ability can become overwhelmed by the added burden of directing their own learning and typically fare better in more tightly structured lessons. An important implication is that it may be necessary to provide low-ability trainees with additional support (e.g., self-tests) or guidance to help them monitor their progress and utilize the learner control afforded by many technology-based training programs (Bell and Kozlowski, 2002a).

A second potentially important individual difference is goal orientation. There are two types of goal orientations that affect how individuals approach difficult learning tasks. First, a mastery goal orientation is characterized by a desire to increase one's competency by developing new skills and mastering new situations. In contrast, a performance goal orientation is characterized by a desire to demonstrate one's competence to others and to be positively evaluated by others (Bell and Kozlowski, 2002b). A trainee's goal orientation has a number of important implications for how he or she approaches training. For example, because mastery-oriented trainees tend to worry less than performance-oriented trainees about their performance and any mistakes they might make, they often have higher and more resilient learning self-efficacy (Kozlowski *et al.*, 2001). In technology-based training, higher self-efficacy may make mastery-oriented trainees more likely to persist through the challenges of self-directed learning and less reliant on an instructor's verbal encouragement. One way to leverage the benefits of a mastery orientation is to design training instructions, goals, and other communications so as to encourage trainees to focus on task mastery and learning, as opposed to performance.

Cognitive ability and goal orientation are two important individual differences, but they are certainly not the only individual characteristics that make a difference in technology-based training environments. Research suggests that trainees with higher levels of prior achievement and knowledge in a subject area perform better in learner control conditions (DeRouin *et al.*, 2004). Trainees who have more previous experience with computers and online learning may experience lower levels of anxiety and greater confidence during training. Trainees who are more conscientious may be more likely to follow instructions and complete the training, and those higher in openness to experience may be more accepting of a novel learning technology. Demographic characteristics, such as age, may also influence individuals' preferences for technology-based learning. Let us hope that future research will detail the role that these and other individual differences play in technology-based training.

Guidelines for technology-based training practices

Drawing on the review of current research and practice in the area of technology-based training presented above, we conclude this chapter with a few guidelines designed to help companies optimize the effectiveness of their technology-based training initiatives. See Table 3.1 for a list of the guidelines.

Leverage the unique instructional capabilities of technology

Learning technologies possess unique pedagogical capabilities that have the *potential* to enhance training effectiveness. This potential can be realized only by moving beyond the practice of repurposing classroom-based training for technological delivery. An alternative approach is needed that involves a detailed assessment of the goals of a training program, identification of the learning experience that will support critical learning processes and facilitate competency development, and careful selection of a learning technology capable of delivering the desired instructional experience (for a more detailed presentation of this approach see Kozlowski and Bell, 2007). Figure 3.1 presents a framework that outlines this alternative approach to technology-based training design. Consistent with recent research that has failed to find that one or more delivery modes (e.g., audio, video)

Table 3.1 Guidelines for technology-based training

1 Leverage the unique instructional capabilities of technology.
   ● Assess the goals of a training program.
   ● Identify the learning experience that will support critical learning processes.
   ● Carefully select a learning technology capable of delivering the desired instructional experience.

2 Adopt a learner-centered perspective.
   ● Deliver personalized learning experiences.
   ● Consider using normative learning curves in an adaptive system.

3 Create a supportive learning environment.
   ● Create an organizational climate that supports delivering training through technology.
   ● Create an environment in which technology-based training is aligned with a company's business and human capital development strategies.

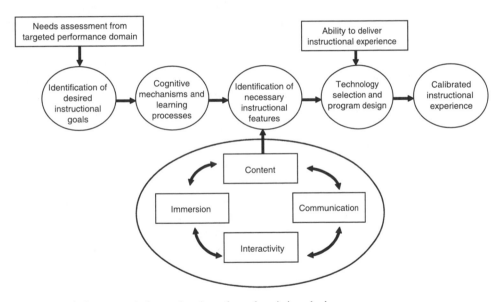

Figure 3.1 A framework for technology-based training design
Source: adapted with permission from Kozlowski and Bell 2002. All rights reserved.

are inherently superior for optimizing learning outcomes (Allen *et al.*, 2004), in this framework training effectiveness is contingent on the alignment of learning considerations with technology selection. Moreover, this framework pushes organizations to think about how the instructional capabilities of learning technologies – in the areas of content, immersion, interactivity, and communication – can be leveraged to create training that goes beyond simply replicating the classroom experience. Ultimately, the key point is summarized well by Burgess and Russell

(2003: 290), "As more organizations and educational institutions adopt distance learning methodologies, it becomes increasingly important to ensure that they are implementing programs that are effective in enhancing employee's skills, rather than simply adopting the latest fad."

Adopt a learner-centered perspective

Even the best-designed technology-based training program will not optimize learning across all trainees. As we discussed earlier, there are a number of individual differences that have the potential to moderate the effectiveness of technology-based training. If one ignores these individual differences, a specific technology-based training program will respond to the needs of only a select portion of the training population. Moreover, those individuals who have the most to gain from training (e.g., inexperienced trainees, low self-efficacy) are the most likely to be left behind. To respond to this issue, companies need to adopt a learner-centered perspective that focuses on leveraging the capability of technology to deliver personalized learning experiences. To date, however, this technological flexibility has been underutilized. This is due, in part, to the fact that the design of personalized instruction remains a time-consuming and resource-intensive endeavor. For example, some estimates suggest that it takes a team of instructional designers and computer programmers between 200 and 1,000 hours to design an hour of intelligent training. Given these high costs, many organizations avoid personalized instruction because they anticipate a negative return on investment. One promising alternative is a strategy referred to as adaptive guidance (Bell and Kozlowski, 2002a). Unlike most efforts at intelligent tutoring, the design premise for adaptive guidance does not require the intensive development of expert models and complex algorithms. Rather, the approach is benchmarked against normative learning curves which are far easier to develop and deploy in an adaptive system. Adaptive guidance and other advisement strategies represent low-cost, flexible tools for assisting trainees in making effective learning choices in technology-based training, which builds confidence and allows trainees to devote more of their attention to the subject matter of the training program (DeRouin et al., 2004).

Create a supportive learning environment

One of the most consistent findings to emerge from the training literature is that a supportive learning environment is critical to training effectiveness. A supportive environment is characterized by clear communication of the value of training and management and peer support that cascades from top management buy-in. Research suggests that a supportive environment is also a key success factor in technology-based training. For example, a 2001 ASTD survey of 700 learners from sixteen US companies found that one of the key drivers of trainees' involvement in an e-learning program was the support they received from co-workers and managers (Sloman, 2002). In addition, Brown (2005) found that employees with greater workloads spent less time in e-learning. He suggests that companies need to create time and space for employees to participate in e-learning and should market the programs through the value of e-learning offerings.

Companies need to approach the transition to technology-based training as a change management initiative (Welsh *et al.*, 2003). In particular, they need to create an organizational climate that supports delivering training through technology. One important step is to highlight the link between human resources and firm success and communicate the role of technology-based training in developing the company's human capital. There also needs to be a strong sense of accountability surrounding technology-based training. The company needs to be held accountable for creating technology-based training programs that help employees address relevant skill gaps. Management needs to communicate the value of the company's technology-based training initiatives and support employees' participation. Finally, employees need to accept responsibility for using technology-based training as a tool for self-managed competency development and career planning. Ultimately, the goal is to create an environment in which technology-based training is aligned with a company's business and human capital development strategies.

Conclusion

Powerful forces are afoot that are pushing organizational training out of the classroom and into workplace technologies. Although this shift in training delivery offers cost-savings and other practical benefits, it also offers the potential to revolutionize training effectiveness by making training better targeted and more learner centered and personalized. Companies that realize this potential will be better positioned to leverage their human capital for sustained competitive advantage.

References

Allen, M., Bourhis, J., Burrell, N. and Mabry, E. (2002) Comparing student satisfaction with distance education to traditional classrooms in higher education: A meta-analysis. *American Journal of Distance Education*, 16: 83–97.

Allen, M., Mabry, E., Mattrey, M., Bourhis, J., Titsworth, S. and Burrell, N. (2004) Evaluating the effectiveness of distance learning: A comparison using meta-analysis. *Journal of Communication*, 54: 402–420.

Anonymous (2004) Blended is better. *T + D*, 58(11): 52–55.

Bell, B.S. and Kozlowski, S.W.J. (2002a) Adaptive guidance: Enhancing self-regulation, knowledge, and performance in technology-based training. *Personnel Psychology*, 55: 267–307.

Bell, B.S. and Kozlowski, S.W.J. (2002b) Goal orientation and ability: Interactive effects on self-efficacy, performance, and knowledge. *Journal of Applied Psychology*, 87: 497–505.

Brown, K.G. (2001) Using computers to deliver training: Which employees learn and why? *Personnel Psychology*, 54: 271–296.

Brown, K.G. (2005) A field study of employee e-learning activity and outcomes. *Human Resource Development Quarterly*, 16: 465–480.

Burgess, J.R.D. and Russell, J.E.A. (2003) The effectiveness of distance learning initiatives in organizations. *Journal of Vocational Behavior*, 63: 289–303.

DeRouin, R.E., Fritzsche, B.A. and Salas, E. (2004) Optimizing e-learning: Research-based guidelines for learner-controlled training. *Human Resource Management*, 43: 147–162.

Galvin, T. (2002) 2002 Industry report. *Training*, 39(10): 24–73.

Global "blended" learning at BP (2003) *Strategic HR Review*, 2(6): 4.

Horwath, A. (1999) Novice users' reaction to a web enriched classroom. *Virtual University Journal*, 2: 49–57.

Kozlowski, S.W.J. and Bell, B.S. (2002) *Enhancing the Effectiveness of Distance Learning and Distributed Training: A Theoretical Framework for the Design of Remote Learning Systems*. Final Report, Contract No. DAAH 04-96-C-0086, TCN: 00156. Research Triangle Park, NC: Battelle Scientific Services.

Kozlowski, S.W.J. and Bell, B.S. (2007) A theory-based approach for designing distributed learning systems. In S.M. Fiore and E. Salas (eds.), *Where is the Learning in Distance Learning? Toward a Science of Distributed Learning and Training*. Washington, DC: APA Books.

Kozlowski, S.W.J., Toney, R.J., Mullins, M.E., Weissbein, D.A., Brown, K.G. and Bell, B.S. (2001) Developing adaptability: A theory for the design of integrated-embedded training systems. In E. Salas (ed.), *Advances in Human Performance and Cognitive Engineering Research, Vol. 1* (pp. 59–123). New York: JAI Press.

Leonard, B. (1996) Distance learning: Work and training overlap. *HR Magazine*, 41(4): 40–47.

Rossett, A. and Schafer, L. (2003) What to do about e-dropouts. *T + D*, 57: 40–46.

Russell, T. (2006) The no significant difference phenomenon. Available http://www.nosignificantdifference.org/ (accessed April 14, 2006).

Salas, E. and Cannon-Bowers, J.A. (2001) The science of training: A decade of progress. *Annual Review of Psychology*, 5: 471–499.

Salas, E., Kosarzycki, M.P., Burke, S., Fiore, S.M. and Stone, D.L. (2002) Emerging themes in distance learning research and practice: Some food for thought. *International Journal of Management Reviews*, 4: 135–153.

Schiflett, S.G., Elliott, L.R., Salas, E. and Coovert, M.D. (eds.) (2004) *Scaled Worlds: Development, Validation, and Application*. Aldershot, UK: Ashgate.

Schramm, J. and Burke, M.E. (2004) *SHRM 2004–2005 Workplace Forecast: A Strategic Outlook*. Alexandria, VA: Society for Human Resource Management.

Sloman, M. (2002) Breaking through the e-barriers. *T + D*, 56(10): 36–41.

Sugrue, B. and Rivera, R.J. (2005) *2005 State of the Industry Report*. Alexandria, VA: American Society for Training and Development.

Sussman, D. (2006) Dividends paid. *T + D*, 60: 26–29.

Webster, J. and Hackley, P. (1997) Teaching effectiveness in technology-mediated distance learning. *Academy of Management Journal*, 40: 1282–1309.

Welsh, E.T., Wanberg, C.R., Brown, K.G. and Simmering, M.J. (2003) E-learning: Emerging uses, empirical results and future directions. *International Journal of Training and Development*, 7: 245–258.

Wisher, R.A. and Priest, A.N. (1998) Cost-effectiveness of audio teletraining for the US Army National Guard. *American Journal of Distance Education*, 12: 38–51.

SEXUAL HARASSMENT TRAINING FOR PROFESSORS

Joseph Shenkel works for the HR department in a large university. The vice-president (VP) of HR decided that it would be a good idea for all faculty and staff to receive annual training on detecting and preventing sexual harassment. Joseph was put in charge of the project. He had to determine the content of training as well as the method. Joseph realized that the spectrum of employees covered was broad, with great diversity in ethnicity, age, backgrounds, and education, ranging from those with PhDs to those without high school diplomas.

Related questions

1 What is it about this context that makes technology-based training especially appropriate or inappropriate?
2 Which training method would be most appropriate?
3 Should the content and/or method be tailored to the employees in this case?

4 New HR challenges in the dynamic environment of legal compliance

TERI J. ELKINS

One of today's most critical HR tasks is reducing the risk of litigation. As discussed in Chapter 1, laws regulating business practices are important components of the general environment's political/legal segment. Due to significant growth in this segment since the 1950s, the legal compliance role of HR has increased in scope, complexity, and importance (Salvatore *et al.*, 2005). Failing to comply with the myriad of business regulations in the United States and Canada can result in a number of negative organizational outcomes including litigation, monetary damages, negative publicity, declines in employee morale and productivity, and reduced investor confidence (Thrasher, 2003). This chapter will examine recent legal developments in the areas of employment discrimination, corporate reform, and alternative dispute resolution. Guidelines will be offered to help HR respond appropriately to new legal requirements and avoid costly negative outcomes.

Sexual harassment

This section looks at recent rulings related to an employer's liability for hostile work environment harassment and provides some guidelines on how organizations can protect themselves in such cases.

Vicarious liability defense

In the United States, sexual harassment is prohibited by the Civil Rights Act of 1964 (Title VII) (42 U.S.C. § 2000e *et seq.*). The US Equal Employment Opportunity Commission (EEOC) was created by Title VII to enforce its provisions. Regulations promulgated by the EEOC have established that an employer is liable for hostile work environment sexual harassment committed by non-supervisory employees when the employer knew or should have known about the harassment and failed to take prompt remedial action (29 C.F.R. § 1604.11(d)). While employers are generally always liable for quid pro quo harassment, which involves an employee with supervisory authority making submission to or rejection of unwelcome sexual conduct a basis for employment decisions (29 C.F.R § 1604.11(a)(2)), employers' liability for hostile work environment created by supervisors was not well defined until recently. In 1998, the US Supreme Court provided clarification, ruling that employers are vicariously liable for a hostile work environment created by a supervisor and providing employers with the following affirmative defense:

> An employer is subject to vicarious liability to a victimized employee for an actionable hostile environment created by a supervisor with immediate (or successively higher) authority over the employee. When no tangible employment action is taken, a defending employer may raise an affirmative defense to liability or damages, subject to proof by a preponderance of the evidence. . . . The defense comprises two necessary elements: (a) that the employer exercised reasonable care to prevent and correct promptly any sexually harassing behavior, and (b) that the plaintiff employee unreasonably failed to take advantage of any preventive or corrective opportunities provided by the employer or to avoid harm otherwise. . . . No affirmative defense is available, however, when the supervisor's harassment culminates in a tangible employment action, such as discharge, demotion, or undesirable reassignment.
>
> (*Faragher v. City of Boca Raton*, at 2292–2293, 1998;
> *Burlington Industries, Inc. v. Ellerth*, at 2270, 1998)

Sexual harassment in the federal jurisdiction of Canada is prohibited by the Canadian Human Rights Act (CHRA) (R.S. 1980–81–82–83, c. 143, s. 7). This Act is enforced by the Canadian Human Rights Commission (CHRC) which identifies behaviors comparable to quid pro quo and hostile work environment harassment in US law as prohibited grounds of discrimination in Canada. Also consistent with US law, the CHRC holds the position that an employer can avoid vicarious liability for harassment committed by its employees or other agents, "if it is established that the employer did not consent to the commission of the act and exercised all due diligence to prevent the act from being committed and, subsequently, to mitigate or avoid its consequences" (Canadian Human Rights Commission, 1998).

Human resource guidelines

Since the *Faragher* and *Ellerth* rulings by the US Supreme Court, lower-level courts and regulatory agencies have begun to provide employers with more specific guidance regarding the defense for vicarious liability. As reflected in the following guidelines, anti-discrimination policies, harassment training, and investigation procedures are critical preventive and corrective actions necessary to avoid liability for hostile work environment sexual harassment.

Guideline 1: Write, communicate, and implement comprehensive anti-harassment policies

Comprehensive anti-harassment policies are essential in demonstrating that an employer has exercised reasonable care to prevent sexual harassment from occurring in the workplace. Enforcement guidance provided by the Equal Employment Opportunity Commission (1999) recommends that anti-harassment policies include:

> a clear explanation of prohibited conduct; assurance that employees who make complaints of harassment or provide information related to such complaints will be protected against retaliation; a clearly described complaint process that provides accessible avenues of complaint; assurance that the employer will protect the confidentiality of harassment complaints to the extent possible; a complaint process that provides a prompt, thorough, and impartial investigation; and assurance that the employer will take immediate and appropriate corrective action when it determines that harassment has occurred.
>
> (Equal Employment Opportunity Commission, 1999, V.C.1)

In addition to content recommended by the EEOC, the CHRC suggests including descriptions of the rights and responsibilities of employees and managers, mechanisms for informal as well as formal complaints, mediation procedures, identification of anti-harassment counselors, and a plan to monitor the policy for effectiveness (Canadian Human Rights Commission, 2005).

Companies not only should create comprehensive anti-harassment policies, but also must ensure that the policies are effectively communicated to employees. US courts have ruled that employers may be liable for harassment if employees are unaware that anti-harassment policies exist (*Miller v. Kenworth of Dothan, Inc.*, 2002). To demonstrate that policies are properly communicated, employers should provide all employees with copies of the policies and require each employee to sign a statement that he or she has read and understood the policy. It is also important to periodically redistribute policies, post them in central locations, and incorporate them into important documents such as employee handbooks (Ludwick, 2004).

Guideline 2: Provide training to all employees regarding the organization's anti-harassment policies and complaint procedures

US court decisions have also indicated that training is an important element of establishing an effective defense for vicarious sexual harassment liability. Companies may be liable for hostile work environment harassment if supervisors are not properly trained to recognize behaviors that constitute sexual harassment (*Hill v. The Children's Village*, 2002) and to effectively handle sexual harassment complaints (*Gaines v. Bellino*, 2002). According to regulatory enforcement guidance and recommendations from legal practitioners, all employees should receive periodic training regarding an organization's anti-harassment policies and complaint procedures to ensure that the policies are understood and taken seriously (Canadian Human Rights Commission, 2005; Equal Employment Opportunity Commission, 1999; Jenero and Galligano, 2003). In terms of training content, all employees should be informed about specific prohibited behaviors, how to report complaints of harassment, and the company's complaint procedures. Managers should also be instructed on how to monitor for sexual harassment, and how to handle complaints, documentation, performance evaluations, counseling, and the company's prohibition against retaliation (Equal Employment Opportunity Commission, 1999; Jenero and Galligano, 2003). Sexual harassment training should be conducted by human resource professionals or others with expertise in harassment law such as attorneys and should be properly documented (Jenero and Galligano, 2003).

Guideline 3: Conduct thorough investigations of harassment complaints and take appropriate corrective actions

According to enforcement guidance from the Equal Employment Opportunity Commission (1999) and the Canadian Human Rights Commission (2005), an impartial, trained investigator should conduct a prompt and thorough investigation after receiving a sexual harassment complaint. The investigator should interview the complainant, the alleged harasser, and any relevant third parties. If there is a conflict in the parties' accounts of events, credibility should be determined based upon plausibility of the accounts, demeanor, motives to lie, corroboration, and past records. Decisions by US courts indicate that failing to conduct proper investigations can result in company liability for compensatory as well as punitive damages (*Coates v. Wal-Mart Stores, Inc.*, 1999).

Based upon evidence gathered in the investigation, the investigator should determine whether sexual harassment occurred, inform the parties of the decision, and take immediate appropriate corrective action. The Equal Employment Opportunity Commission (1999) views appropriate action as that which will stop the harassment and prevent future harassment from occurring. This may include a written/oral reprimand, demotion, decrease in salary, suspension, termination, training, and monitoring. Additionally, action should be taken to correct the effects of the harassment on the victim through apologies, counseling, monitoring, and compensation for losses. It is also important for the investigator to document the investigation by taking notes and providing a written report that describes the investigation process, decision, and recommended corrective action (Canadian Human Rights Commission, 2005). After the investigation, the company should follow up to ensure that the victim has not been retaliated against in any way (Oppenheimer, 2004).

Age discrimination

This section looks at recent rulings related to an employer's liability for disparate impact claims of age discrimination and provides some guidelines on how organizations can protect themselves in such cases.

Disparate impact claims

Because of the aging workforce and possible labor shortages, issues related to age discrimination are of current concern to companies. Human rights legislation prohibiting employment discrimination based on age exists in all Canadian jurisdictions (Gunderson, 2003). The Canadian Human Rights Act (R.S., 1985, c. H-6) protects employees from age discrimination in the federal jurisdiction and prohibits both the intentional differential treatment of an individual because of age and unintentional discrimination resulting from a neutral policy or practice. The Age Discrimination in Employment Act (ADEA) of 1967 (29 U.S.C.S. § 621) prohibits US employers from discriminating against individuals of 40 and older because of their age. Until recently, however, ADEA claims could only be based upon a disparate treatment theory of intentional discrimination.

In 2005, the US Supreme Court ruled that ADEA claims can also be brought under a disparate impact theory of unintentional discrimination in which a neutral policy adversely affects those aged 40 and older (*Smith v. City of Jackson*, 2005). The defendant in *Smith* made modifications to its compensation plan for police officers, providing all officers with raises that were designed to bring starting salaries closer to regional averages. The new plan resulted in officers with five years or less seniority receiving proportionately larger raises than those with more seniority. A group of officers filed suit claiming age discrimination because most of the officers with more than five years seniority were over 40 years of age. The Supreme Court ruled that although a disparate impact claim could be brought, a company can defend itself by providing a reasonable factor other than age (RFOA) for the policy. In ultimately finding that age discrimination did not occur, the court ruled that although the defendant could have used other methods of making starting salaries more competitive, the method it used was not unreasonable.

Human resource guidelines

The ability to file disparate impact age discrimination claims presents a threat of increased litigation and defense costs for organizations (Reilly *et al.*, 2006). Legal scholars also believe that the ruling makes it easier for employees to file class action age discrimination claims since such claims are based upon statistical analysis rather than proof of intent (Clark, 2005). Thus, it is critical that companies assess and minimize their potential age-related disparate impact liability.

Guideline 4: Review HR policies and practices for disparate impact based upon age

Human resource policies and practices should be reviewed to determine if disparate impact based on age is occurring or could potentially occur. Specific policies and practices that should be evaluated include benefit plans, layoffs, retirement/pension plans, compensation systems, restructuring, and hiring and promotion policies (Clark, 2005).

Guideline 5: Identify and document reasonable factors other than age for problematic policies

If disparate impact based upon age is found in human resource policies or practices, companies should identify and document reasonable factors other than age to explain the disproportionate effects. For example, salary competitiveness was considered a reasonable justification for the defendant's revised raise policy in *Smith*.

Alternative dispute resolution

This section looks at recent rulings related to the legality of using mandatory arbitration agreements and provides some guidelines on how organizations can use such agreements to their benefit.

Mandatory arbitration agreements

Changes and uncertainty in employment laws can increase the risk of litigation. In fact, employment suits have increased by 400 percent since the mid 1980s (Thrasher, 2003). Because of the high costs associated with employment litigation, some companies have begun using arbitration to resolve employment claims. Arbitration not only is less expensive than most litigation, but also can be a much faster mechanism for resolving disputes than the trial process (Camardella, 2001). Overall, federal statutory law and court decisions in the United States have been favorable toward mandatory arbitration clauses in which, as a condition of employment, employees and applicants agree to arbitrate claims against employers and waive their right to litigation.

Mandatory arbitration is explicitly permitted for commercial transactions by the Federal Arbitration Act (FAA) of 1925 (9 U.S.C. Section 1 *et seq.*) which states:

> A written provision in any maritime transaction or a contract evidencing a transaction involving commerce to settle by arbitration a controversy thereafter arising out of such contract or transaction, or the refusal to perform the whole or

any part thereof, or an agreement in writing to submit to arbitration an existing controversy arising out of such a contract, transaction, or refusal, shall be valid, irrevocable, and enforceable, save upon such grounds as exist at law or in equity for the revocation of any contract.

(9 U.S.C. Section 2)

The US Supreme Court first addressed whether mandatory arbitration agreements are enforceable under the FAA for statutory employment discrimination claims in *Gilmer v. Interstate/Johnson Lane Corp.* (1991). In this case, the Supreme Court ruled that an arbitration agreement signed by Mr. Gilmer as part of a securities registration application was enforceable for a claim of discrimination under the ADEA. Upon being hired as a financial services manager, Mr. Gilmore was required to register as a securities representative with a number of stock exchanges. This process involved completing an application that included an agreement to arbitrate disputes as required by the rules of the various exchanges. The New York Stock Exchange rules require arbitration of "any controversy between a registered representative and any member or member organization arising out of the employment or termination of employment of such registered representative" (*Gilmer v. Interstate/Johnson Lane Corp.* at 23). After working for the company for six years, Mr. Gilmer was dismissed and his duties were given to a 28 year old. As a result, he filed an age discrimination claim with the EEOC which then filed suit against the company in federal court. In granting the company's motion to compel arbitration under the FAA, the Supreme Court indicated that neither the ADEA nor its legislative history explicitly precludes arbitration and that arbitration is not inconsistent with the ADEA's purposes. Ten years later, in *Circuit City, Inc. v. Adams* (2001), the US Supreme Court ruled that arbitration agreements that are part of an employment contract are also enforceable under the FAA for statutory claims.

In *EEOC v. Waffle House, Inc.* (2002), the US Supreme Court addressed whether arbitration agreements signed by employees prohibit the EEOC from litigating claims on the employee's behalf. In this case, the plaintiff applied to be a grill operator at Waffle House and was required to sign an application containing a mandatory arbitration agreement which stated:

> The parties agree that any dispute or claim concerning Applicant's employment with Waffle House, Inc., or any subsidiary or Franchisee of Waffle House, Inc., or the terms, conditions or benefits of such employment, including whether such dispute or claim is arbitrable, will be settled by binding arbitration. The arbitration proceedings shall be conducted under the Commercial Arbitration Rules of the American Arbitration Association in effect at the time a demand for arbitration is made. A decision and award of the arbitrator made under the said rules shall be exclusive, final and binding on both parties, their heirs, executors, administrators, successors and assigns. The costs and expenses of the arbitration shall be borne evenly by the parties.

(*EEOC v. Waffle House, Inc.* at 758)

Shortly after the employee was hired, he had a seizure at work and was dismissed. He then filed a claim of disability discrimination with the EEOC. After an investigation, the agency found probable cause that discrimination had occurred and filed suit against Waffle House. The EEOC was named as the plaintiff in the suit; the employee was not a party. The agency sought compensatory and punitive damages on the employee's behalf and Waffle House moved to compel arbitration. The Supreme Court ruled that the EEOC was not a party to the arbitration agreement and was given the power by Title VII and the Civil Rights Act of 1991 (42 U.S.C. 1981) to sue and seek victim-specific relief such as backpay, reinstatement, etc. Thus, regulatory agencies such as the EEOC can sue companies on behalf of an employee as part of the agency's enforcement duties even if the employee has signed a mandatory arbitration agreement with the employer.

While mandatory arbitration agreements between employers and their employees are not as prevalent in Canada as in the United States, their popularity is rising (Alexandrowicz, 2005). Although federal and provincial statutes exist that regulate arbitration agreements between private parties in Canada, the statutes do not address agreements between employees and employers. Because courts interpreting these statutes generally presume the validity of arbitration agreements in commercial contexts, legal scholars have predicted that employment arbitration agreements will be viewed as enforceable unless they are unconscionable (Alexandrowicz, 2005). That is, Canadian courts are likely to evaluate mandatory arbitration agreements in employment contexts in much the same way as the US Supreme Court in *Gilmer* and *Circuit City*.

Human resource guidelines

Considering the legal support that exists for mandatory arbitration, it is likely that an increasing number of employers in North America will implement mandatory arbitration agreements for the resolution of employment disputes (Spognardi and Ketay, 2002). The FAA and the US Supreme Court decisions indicate that arbitration agreements will be upheld if they are fair. Subsequent lower court decisions have begun to provide guidance regarding the execution and content of legally enforceable fair arbitration agreements.

Guideline 6: Follow contract law principles when executing a mandatory arbitration agreement

Mandatory arbitration agreements are contracts and should be separate from the application and other employment agreements. To ensure that employees and applicants fully understand the implications of mandatory arbitration, they should be given time to read the agreement and ask questions before signing it. Employers should also establish that consideration exists by providing money or some other tangible job benefit in exchange for the signing the agreement (Spognardi and Ketay, 2002).

Guideline 7: Establish terms and conditions in mandatory arbitration agreements that ensure procedural and substantive fairness

To maximize the enforceability of mandatory arbitration agreements, their content should clearly define the types of claims subject to arbitration and provide a detailed description of the arbitration process. In defining a fair arbitration process, courts have indicated that employees should participate in selecting a neutral arbitrator (*Hooters of America v. Phillips*, 1999), the costs of arbitration should not be burdensome to the employee (*McCaskill v. SCI Mgt. Corporation*, 2002), and the arbitrator should be able to provide the same remedies that are available through litigation (*Circuit City, Inc. v. Adams*, 2002). It has also been recommended that companies require written opinions from arbitrators, provide for adequate discovery, and allow representation by an attorney at the employee's expense (Spognardi and Ketay, 2002).

Corporate reform

The Sarbanes–Oxley Act of 2002 (SOX) (15 U.S.C. 1701) was passed in the United States in response to recent corporate financial scandals. (See Chapters 6 and 9 for more discussions related to this.) Although it was initially believed that the legislation would have very little impact on the human resource function in organizations, HR is now actively involved in SOX compliance activities (Grossman, 2005a). The following sections will identify portions of SOX and comparable provisions of Canada's Multilateral Instrument 52–111 that have the greatest effects on HR, and make recommendations regarding compliance.

Internal control requirements and human resource guidelines

Section 404 of SOX focuses on the assessment of internal controls. Specifically, the act states that annual reports required by the Securities and Exchange Act of 1934 must include internal control reports that:

- state the responsibility of management for establishing and maintaining an adequate internal control structure and procedures for financial reporting; and
- contain an assessment, as of the end of the issuer's fiscal year, of the effectiveness of the internal control structure and procedures of the issuer for financial reporting.

(15 U.S.C. 7201, Sec. 404 (a)(1) and (2))

The Canadian Securities Administrators (CSA) proposed Multilateral Instrument 52–111 and released it for public comment in February 2005. The rule essentially mirrors the requirement of SOX Section 404. Under the proposed rule, employers were originally required to report on the effectiveness of their internal controls over financial reporting for financial years ending on or after June 30, 2006. In July 2005, the CSA extended this implementation by one year to allow more time to consider comments submitted regarding the proposed rule and the impact of SOX implementation in the United States (Canadian Securities Administrators, 2005).

Guideline 8: Work with the company's finance department to comply with financial control requirements

Because HR is responsible for a number of functions that affect internal controls managed by finance, human resource professionals have estimated that HR will spend 80 percent of its SOX compliance efforts on Section 404, working closely with chief finance officers (CFOs) and auditors (Grossman, 2005a). Thus, HR should work closely with finance to develop documentation that will be requested by auditors (Dailey and Brookmire, 2005). Specific areas in which HR can expect to be heavily involved include: compensation and benefits (ensuring the accuracy of pension expense accruals and liabilities), payroll (validation and reconciliation of payroll amounts), operations (review of complaint management processes to assess legal liability), and confidentiality (ensuring that confidential employee information is secure) (Grossman, 2005a). The US Securities and Exchange Commission (SEC) is tasked with enforcing SOX and has suggested that employers utilize the COSO (Committee of Sponsoring Organizations of the Treadway Commission) internal control framework to assist with Section 404 compliance (Securities and Exchange Commission, 2005). According to the COSO framework, effective internal control can be achieved by focusing on the following components: the control environment (ethical values of the company), risk assessment (internal and external sources of risk), control activities (managerial policies and procedures), information and communication (operational, financial, and compliance data), and monitoring (control system assessment) (COSO, 2005).

Code of ethics requirements and guidelines

Section 406 of SOX requires companies to adopt a code of ethics aimed at senior financial officers and specifies that the code should promote:

- honest and ethical conduct, including the ethical handling of actual or apparent conflicts of interest between personal and professional relationships;
- full, fair, accurate, timely, and understandable disclosure in the periodic reports required to be filed by the issuer; and
- compliance with applicable governmental rules and regulations.

(15 U.S.C. 7201 Sec. 406 (c)(1)–(3))

Guideline 9: Write, communicate, and implement a comprehensive code of ethics

Most companies have codes of ethics in place. To ensure compliance with Section 406, the content of the codes should be reviewed for their focus on financial issues. Companies should ensure that their codes require compliance of all employees, describe specific prohibited behaviors, create confidential reporting mechanisms, identify investigation procedures, and protect whistleblowers (Dailey and Brookmire, 2005). In addition to revising the content, companies should document that employees have received the new codes, and provide all employees with training focused on ethics code compliance (Grossman, 2005b). See Chapter 6 for more on codes of ethics.

Complaint process requirements and guidelines

SOX Section 301 requires audit committees of the board of directors to establish procedures for:

- the receipt, retention, and treatment of complaints received by the issuer regarding accounting, internal accounting controls, or auditing matters; and
- the confidential, anonymous submission by employees of the issuer of concerns regarding questionable accounting or auditing matters.

(15 U.S.C. 7201 (4(A)(B)))

This section also gives the audit committee the authority to appoint advisors to assist in carrying out its duties. Because HR is traditionally responsible for internal investigations of potential illegal activity, they are likely to be involved in the investigation of SOX complaints (Grossman, 2005b).

Guideline 10: Establish procedures for reporting and investigating complaints of SOX violations

Legal experts have recommended establishing confidential complaint mechanisms such as hotlines, helplines, and web sites and making complaint systems available to a wide range of stakeholders including current and former employees, customers/clients, and public interest groups (Grossman, 2005b). The investigation of complaints should be approached in ways similar to complaints of discrimination. Refer to Guideline 3 for a discussion of sexual harassment investigations. When investigating allegations of wrongdoing committed by officers or directors, companies should consider using third parties such as an accounting or law firm (Felsberg, 2005).

Compensation and benefits requirements and guidelines

Two SOX sections focus on compensation and benefits requirements that have implications for HR. Section 402 prohibits companies from making personal loans to executive officers and members of the board of directors. Many companies are banning loans to all employees as a result of this provision (Grossman, 2005b). Section 306 prohibits officers, directors, and other insiders buying or selling stock during pension fund blackout periods and requires that officers, directors, employees, and the SEC be given notice of blackouts.

Guideline 11: Review and monitor compensation and benefits policies for compliance

To ensure that compensation and benefits policies comply with SOX, HR should conduct a thorough review and stop illegal practices such as making personal loans to executives, officers, and directors and trading during blackout periods. Additionally, human resource executives have suggested that HR monitor judicial interpretations of compensation and benefits policies including: contributions to split-dollar life insurance policies, margin call loans, relocation loans, cash advances for business expenses, and 401(K) loans (Dailey and Brookmire, 2005).

Conclusion and summary of guidelines

One of today's most critical HR functions is legal compliance (Thrasher, 2003). Ineffective compliance efforts can be very costly. In a survey of corporate attorneys and human resource managers, 57 percent of the respondents reported that their company had been a defendant in employment-related litigation in the past year (Jackson Lewis, 2005). Jury verdict statistics indicate that the mean compensatory jury award for employment cases is $250,000 (Jury Verdict Research, 2004). Violations of SOX requirements can result in substantial civil monetary penalties as well as criminal sanctions. As new laws are passed and courts provide interpretations of statutory provisions and apply statutes to novel situations, compliance becomes more difficult and potentially more costly.

Guideline 12: Utilize the outreach and training functions of administrative agencies to monitor changes in the legal environment

Agencies such as the EEOC, CHRC, and SEC provide a number of services to help companies comply with complex and changing business regulations. While the guidelines presented in this chapter and summarized in Table 4.1 may assist HR in current compliance activities, the dynamic legal environments in both the United

States and Canada require continuous monitoring to avoid costly outcomes. Administrative agencies can be of tremendous assistance to HR in keeping abreast of new legal requirements.

Table 4.1 Guidelines for complying with current legal developments

Sexual harassment

1 Write, communicate, and implement comprehensive anti-harassment policies.
2 Provide training to all employees regarding the organization's anti-harassment policies and complaint procedures.
3 Conduct a thorough investigation of sexual harassment complaints and take appropriate corrective action.

Age discrimination

4 Review human resource policies and practices for disparate impact based upon age.
5 Identify and document reasonable factors other than age for policies and practices that create a disparate impact based upon age.

Mandatory arbitration agreements

6 Follow contract law principles when executing mandatory arbitration agreements.
7 Establish terms and conditions in mandatory arbitration agreements that ensure procedural and substantive fairness.

Sarbanes–Oxley

8 Work with the company's finance department to comply with financial controls requirements.
9 Write, communicate, and implement a comprehensive code of ethics.
10 Establish procedures for reporting and investigating complaints of SOX violations.
11 Review and monitor compensation and benefits policies for compliance.

Monitoring the legal environment

12 Utilize the outreach and training functions of administrative agencies to monitor changes in the legal environment.

References

Alexandrowicz, J. (2005) A comparative analysis of the law regulating employment arbitration agreements in the United States and Canada. *Comparative Labor Law and Policy Journal*, 23: 1007–1055.
Burlington Industries, Inc. v. Ellerth, 118 S.Ct. 2257 (1998).
Camardella, M.J. (2001) Should your organization require arbitration of employment disputes? *Employment Relations Today*, 28: 139–142.

Canadian Human Rights Commission (1998) Harassment and the Canadian Human Rights Act. Available http://www.chrc-ccdp.ca/publications/harassmentchra-en.asp (accessed April 23, 2006).

Canadian Human Rights Commission (2005) Anti-harassment policies for the workplace: An employer's guide. Available http://www.chrc-ccdp.ca/publications/anti_harassment_toc-en.asp#part2 (accessed March 4, 2006).

Canadian Securities Administrators (2005) Regulators revise timeline for internal control reporting project. Available http://www.csa-acvm.ca/html_csa/news/05_15CSA52–111.htm (accessed March 8, 2006).

Circuit City, Inc. v. Adams, 121 S.Ct. 1302 (2001).

Circuit City, Inc. v. Adams, 279 F.3d 889 (2002).

Clark, M. (2005) ADEA prevention not panic. *HR Magazine*, 50: 58–62.

Coates v. Wal-Mart Stores, Inc., 976 P.2d 999 (N.M. 1999).

COSO (2005) Internal control: Integrated framework. Available http://www.coso.org/publications/executive_summary_integrated_framework.htm (accessed March 2, 2006).

Dailey, P.R. and Brookmire, D.A. (2005) Back to our future: Challenging new compliance and leadership accountabilities for human resources, courtesy of Sarbanes–Oxley. *Human Resource Planning*, 28: 38–44.

Equal Employment Opportunity Commission (1999) Enforcement guidance: Vicarious employer liability for unlawful harassment by supervisors. Available http://www.eeoc.gov/policy/docs/harassment.html (accessed May 3, 2006).

Equal Employment Opportunity Commission v. Waffle House, Inc., 122 S.Ct. 754 (2002).

Faragher v. City of Boca Raton, 118 S.Ct. 2275 (1998).

Felsberg, E.J. (2005) Understanding retaliation and whistleblowing claims. *Employment Relations Today*, 32: 91–96.

Gaines v. Bellino, 801 A.2d 322 (N.J. 2002).

Gilmer v. Interstate/Johnson Lane Corp., 500 U.S. 20 (1991).

Grossman, R.J. (2005a) Demystifying Section 404. *HR Magazine*, 50: 46–53.

Grossman, R.J. (2005b) Are you clear? *HR Magazine*, 50: 54–58.

Gunderson, M. (2003) Age discrimination in employment in Canada. *Contemporary Economic Policy*, 21: 318–328.

Hill v. The Children's Village, 196 F.Supp. 2d 389 (S.D. N.Y., 2002).

Hooters of America v. Phillips, 173 F.3d 933 (4th Cir. 1999).

Jackson Lewis (2005) Findings from 2004 workplace survey reveal changing trends, attitudes in corporate America. Available http://www.jacksonlewis.com/legalupdates/article.cfm?aid=732 (accessed April 25, 2006).

Jenero, K.A. and Galligano, M.L. (2003) Courts continue to emphasize importance of policy development and training. *Employee Relations Law Journal*, 28: 113–124.

Jury Verdict Research (2004) JVR news release. Available http://www.juryverdictresearch.com/Press_Room/Press_releases/Verdict_study/verdict_study9.html (accessed March 23, 2006).

Ludwick, K.D. (2004) Minimizing punitive damages exposure in employment cases: Post-Kolstad case law lessons. *Employee Relations Law Journal*, 29: 69–93.

McCaskill v. SCI Mgt. Corporation, 285 F.3d 623 (7th Cir. 2002).

Miller v. Kenworth of Dothan, Inc., 277 F.3d 1269 (11th Cir. 2002).

Oppenheimer, A. (2004) Investigating workplace harassment and discrimination. *Employee Relations Law Journal*, 29: 56–68.

Reilly, D.M., Valaas, K.E. and Powell, L. (2006) The ADEA, disparate impact claims, and compensation adjustments. *Compensation and Benefits Review*, 38: 37–43.

Salvatore, P., Halem, D., Weitzman, A., Smith, G. and Schaefer, L. (2005) How the law changed HR. *HR Magazine*, 13: 47–56.

Securities and Exchange Commission (2005) Statements of SEC Chief Accountant Donald Nicolaisen and Corporation Finance Division Director Alan Beller regarding new COSO

Guidance on Section 404 compliance. Available http://www.sec.gov/news/press/2005–153.htm (accessed April 13, 2006).

Smith v. City of Jackson, 544 U.S. 228 (2005).

Spognardi, M.A. and Ketay, S.L. (2002) Having your waffle and eating it too: The EEOC's right to circumvent arbitration agreements. *Employee Relations Law Journal*, 28: 115–127.

Thrasher, K. (2003) Employment practices compliance systems can help provide support to HR. *Employment Relations Today*, 30: 61–68.

THE SALARY THAT DOESN'T COMPUTE

Ken Longhectar is a 43-year-old programmer who has worked for a medium-sized high-technology firm for twenty years. The company tends to promote from within, and hire recent college graduates for their entry-level positions. The company has had to substantially increase wages for these entry-level positions over the past several years, to keep up with the external market. As a result many of the newer employees are earning more than the senior employees, although the new employees have less experience and are frequently poorer performers than their more senior counterparts. Ken recently learned that he is making substantially less than most new hires and has brought this discrepancy to the HR manager's attention.

Related questions

1 What potential discrimination claims might Ken have against the company?
2 Does the company have any valid defenses to such claims?
3 What can the company do to avoid future discrimination claims based upon its compensation policies?

5 The changing family and HRM

PAMELA L. PERREWÉ

> The wave of the future is not the conquest of the world by a single
> dogmatic creed but the liberation of the diverse energies of free nations
> and free men.
>
> John F. Kennedy

In the 1970s, Kanter (1977) recognized that traditional organizations were designed as if workers did not have families or personal demands – she termed this the "myth of separate worlds." Employees were expected to make work a priority and not to bring family responsibilities into the organizational setting. Families were structured such that males were the primary (often only) breadwinners. Because the structure of the organization and the family were well defined, little ambiguity existed over roles and there was very little flexibility in the system. Society has evolved such that we no longer have well-defined, "one size fits all" organizational and family structures. This progress, however, has led to more complexity as well as uncertainty.

Environmental changes continue to impact work–life issues. This chapter examines general environmental trends, specifically globalization and technological advancements, as well as labor market factors such as the changing demographics of the workforce, and how these changes affect employees as well as HRM. Labor market topics include the increase in dual-careers, childcare requirements, elder care issues, multiculturalism, same-sex parents, and blended families. Although each of these issues affects the work–life interface, these changes do not need to be deemed negative for the employee or the organization. In fact, there is nothing inherently stressful about juggling more than one role – we simply need to know how to manage these roles. The HR professional's response to these changes can lead to positive outcomes for both the employee and the organization. This chapter concludes with some specific guidelines on how HR can help the employee and the organization to better adapt to the changing workforce.

Changes in the environment

Dramatic changes have occurred in both the general environment and the labor market related to the changing family.

General factors

Changes in globalization and technology have strongly affected HRM and the family.

Globalization

Chow (2003: 444) defines globalization as "the complex and multifaceted processes of worldwide economic, social, cultural and political expansion and integration which have enabled capital, production, finance, trade, ideas, images, people and organizations to flow transnationally across the boundaries of regions, nation-states, and cultures." (See Chapter 2 for a more detailed discussion of globalization.) With the increase in globalization, we need to be aware of the wider international and cultural context of work and the implications for work–life integration. The European Union (EU) has been active in promoting policies that emphasize issues regarding gender. At a minimum, these policies promote equal opportunities for women globally. However, many argue that these policies do not go far enough and should be more radical by including and considering the work–family interface (Lewis and Haas, 2005).

Those outside the United States have different values and attitudes about work. Some do not agree with the ways the United States does business and become hostile when it attempts to impose US solutions on them. Further, some US ideas do not translate well into other countries. For example, many US businesses encourage "affinity groups" whose purpose is to serve as a voice for minority groups. This is not popular in South Africa as the separation of people by color is reminiscent of apartheid (Sherwood, 2006).

The United Nations (UN) and the EU have impacted policies regarding work–family issues such as the stated emphasis on societies' responsibility to provide childcare for employees as well as the importance of both parents sharing the responsibilities of work and family. EU directives include employee rights for both men and women regarding parental leave and part-time employment. International social policies are now recognizing the need for more attention to the work–life interface throughout the world. The hope is that these social policies will eventually aid global organizations to have some consistency regarding work–life policies, regardless of the country in which the organization is based or is operating.

Technology

Advances in telecommunications and information technology have given some flexibility as to how organizations are structured and the way work can be organized. Technology can provide options for organizations and employees to better manage work–life responsibilities. Of course, technology can also be viewed as creating an environment of entrapment such that employees are always available to organizational as well as family requests with no time to simply focus on one domain. New technologies such as palm pilots, laptop computers, and pagers, and advances in cellular phones create an environment where individuals are expected to always be available.

On the other hand, technology allows individuals flexibility as to where and even when to work. Employees may have opportunities to work from home or another remote location by using laptop computers, for example. This allows them to work around their family responsibilities and schedules. Teleworking (i.e., working part of the time from home and part of the time in the organization) has been touted as one way to attract and retain top employees who desire a balance between work and family life. However, research has indicated that employees are working more than ever before by bringing work into the family domain (Valcour and Hunter, 2005). Work and family domains are being blurred by the expectation that individuals should be available all of the time. Thus, although technology can add flexibility to individuals' lives, it can also, simultaneously, create conflicts between work and family domains by encouraging individuals to be available to work and family requests continually.

Labor market factors

Dual-career families, the changing shape of families, the aging workforce, and increased diversity are all aspects of changing labor market factors.

Dual-career families

According to the Employment Policy Foundation's Center for Work and Family Balance in 1940, approximately 66 percent of the working households had only one wage earner. Today, that number is fewer than 25 percent of all households. Further, it is estimated that by 2030, only 17 percent of all households will have the traditional one wage earner – the majority of the households today consist of two wage earners and it appears that this trend is going to continue (Clay, 2005). As the number of families with both parents working continues to soar, much of the research on the phenomenon has focused on the time pressures, demands, role juggling, and work–family conflicts that can lead to stress for working parents.

Although juggling too many roles with too many demands can be stressful, recent research suggests that engaging in multiple roles (e.g., mother, wife, and manager) may actually be viewed as positive. Multiple roles can aid in psychological as well as monetary rewards. Research has shown that working mothers are less distressed than stay-at-home mothers (Barnett *et al.*, 1995). Thus, organizations and employees should be concerned about the upper limits of juggling roles, but should not assume that engaging in multiple roles is inherently bad.

The changing shape of families

The structure of the family and the roles of parental involvement continue to change and evolve. For example, one in every three Americans is part of a stepfamily (DeAngelis, 2005). These blended families can bring about additional complexities in the work–life interface, especially because in about one-quarter of these unmarried parents head families. Being in blended families or single parenting can bring about pressures at home that spill over into the workplace. Further, parenting roles continue to change.

Just as women want balance in their work and family, so do men. Fathers are no longer satisfied with playing a peripheral role in their children's lives. More and more, fathers are demanding a significant role in care-giving for their children and they have become a major force in child-rearing early in their children's lives.

Finally, more people are choosing to begin families in the context of two gay or lesbian parents (Dingfelder, 2005). Gay and lesbian parents have additional stressors that traditional parents (i.e., one man and one woman) do not endure. They are concerned about not giving their children both a male and a female role model (although this concern is also shared by single parents); they are concerned about their children being teased or bullied as a result of having gay or lesbian parents; and they are concerned about legal issues as some states do not allow gay or lesbian parents to be recognized, giving them no rights to important things like spousal health insurance. The demands and stressors associated with family roles and the changing shape of families will continue to affect the interface between work and family.

The aging workforce

In general, the US population is becoming older and the most significant population trend of the twentieth century was the baby boom after World War II. Based on the "graying of America," two issues relevant to HR professionals are clear. First, employees are working longer than ever before. Reasons for employees working beyond the typical retirement age of 65 stem from individuals living longer, healthier lives and wanting to continue to make significant contributions to the working world, and needing to work due to financial concerns. Indeed, only a small proportion of aging employees expect not to work at all during retirement, with most citing financial obligations as the reason to remain in the workforce (Reynolds *et al.*, 2005). For whichever reason, organizations have an older workforce with which to contend. Second, many of those in the baby boom generation are finding themselves responsible for the care of their parents or other elderly individuals. Elder care for family members is becoming an issue of ever-increasing importance to workers.

Diversity

The demographic profile of the US workforce has changed; there are greater numbers of women and minorities in the workplace. For example, it is projected that early in the twenty-first century, the majority of first-time job seekers will be minorities, and the percentage of married women entering the workforce will surpass 70 percent, up from 35 percent in 1966 (Mische, 2000). Immigration has also magnified diversity issues. During the twentieth century, laborers were predominantly African Americans, Asian Americans, and Chicanos (Glenn, 2001). However, as these groups have moved up the labor market, immigrants have taken over the lower-level laborer role (Poster, 2005). Finally, there has been a steady increase of international as well as transracial adoptions (Chamberlin, 2005). Adoption is playing an important role in the increase of diversity in families. All of these trends have impacted the diversity and multiculturalism of the family and the organization.

HRM responses

The environmental changes just examined affect working individuals as well as the organization. The prevalence of dual-careers, an aging workforce, and an increase in diversity and multiculturalism all call for some type of response from the organization to help with work–family balance issues. I examine workplace flexibility, tolerance, and work–life programs as positive responses that organizations can have to these environmental changes.

Flexibility in the workplace

More and more companies are using flexible work schedules and find that workers like the change. Many employees desire or need a nontraditional work arrangement, such as compressed work weeks, job sharing, flextime, and paid or unpaid leaves of absence. Compressed work schedules allow for a forty-hour work-week in fewer than the traditional five days. Compressed work schedules might have employees working ten hours for four days, allowing the employee to have three days off each week. Job sharing work schedules allow employees to share one job. This works very well for individuals who want to work part time when the organization needs to have the position filled full time. Essentially, two part-time employees share one full-time job.

Flextime is another popular option in which a work schedule gives employees some control over when they begin and end their work day. This can be particularly helpful to employees who may have family responsibilities in the late afternoon or early morning. Finally, paid or unpaid leave of absence is another strategy that allows flexibility to the employee. Sometimes employees need to take leave from their job to take care of family responsibilities such as a new baby or elder care. During this time, employees may or may not be paid, but they normally retain their health benefits.

Teleworking, in which an employee can work from home or another remote location through electronic media, can offer autonomy to employees as they are not tied to working during specified times within the organization. However, as mentioned earlier, it is important to recognize that teleworking might lead to the expectation that employees are always available because their hours are not necessarily restricted to an organization's traditional work week. It is important for HR professionals to make sure employees are not always on call.

Further, it is important that employees who take advantage of these opportunities are not punished. For example, some employees might not take advantage of paternity leave because they believe management will think they are not serious about their work or are not committed to the organization. The negative attitudes of management toward these types of flexible working arrangements can essentially eliminate any of the positive results these programs should produce. Top management will need to ensure that the organizational culture is tolerant of alternative work schedules.

Diversity and tolerance

In regard to managing global diversity, HR management should not begin with the assumption that US or Canadian solutions are universally accepted and universally applicable. Perhaps the most fundamental lesson of US and Canadian diversity practices is to listen to others, include their viewpoints, and allow them involvement and ownership of their solutions (Sherwood, 2006). Although globalization has been a popular concept for a long time, the idea of global diversity management is still in its infancy.

It is important not to assume that your values are the best for the organization. For example, in the United States and Canada, the culture is more individualistic which is often viewed as productive. While individual competition can be positive to some degree, cultural values in other countries, such as China, emphasize the importance of family, friends, and social relationships. Loyalty to the organization is more common in China than in North America, for example.

In regard to culture within an organization, developing a culture of tolerance is important due to the diversity inherent in organizations today. Diversity involves not only racial and ethnic differences, but also gender, age, and lifestyle differences. In organizations, diversity is often considered a strategy for improving employee retention and increasing consumer confidence and, thus, the reputation of the firm. In a global and diverse marketplace, an organization whose makeup mirrors the makeup of the marketplace it serves is better equipped to do well than an organization whose makeup is homogeneous.

It is important, however, for an organization to utilize its diversity – this is called inclusion. If an organization is diverse, but all of the decisions are made by one primary, homogeneous group, diversity is not going to add much value to the organization. Thus, organizational cultures need to be tolerant of others in the workplace. Tolerance means employees do not persecute or discriminate against those who may believe or behave in ways which they may not agree with. Further, for diversity to be effective, cultural tolerance is really the minimum requirement – organizational cultures should embrace diversity and utilize it.

The benefits of a diverse workforce are becoming better understood. Research suggests that a diverse workforce provides economic rewards because diverse and heterogeneous groups bring different perspectives to bear on problems, helping creativity and innovation (Crosby *et al.*, 2003). However, managing diversity can be a challenge for organizations as the variety in the demographic profile is reflected in the range of employee attitudes and values. By and large, this is a complex problem; the similarity among workforce participants is decreasing, thus requiring unique interactions by leaders tailored to the specific needs of diverse organizational members. Diversity consultants and trainers are available to help organizations develop a strong culture of tolerance and diversity.

Work–life programs

Work–life programs are important tools HR professionals can use to attract and retain top employees. Employees experiencing work or family stress could benefit from having access to a fitness center, childcare benefits, and seminars on topics like elder care, financial planning, or professional counseling services. These types of benefits for employees are often very cost effective for organizations. For example, fitness centers have been shown to be very cost effective for organizations by lowering absenteeism due to illness (Feinstein, 1990). This is not to say that all organizations need to develop a fitness center on site – this may not be practical. However, encouraging good nutrition and exercise is not very costly. For example, organizations might be able to help their employees by partially funding their memberships to local fitness centers.

Working parents with small children are commonplace in our society. The costs of daycare and the inconvenience of taking and picking up children are barriers to many working parents. To support these individuals, some organizations have opened on-site daycare programs or partially subsidize daycare in a nearby facility. It is important to remember, however, that childless workers might believe they are subsidizing benefits for working parents and may be disgruntled. To help this situation, some companies have gone to a cafeteria plan of benefits that allows employees to pick and choose from a variety of benefit options. For example, a young, single parent might place a greater value on childcare than an older worker, who might place a higher value on retirement and long-term health insurance benefits.

Finally, organizations can develop programs or bring in consultants to present seminars that are important to the work–life initiative. Not only can seminars on topics such as financial planning, elder care, and managing stress help employees gain important information, but also these types of activities demonstrate that the organization is concerned about the employee both on and off the job. Whether the organization is providing programs for employees, developing diverse benefit plans, or creating new work scheduling options, the importance of employee involvement in determining the types of strategies and programs an organization embraces cannot be overstated.

Employee involvement has been shown to provide great benefits to the employee and the organization. Employee involvement is based on two principles that managers have been familiar with for many years. First, employees tend to support what they helped to create. For example, if employees are involved with developing flexible scheduling programs, they are more likely to be committed to these programs and more likely to take advantage of these programs. Second, employees who know most about the inner functioning of an operation are those who actually perform the work. Asking for information about, for example, flexible scheduling, and participation of the people actually performing the job can provide insights not available from managers or consultants.

Outcomes of HR responses

The outcomes of HR responses will affect the employees as well as the organization directly. Responses that include flexibility, diversity, and tolerance, and work–life programs will likely lead to positive outcomes for the employee and employing organization. One of the goals of these responses is to better the person–environment fit. In other words, these HR responses are an attempt to ensure that the needs of the person are met by the organization and vice versa. Person–environment fit theory states that stress arises not from the person or environment separately, but rather from the misfit between the person and the environment (Edwards and Rothbard, 2005).

Flexible work schedules have been found to increase productivity and job satisfaction (Baltes *et al.*, 1999). Further, schedule flexibility regarding work arrangements gives employees greater control over work and family matters, thereby helping employees manage the often conflicting demands of work and family. Interestingly, simply offering flexible work schedules may not convince employees to take advantage of scheduling options, particularly if they do not believe management supports these types of programs. In other words, employees may be concerned that their supervisor may not view using a flexible work schedule favorably. For example, Kossek *et al.* (1999) found that when managers provide an example and make visible to others that flexible work arrangements are viable options for employees, employees are more likely to use such schedules themselves. It has also been proposed that flexible work schedules lead to better employee attitudes, more loyalty and commitment to the organization, lower levels of turnover, higher job satisfaction, and higher performance (Kossek *et al.*, 2005).

As mentioned earlier, an organization whose makeup mirrors the makeup of the marketplace it serves is better equipped to do well than an organization whose makeup is homogeneous. It makes sense that a diverse workforce would be more in touch with a diverse marketplace. Not only does developing a culture of diversity and tolerance help the organization connect with its market, but also this type of culture is the best at retaining top employees. The reputation of the organization is often enhanced when consumers see an effort by the organization to embrace diversity. Diversity can serve as a positive recruiting tool that allows companies to attract the best applicants. Companies included in *Fortune*'s or *Business Week*'s lists of the top companies for women, ethnic and racial minorities, people with disabilities and/or the general population, attract more applicants than do their competitors.

Finally, programs aimed at helping employees by giving them information on topics such as work–family balance, financial planning, and fitness are ways to increase employee commitment as well as fit with the organization. Be sure to ask the employees about the types of programs they would like to have. The benefits of involving employees in the decisions about these programs and initiatives are huge. Employee involvement provides employees with a greater understanding of why decisions are made. Involvement has been shown to lead to higher employee commitment to the organization as well as higher productivity. Employee involvement simply helps to produce better decisions.

Moderating factors

Factors that may affect the relationship between HR responses and outcomes include the resources within the firm to allow parental leave, the job design of the firm to allow flexibility in working hours, and the ability and willingness of management to embrace change. Thus, even if the HR professionals would like to implement flexible work scheduling, leaves of absence, and diversity and work–life training programs, factors beyond their control may hinder their efforts. It is important for HR professionals to work closely with others in top management to make sure not only that any programs developed are accepted, but also that they are viable for the organization.

Summary and guidelines

The modern North American workforce and the modern North American family are rapidly changing. At no other point in history have older employees and dual-earner families been as prevalent in the workforce as they are today. Furthermore, increased life expectancies have created the first "sandwich" generation of employees, simultaneously moving between care-giving roles for children and for aging loved ones. Intuitively, these additional role demands have contributed to shifting attitudes toward retirement and the changing roles of older employees. As care-giving roles change, it is increasingly likely that older employees will experience the inter-role conflict inherent in the interaction of the work and family domains. Further, with globalization at an all-time high, concern for diversity and tolerance becomes paramount for success.

This chapter has focused on what organizations and HR professionals can do to help work–life integration for employees; however, it is also important for employees to help themselves. If employees would like more control over their work environment and work schedule, it is important for them to speak up for themselves. Recent research describes the linkages between employees speaking up and flexible work scheduling compromises being developed between employees and top management (Edmondson and Detert, 2005). Conflicts between work and non-work demands occur frequently in organizations and employees need to express their needs in order to have the type of work schedule and autonomy they desire. Of course, a critical component to this being effective is having a management culture that is tolerant of these types of requests. Also, top management will need to create conditions under which employees are able to make contributions to the collective work outside of the traditional work week and this may require management to redesign some of the jobs.

Employees may also benefit from received social support from others in a similar situation. Social support from others can help reduce distress experienced from work–life demands. In a general sense, social support can be delineated into instrumental support and emotional support. Instrumental support refers to the availability of tangible resources via other people whereas emotional support refers to the act of talking with others who listen with caring ears; this subsequently places individuals in a positive mood. Emotional support is a necessary precursor to instrumental support because individuals who are willing to lend tangible resources (e.g., money or temporary housing) must first understand the needy individuals' plight. As such, supportive individuals who are willing to provide instrumental support are also likely to be emotionally available to needy individuals.

Table 5.1 Guidelines for addressing the changing family

1 Involve employees in work–life initiative programs and allow them to help develop the topics.
2 Technology may not be a liberating force for work–life integration, thus HR management must be concerned with technology as a means for autonomy, not as a means to expect employee availability at all times.
3 Encourage support networks and social relationships such that individuals with similar needs can find each other.
4 Encourage stress reduction and fitness programs for employees.
5 Create alternative work schedules that give employees autonomy over when and, if possible, where they work.
6 Ensure that employees do not incur any negative repercussions as a result of taking advantage of alternative work schedules.
7 Employees should learn to speak up regarding their needs in order to have alternative work schedules or other benefits.
8 Employees should seek social support from others in similar situations.
9 Develop diversity training programs for managers and employees.
10 In regard to global diversity management, listen to those in other countries and allow them ownership over their solutions.

One example of social support comes from a group of female attorneys in Miami, Florida who have developed a formal initiative called "Focus on Women" that is aimed at sharpening their business and networking skills. The basic idea is to make business development a team effort with events that connect women attorneys and powerful women executives. Most of these women have children under 18 years of age and are fighting the misperception that too much of a focus is on children, aging parents, or other perceived "women's issues." Building relationships with others in similar situations not only is good for social support, but also makes good business sense.

See Table 5.1 for a list of specific guidelines, based on this discussion, offered to the employee and the organization. By following these guidelines, employees and employers will help increase the likelihood of positive outcomes to their responses to the changing family.

References

Baltes, B.B., Briggs, T.E., Huff, J.W., Wright, J.A. and Neuman, G.A (1999) Flexible and compressed workweek schedules: A meta-analysis of their effects on work-related criteria. *Journal of Applied Psychology*, 84: 496–513.
Barnett, R.C., Raudenbush, S.W., Brennan, R.T., Pleck, J.H. and Marshall, N.L. (1995) Change in job and marital experiences and change in psychological distress: A longitudinal study of dual-earner couples. *Journal of Personality and Social Psychology*, 69(5): 839–850.

Chamberlin, J. (2005) Adopting a new American family. *Monitor on Psychology*, 36: 70–71.

Chow, E.N. (2003) Gender matters: Studying globalization and social change in the 21st century. *International Sociology*, 18(3): 443–460.

Clay, R.A. (2005) Making working families work. *Monitor on Psychology*, 36: 54–56.

Crosby, F.J., Iyer, A., Clayton, S. and Downing, R.A. (2003) Affirmative action: Psychological data and the policy debates. *American Psychologist*, 58: 93–115.

DeAngelis, T. (2005) Stepfamily success depends on ingredients. *Monitor on Psychology*, 36: 58–61.

Dingfelder, S.F. (2005) The kids are all right. *Monitor on Psychology*, 36: 66–68.

Edmondson, A.C. and Detert, J.R. (2005) The role of speaking up in work–life balancing. In E.E. Kossik and S.J. Lambert (eds.), *Work and Life Integration: Organizational, Cultural, and Individual Perspectives* (pp. 401–427). London: Lawrence Erlbaum.

Edwards, J.R. and Rothbard, N.P. (2005) Work and family stress and well-being: An integrative model of person-environment fit within and between the work and family domains. In E.E. Kossik and S.J. Lambert (eds.), *Work and Life Integration: Organizational, Cultural, and Individual Perspectives* (pp. 211–242). London: Lawrence Erlbaum.

Feinstein, S. (1990) Health promotion brings dollar-and-cents return, a study shows. *The Wall Street Journal*, September 18: A1.

Glenn, E.N. (2001) Gender, race, and organization of reproductive labor. In R. Baldoz, C. Koerber and P. Kraft (eds.), *The Critical Study of Work* (pp. 71–82). Philadelphia, PA: Temple University Press.

Kanter, R. (1977) *Men and Women of the Corporation*. New York: Basic Books.

Kossek, E.E., Barber, A.E. and Winters, D. (1999) Using flexible schedules in the managerial world: The power of peers. *Human Resource Management*, 38: 33–46.

Kossek, E., Lautsch, B. and Eaton, S. (2005) Flexibility enactment theory: Relationships between type, boundaries, control and work–family effectiveness. In E.E. Kossek and S. Lambert (eds.), *Work and Life Integration: Organizational, Cultural and Psychological Perspectives* (pp. 243–262). Mahwah, NJ: Lawrence Erlbaum.

Lewis, S. and Haas, L. (2005) Work–life integration and social policy: A social justice theory and gender equity approach to work and family. In E.E. Kossik and S.J. Lambert (eds.), *Work and Life Integration: Organizational, Cultural, and Individual Perspectives* (pp. 349–374). London: Lawrence Erlbaum.

Mische, M.A. (2000) *Strategic Renewal: Becoming a High Performance Organization*. Upper Saddle River, NJ: Prentice Hall.

Poster, W.R. (2005) A transnational approach to work–life policy. In E.E. Kossik and S.J. Lambert (eds.), *Work and Life Integration: Organizational, Cultural, and Individual Perspectives* (pp. 375–400). London: Lawrence Erlbaum.

Reynolds, S., Ridley, N. and Van Horn, C.E. (2005) A work-filled retirement: Workers' changing views on employment and leisure. *WorkTrends: Americans' Attitudes about Work, Employers, and Government*. Center for Survey Research and Analysis, University of Connecticut and the J.J. Heldrich Center for Workforce Development, Rutgers University.

Sherwood, S. (2006) Global diversity management: Cultures in dialogue. *DiversityInc.*, January/February: 24–30.

Valcour, P.M. and Hunter, L.W. (2005) Technology, organizations, and work–life integration. In E.E. Kossik and S.J. Lambert (eds.), *Work and Life Integration: Organizational, Cultural, and Individual Perspectives* (pp. 61–84). London: Lawrence Erlbaum.

RETAINING NEW MOTHERS

Leslie Quest is the HR manager for a medium-sized firm in Texas. She has noticed that they have lost numerous upwardly mobile professional female employees who had just had children. Although most intended to return to work after they had children, many did not. The company follows all Family Medical Leave Act regulations and provides some flextime.

Related questions

1 What other benefits could Leslie introduce that may help retain new mothers?
2 What are the potential legal liabilities of introducing these benefits?
3 What are the other potential advantages and disadvantages of such benefits?

Part II

Areas of increased importance

6 Ethics and HRM

K. MICHELE KACMAR

Formally defined, ethics is the study of morality (Velasquez, 2002). Morality, or morals, are the standards by which you judge right from wrong. The standards you use to judge a behavior are set by the values you hold. Values are the degree of conviction you have to the way you conduct your life. They are the basic convictions that a specific mode of conduct or end-state of existence is preferable to an opposite or converse mode of conduct or end-state of existence (Rokeach, 1968). The degree of conviction to your values can be described as primary, secondary, or peripheral. Primary or core values are the values or convictions you have that are unwavering. These values define who you are. When others are asked to describe you, they do so by describing your core values. For instance, individuals who take good care of their bodies and work out religiously will always make time to go to the gym because they value their health and the benefits they receive from being healthy. Secondary values are those that are important to you, but that you would forgo under certain circumstances. Individuals who enjoy working out but who are willing to miss a workout or two would fall into this category. Finally, peripheral values are those that you recognize, but do not live by. Individuals who know where the gym is but have never set foot in it would hold working out as a peripheral value. As hinted above, your values determine your behavior. This can be seen in how people spend their free time. Activities engaged in when no parameters exist reflect an individual's value system.

The relationship between ethics, moral standards, values, and behavior is diagrammed in Figure 6.1. Since values are a key component to ethics, let's look at these more closely. Values cannot be seen. Instead, values are implied through your behavior. The degree of commitment people have to their values separates those who are willing to stand on the side of the road holding a sign in support of a cause they value from those who drive by and wonder what would possess someone to stand on the side of the road and hold a sign. Many of your values, especially your core values,

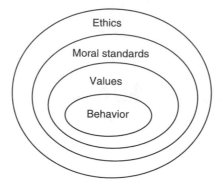

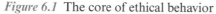

Figure 6.1 The core of ethical behavior

were learned early in life from key role models such as your parents, family, and friends. However, experiences you have had, exposure to the media, and emotional and intellectual development may have reshaped your values (Kohlberg, 1976). Let's say that you grew up in a strictly Democratic household. Everyone in your family voted Democratic for as far back as anyone can remember. Thus, as you grew up, you saw yourself as a Democrat. While in college you met a person who captivated you. Unfortunately, this person was extremely active in the Young Republicans Association. In order to be with this person, you were forced to spend time at Republican rallies. At one such rally, you heard a Republican candidate speak. Given that you are a Democrat, you were surprised by how much the candidate's message resonated with you. This experience made you begin to question your commitment to the Democratic Party. Such a response suggests that the experience of being exposed to Republicans may help to move being a Democrat from a primary value to a secondary value.

Explosive and devastating outcomes can occur when individuals hold conflicting core values. Doctors who value choice and who are willing to conduct abortions become targets of individuals who value life enough to bomb an abortion clinic or shoot doctors who perform abortions. In the business world, top officials who value their own success over the success of their company can run a firm into bankruptcy if someone does not stop them in time. Business scandals reported on the news and in the *Wall Street Journal* on a daily basis occur because people hold different values. One person will look at a situation and see an opportunity to make money while another sees a loophole that needs closing. The strength of commitment an individual has to his or her values is what makes one person a willing participant in a shady deal and another a whistleblower.

Environmental factors

Since the mid 1990s, ethical scandals in business have been on the rise. Familiar examples of major corporations that have been involved in scandals include Enron,

WorldCom, Tyco, and HealthSouth. In virtually all of these cases top officials including Ken Lay, Bernard Ebbers, Dennis Kozlowski, and Richard Schrushy pleaded ignorance to knowledge of, or involvement in, any corrupt activities in their organizations. Whether or not their pleas were true, ethical problems at the top are clearly evident in each of these cases. If these men were aware of and/or participated in the dishonest activities in their organizations and lied about it, changes are needed to limit the possibility of this occurring in the future. Further, if it is true that these top officials were unaware of the ethical scandals within their organizations then changes are needed so that future CEOs will make it their job to be more aware. This begs the question of how to prevent and deter unethical and illegal activities from occurring in organizations. Research has shown that a combination of external regulations and compliance programs and voluntary corporate ethics programs is the most effective way to combat inappropriate corporate behavior (Trevino *et al.*, 1999).

With respect to external regulations and compliance, in 2002 the US Congress passed the Sarbanes–Oxley Act (SOX). (See Chapters 4 and 13 for further discussions of SOX.) This legislation was designed to protect the public from top officials who knowingly or unknowingly allow unethical and illegal behaviors to occur in their organizations. One key provision of SOX is the requirement that CEOs and chief financial officers (CFOs) sign statements making them personally responsible for the accuracy of the quarterly financial statements. Knowingly misrepresenting the financials opens them up to punishments including fines and jail time. Adding this requirement to SOX was designed to eliminate the claims of ignorance described above. SOX also requires that financial officers develop, sign, and follow a code of ethics that is registered with the Securities and Exchange Commission (SEC). Another important aspect of SOX is that it provides protection for whistleblowers, which may encourage more people to report activities they know are wrong without fear of retaliation or retribution.

There are a variety of other external regulations that help to encourage members of organizations to act ethically. Examples include compensation laws that specify the minimum an organization can legally pay its employees as well as laws that specify overtime pay requirements (Anthony *et al.*, 2006). Other key HR regulations that promote the ethical treatment of employees include discrimination and affirmative action laws, safety and health regulations, dismissal requirements, and privacy issues. However, not all companies abide by the laws on the books. Wal-Mart has faced multiple law suits regarding treatment of women and minorities (Zehr, 2001) and its pay policies (Armour, 2003). One such claim stemmed from pushing its low-cost strategy down to its suppliers. This required some of its suppliers to operate under sweatshop conditions in order to turn a profit. Employees of Wal-Mart's suppliers claimed to have been paid less than the minimum wage and to have been forced to work overtime for no pay, a practice for which Wal-Mart has been repeatedly sued. One of the lawsuits filed against Wal-Mart claimed that it is reasonable to assume that Wal-Mart would have known that its suppliers had to violate workers' rights to meet Wal-Mart's demands. Wal-Mart denied knowledge and stated that it strives to do business only with factories that are run legally and ethically. Let us hope that being publicly found to have failed in this goal will help Wal-Mart do better in the future.

Responses

One response organizations are showing to the increased pressure to act ethically is the voluntary creation of an internal ethics program. One of the key components of an internal ethics program is the development and dissemination of a corporate code of ethics. Codes of ethics range in type and content. At one end of the spectrum are codes of ethics that lay out standards of acceptable behaviors or policies that must be followed. Thus, when employees face an ethical dilemma, there is no question about how they should behave. An example of such a code of ethics would be when firms set monetary limits on gifts that employees can accept. Any gift that exceeds the established limit must be declined. Failure to decline such gifts can lead to reprimands or dismissal. Obviously, not every possible ethical dilemma can be covered in procedural codes of ethics. Thus, this type of ethical code is often paired with another type, a corporate values statement.

A corporate values statement clearly describes the core values the company wants its employees to exhibit. Frequently included in core values statements are descriptions of how employees are to treat one another as well as the firm's primary and secondary stakeholders (e.g., stockholders, customers, communities). To be most effective, the values statement must come from the top with the CEO being directly involved in its development. Top management must also actively disseminate the values statement and then live by it. Without demonstrated buy-in from the top, a values statement will not produce the type of behavior it was designed to elicit. Finally, the more focal the values statement is in the organization, the more useful it will be in creating and sustaining acceptable behavior. Thus, it is critical to disseminate it widely and to frequently follow up to ensure everyone is aware of and abiding by the corporate values. To ensure that its purpose, values, and principles are understood and used by all its employees, Procter and Gamble routinely surveys its employees. The questions asked focus on whether employees at all levels (e.g., high-level leaders, their direct managers, other employees in their area) consistently follow the company's purpose, values, and principles.

HR responses and ethics

Many of the key activities HR traditionally engages in help to uniquely position it to be able to create and maintain an ethical environment. For instance, one of the most important steps is understanding the organization's ethical climate. To accomplish this, an organization must formally assess its culture. HR departments traditionally charged with conducting employee surveys can use their expertise to discover what behaviors are routinely being rewarded and reinforced, what values and attitudes are prevalent, and how strong the pressure to engage in misconduct is. Once the current culture is uncovered, steps can be taken to eliminate and discourage reasons for misbehavior and introduce and encourage reasons to behave ethically.

A second natural connection between ethics and HR is training. It is simply not enough to create and post a code of ethics. For the code to become instilled enough in the minds of the employees to provide them guidance for making business decisions on a daily basis, training is needed. One example of how this can work is the Club Aluminum Company. In the early 1930s, Herbert Taylor was the CEO of the struggling Club Aluminum Company based in Chicago. In an effort to turn his company around, Taylor penned a code of ethics that he required be used to make any and every corporate decision. Applying Taylor's code of ethics required that employees ask themselves four simple questions: Is what you are saying the truth? Is it fair to all concerned? Will it build goodwill and better friendships? Will it be beneficial to all concerned? A decision was acceptable only when the employee could answer yes to all four questions. Training Club Aluminum employees to internalize and apply this code of ethics to every decision made is credited with turning the company around. Interestingly, the Rotary Club, a worldwide organization composed of business and professional leaders that provides humanitarian service and encourages high ethical standards in all vocations, adopted Taylor's code of ethics as its own. Dubbed the 4 Way Test, it today stands as one of the Rotary Club's hallmarks.

Still another HR component that helps instill ethics in the workplace is the performance appraisal process. Individuals work for rewards, whether they be monetary, physical, or emotional. Developing an appraisal system that rewards individuals for ethical behaviors and punishes those who act unethically helps to reinforce the ethical climate. Incorporating the enforcement of ethical behavior into the reward structure of managers also will help to encourage a unified message. For instance, managers whose areas meet their quarterly numbers, but do so by engaging in unethical means, could be treated as though they had missed their target. Alternatively, an area that missed its numbers, but did so because it acted in a benevolent and ethical manner (e.g., donated stock to flood victims rather than selling it), may be treated as though it had made its goal.

Finally, HR can use its expertise in communicating with the workforce to get out the ethical message. Newsletters and intranets can be used by HR to publicize the importance of ethical behavior in the organization. It is imperative that the ethics message comes from the top as key officials set the ethical tone for the entire organization. This is known as "tone at the top." Publicly interviewing top officials about their views on ethics and the importance of employees acting ethically can help to reinforce the message. This approach also can be used to change the organizational culture by introducing stories of heroic ethical behavior enacted by key officials in the organization. These stories will be shared with others and become part of the evolving ethical culture.

The outcomes of corporate ethics responses: costs and benefits

Many believe that the cost of allowing unethical behavior to occur in organizations is too high not to respond. Estimates of the costs associated with recent business scandals (e.g., Enron, Tyco, WorldCom, HealthSouth) top $7 trillion in stock market losses (Heffes, 2003). This cost does not include the cost incurred by employees in these firms who lost their jobs and their retirement savings. However, there are others who argue that the government went too far with SOX and that the costs of implementing and maintaining compliance to create an ethical business environment is too high. Results from a survey by Financial Executive International found that firms with $5 billion in revenue could expect to spend an average of $4.7 million implementing the internal controls needed to comply with SOX and an additional $1.5 million a year to maintain compliance (Volcker and Levitt, 2004). Using these numbers to calculate a national total, the costs of SOX come to $5.5 billion per year (Cavanaugh, 2006). Most believe that such expense is needed to make investors trust in business again.

In addition to the monetary costs are human costs. Working in an unethical environment can demotivate individuals. For instance, those who know that reporting their legitimate sales will not be sufficient to receive their annual bonus face a choice. They can receive their bonus by pre-booking sales or shipping unordered merchandise to a customer with a note telling them to return what they do not want after the end of the quarter (Silver, 2002) or they can report their actual sales and forgo their bonus. If creative reporting practices are ignored and not punished, there is little incentive for sales people to actually sell anything. Further, such environments encourage ethical sales people to self-select themselves out of the organization and attract those who prefer creative accounting to making sales. Clearly, this is the opposite of what a company would want to happen.

Other human costs stemming from an unethical workplace include the lack of trust and loyalty of the employees to one another and to the firm. When individuals work to better themselves, the firm's goals fall by the wayside. Such environments are ripe for failure. The failure can stem from individuals' self-focused behaviors undermining the corporate goals (Ferris *et al.*, 1989), reduced productivity due to the lack of trust and cooperation among workers (Kacmar *et al.*, 1999), or top management entering into lucrative contracts that they knowingly cannot fulfill.

Many of the recent public displays of unethical behavior exhibited by corporations have led some to suggest that taking the high road in all business decisions is the best long-term business strategy to adopt (Velasquez, 2002). Just as Club Aluminum found back in the 1930s, sustained ethical behavior can benefit firms. These benefits can be seen through increased profits, loyal, repeat customers, lack of SEC inquiries, fewer law suits, and highly motivated and committed employees. Granted, there will be times when doing the right thing will result in losing a lucrative contract or a valued employee. However, sustained unethical behavior will eventually be discovered, often with catastrophic consequences. In the long run, the companies with managers who remain true to their moral and ethical convictions will flourish.

Guidelines for fostering an ethical culture

The Ethics Resource Center, the oldest non-profit organization in the United States devoted to organizational ethics, has developed a variety of tools and suggestions for helping to foster an ethical climate in organizations. One such tool, the Ethics Effectiveness Quick-Test, can be found on its website (http://www.ethics.org/quicktest/index.cfm). This test asks eight questions about twelve different areas that can help to increase the ethical effectiveness in an organization. Some of the areas include rewarding ethical behavior, creating ethical policies and procedures, ethics training, and making sure those in positions of leadership lead in an ethical manner. By taking the test, managers are able to identify, from an ethical perspective, what is working well within their organizations and where improvement might be required.

When no policies and procedures exist to help structure employees' behaviors, they are free to act as they wish (Kacmar and Baron, 1999). The lack of a well-developed policy and procedures manual allows individuals the opportunity to take advantage of situations that present themselves. For instance, if a supplier offers free tickets to a sold-out concert or sporting event, some employees may be tempted to accept them. However, accepting such a gift may create a conflict of interest. In other words, the employee may feel obligated to help the supplier in the future by offering them better terms to pay them back for the tickets. All of this can be avoided by having a policy about accepting gifts. Many firms allow employees to accept small gifts (e.g., up to $50) as long as they inform their supervisor. The amount set is one that all could agree would not create a feeling of indebtedness. When the gift exceeds the set price, as the tickets in our example most likely would, it must be turned down.

While having a strong policy and procedures manual in place can go a long way in creating an ethical environment, the policies are useful only if they are enforced. Thus, any individual who accepts a gift that exceeds the limit must be dealt with according to the policy. This may mean reprimanding the individual verbally or in writing, or even dismissing him or her if the gift is sufficiently large. On the flip side, when individuals adhere to the policies and procedures they need to be rewarded. Individuals who report to their supervisor that a supplier was trying to give them tickets will be heralded as a model employee and this action also will allow the company to address the issue with the supplier.

Another way to foster an ethical culture is to recruit employees with strong moral character. Individuals who are described as having a good character are those who are viewed as having integrity, trust, and loyalty (Wolfe, 2002). Such characteristics also can be developed and reinforced after an employee is hired. The need to have all employees demonstrate strong character is critical for developing and maintaining an ethical culture. Only in such an environment will employees cooperate with one another, build a trusting work environment, and become committed to the organization and its mission.

Creating a corporate division responsible for the ethical tone of the firm speaks volumes about its perspective on doing the right thing. Rather than simply offering lip service to taking the high road, developing a division and appointing a high-ranking official to oversee the unit greatly elevates the importance of ethics in the organization. One example of how this can be done effectively is in Ernst and Young. In 2003, Ernst and Young, through an in-depth eighteen-month procedure, created a values statement that explains who they are and what they do. Following this, they turned to the job of creating a Code of Conduct that outlined how Ernst and Young employees should approach their jobs. Rather than being rules or procedure based, the Code of Conduct is values based which helps individuals to think about and select their own way of fulfilling the Code of Conduct. Ernst and Young's Values Statement is reproduced in Table 6.1. Finally, in order to keep the values and Code of Conduct alive in the minds of Ernst and Young employees, they created an Ethics and Oversight Board who conduct a gap analysis to determine how closely the day-to-day behaviors map to the Code of Conduct. Finally, they appointed an Ethics and Compliance Officer to set and advertise the tone at the top. Since his appointment, Jeffrey Hoops has focused on developing tools for the employees at Ernst and Young to allow them to live by the firm's Code of Conduct.

See Table 6.2 for a list of specific guidelines, based on this discussion, to help organizations foster an ethical climate.

In closing I'd like to offer one final suggestion designed to encourage everyone to take the high road when making decisions in life. Whenever you are required to make a difficult decision, especially one that is ethically challenging, select an option that you would be comfortable describing to the nation on the evening news. We can all be confident that if the individuals responsible for Enron, WorldCom, Tyco, and

Table 6.1 Values statement of Ernst and Young

Our Values Statement
(Who we are and what we stand for)
People who demonstrate integrity, respect, and teaming. People with energy, enthusiasm, and the courage to lead. People who build relationships based on doing the right thing.
When we developed our Values Statement, we asked hundreds of our people across the world to tell us what they thought about *who we are and what we stand for*, as individuals and as an organization. There was a remarkable level of consistency in their responses. We built our Values Statement on those responses. That's why we know that it truly reflects the way our people act and behave worldwide.

Source: http://www.ey.com/global/content.nsf/International/About_EY_-_Values

Table 6.2 Guidelines for fostering an ethical climate

1 Measure your organization's ethical effectiveness.
2 Develop policies and procedures that provide strong ethical guidelines.
3 Enforce those policies and procedures by disciplining employees who violate them and rewarding employees who follow them.
4 Recruit and hire employees with strong moral character.
5 Develop and reinforce ethical behaviors after an employee is hired.
6 Create a corporate department responsible for the ethical tone of the firm.
7 Develop a values statement and codes of conduct.

HealthSouth had followed this rule, the ending to the story for each of these companies would have been different.

References

Anthony, W.P., Kacmar, K.M. and Perrewé, P.L. (2006) *Human Resource Management: A Strategic Approach.* Mason, OH: Thomson Custom Solutions.

Armour, S. (2003) Wal-Mart take hits on worker treatment. *USA Today*, February 10: 1.

Cavanaugh, G.F. (2006) *American Business Values.* Upper Saddle River, NJ: Prentice Hall.

Ferris, G.R., Russ, G. and Fandt, P. (1989) Politics in organizations. In R.A. Giacalone and P. Rosenfeld (eds.), *Impression Management in the Organization* (pp. 143–170). Hillsdale, NJ: Lawrence Erlbaum.

Heffes, E.M. (2003) Restoring corporate integrity and public trust. *Financial Executive*, June: 18–20.

Kacmar, K.M. and Baron, R.A. (1999) Organizational politics: The state of the field, links to related research, and an agenda for future research. In G.R. Ferris (ed.), *Research in Personnel and Human Resources Management* (vol. 17, pp. 1–39). Greenwich, CT: JAI Press.

Kacmar, K.M., Bozeman, D.P., Carlson, D.S. and Anthony, W.P. (1999) An examination of the perceptions of politics model: Replication and extension. *Human Relations*, 52: 383–416.

Kohlberg, L. (1976) Moral stages and moralization: The cognitive-development approach. In T. Lickona (ed.), *Moral Development and Behavior: Theory, Research, and Social Issues* (pp. 31–53). New York: Holt, Rinehart, and Winston.

Rokeach, M. (1968) *Beliefs, Attitudes, and Values.* San Francisco, CA: Jossey-Bass.

Silver, D. (2002) *Cookin' the Book$.* Los Angeles, CA: Adams-Hall.

Trevino, L.K., Weaver, G.R., Gibson, D.G. and Toffler, B.L. (1999) Managing ethics and legal compliance: What works and what hurts. *California Management Review*, 41(2): 131–151.

Velasquez, M.G. (2002) *Business Ethics: Concepts and Cases*, 5th edn. Upper Saddle River, NJ: Prentice Hall.

Volcker, P. and Levitt, A. Jr. (2004) In defense of Sarbanes–Oxley. *Wall Street Journal*, June 14: A16.

Wolfe, A. (2002) *Moral Freedom: The Search for Virtue in a World of Choice.* New York: Norton.

Zehr, D. (2001) Wal-Mart agrees to pay $6.8 million to settle disabilities lawsuits. *Arkansas Democrat-Gazette, Little Rock Knight Ridder/Tribune Business News*, December 18.

THE TRAVELING EMPLOYEE

James Philips is the supervisor for several employees who regularly travel to other countries as part of their job duties. James heard through informal channels that one of his employees was routinely visiting hashish houses and prostitutes whenever his work brought him to Amsterdam. Although illegal in the United States, both are legal in Amsterdam. The company had no policies regarding such behavior.

Related questions

1 What should James do in this case?
2 Should companies be concerned about what employees do during non-work hours?
3 Should employees be held to host country or home country ethical standards when traveling?

7 Health, safety and HRM

LOIS E. TETRICK AND MICHAEL T. FORD

In 1970, the US Congress enacted the Occupational Health and Safety Act requiring employers to provide safe and healthy work environments for their employees and, in turn, for employees to comply with existing standards applicable to their work. While the Act does mention psychological factors resulting from exposures at work, the focus of this legislation was on the existence and elimination of physical injuries and occupational illnesses. Therefore, much of the focus on health and safety in the workplace historically has focused on safety engineering, industrial hygiene, and occupational medicine and nursing. As a result, the responsibility for health and safety has traditionally been located outside of human resources, and instead centered in divisions and departments directly related to production. However, given the nature of today's and tomorrow's workplace, there are a number of current issues related to health and safety that should be of particular concern to human resource management, many of which are outlined here. These include external factors involving legal, demographic, and market trends, as well as internal factors such as employee stress, work and family issues, and workplace violence and incivility.

First, however, we must *define* health in organizations. The definition of health has undergone a metamorphosis at both the individual employee level and the organizational level (Hofmann and Tetrick, 2003). There is a growing recognition that health at the individual employee level is not only the absence of illness but also includes positive health or optimal functioning, and that psychosocial factors in the workplace can and do affect the health of employees and their families. At the same time, the definition of health at the organizational level has moved from focusing almost exclusively on return-on-investment and other financial indicators to include human resource factors such as turnover rates, the number of grievances, and the overall morale of employees of the organization. Healthy organizations are said to retain their employees, have fewer employee complaints, and maintain high workforce commitment and positive attitudes. The common elements among the definitions of both individual employee health and organizational health are the explicit recognition of environmental factors contributing to both ill-health and positive health and the acknowledgment of the relation between employee health and organizational health.

The purpose of this chapter is to discuss some of the current trends that are increasing the importance of health and safety in the workplace, and then describe some of the HR responses to these trends. In addition, we will provide some guidelines for HR departments in addressing health and safety issues in the workplace.

Environmental factors relative to health and safety

As suggested above, health and safety has continued to gain importance for organizations, based on several internal and external environmental factors. The division between internal and external is sometimes not clear, as the etiology of the factors might arguably arise both internally and externally. However, we have tried to identify some that are more external and those that are more internal to organizations and explain reasons for their relevance to workforce health and safety.

External environment

Americans with Disabilities Act

One external factor relative to the importance of health and safety to organizations is the enactment of the Americans with Disabilities Act of 1990 (ADA). The ADA was designed to promote the employment of individuals with disabilities. Disabilities in this sense are defined as impairments that limit one or more major life activities but do not prevent individuals from performing the essential duties of the job (Tetrick and Toney, 2002). A lack of adherence to the ADA can lead to litigation, which is likely to be costlier than making reasonable accommodations; some reports suggest the costs of reasonable accommodations are relatively nominal with many being $500 or less. National data do not appear to be available to assess national trends in the number of workers with disabilities in the workforce. However, the working conditions of individuals with disabilities who are employed do not appear to differ from those without disabilities (Yelin and Trupin, 2003), although according to the California Work and Health Survey, individuals with disabilities have lower employment rates and lower job security.

The ADA applies both to the selection of employees with disabilities and to employees who subsequently develop disabilities, requiring employers to provide reasonable accommodations to employees with disabilities. Given the aging workforce (see below and Chapter 5), the fact that the ADA applies to employees who may have been on the job for several years suggests that it is in the interest of employers to be concerned about the health and safety of their employees.

Family and Medical Leave Act

The Family and Medical Leave Act of 1993 (FMLA) requires employers to provide up to twelve weeks of job-protected leave for employees who need it for family or medical crises. The Act does not require employers to provide employees with pay while they are on leave, but does require them to allow employees to return to their job at the end of that leave. Only 16 percent of all employees took leave in 2000, which was about the same as in 1995, although according to Waldfogel (2001), older employees, married employees, and those with children were all more likely to take leave under the FMLA in 2000 than in 1995. One reason for low participation found in Waldfogel's study may lie in the fact that in 2000, approximately 40 percent of those surveyed had not heard of the FMLA and 50 percent didn't know whether they were covered by the FMLA.

The FMLA may contribute to employers' increased attention to health and safety in the workplace, while it is also likely that the enactment of this legislation makes salient the importance of employees' non-work life. Employers are increasingly concerned about work–family balance, especially as it affects their ability to attract and retain employees. (See Chapter 5 for more on work–life balance.)

Rising health care insurance costs

A third external factor that appears to have increased employers' attention to health and safety issues is rising health care insurance costs. Per capita health care expenditures increased between 5 and 9 percent per year between 1993 and 2002 (Buckley and Van Giezen, 2004). (See Chapter 11 for more on the rising costs of health care.) Legislative reforms in some states have provided health care cost reduction incentives for high-quality safety programs. For most organizations the cost of health care coverage for their employees is based on their experience levels, with insurance companies providing incentives and support to reduce accidents and illnesses. Several health promotion and wellness programs in organizations have been sold to management as a cost reduction effort. Hence it appears that there are increased incentives to reduce the risk of employee health decrements due to injuries and illnesses.

General workforce trends

Nationally, the North American workforce is becoming older, includes more women, and is ethnically and racially diverse. The diversity of the pool of qualified applicants has resulted in pressures to attract and retain employees. This, in and of itself, has not necessarily increased employers' concerns about health and safety, but it does play out in internal factors that may have increased such concerns. (See Chapter 5 for details on general workforce trends.)

Internal environment

Job stress

There is evidence that employees are experiencing more distress than ever before. A 2002 national survey found that half of all workers see job stress as a major problem, which is over double the proportion who expressed this view just ten years earlier (National Institute for Occupational Safety and Health (NIOSH), 2004). This may be attributed in part to the increased emphasis on lean production and the corresponding increases in employee workload. A $10 billion per year stress management industry has emerged out of the increased prevalence and salience of workplace stress. Management and the control of job stress therefore has become increasingly important for organizations in dealing with traditional role stressors and newly emerging phenomena.

Traditionally, key role stressors for employees include ambiguity, conflict, and overload (Kahn, 1980). Role ambiguity reflects a lack of clarity and specificity about one's occupational role responsibilities. Role conflict is the presence of competing or incompatible role demands. Role overload is created by having too much work to do, too little time to do that work, and/or not having the resources to complete the work required. There is evidence that these role demands are as high as ever, with more employees indicating they do not have enough time to meet all of the work demands with which they are confronted (Bond *et al.*, 1998).

While these traditional work role stressors are still an important part of today's business environment, other stressors have received attention in recent years. One emergent stressor is the conflict between work and family roles, which is prevalent today, with far more dual-earning couples in the United States now than there were even in the mid 1970s. Particularly important to organizations is the influence of family-related demands and other stressors on employee performance, health, and tenure. Work–family conflict is associated with psychological strain, depression, burnout, a higher intent to leave the organization, and lower job performance (Allen *et al.*, 2000); such consequences are important both to individual employees and organizations.

Technological advances also have impacted the nature of the stress that employees experience. For example, the telecommuting and other off-site work options that are now available may create isolation for participating employees. This in turn reduces the social interaction of these employees and the support they receive from their co-workers. Electronic communication can also blur the distinction between work and non-work due to increased expectations that workers check email and voice-mail accounts outside of normal office hours (Coovert and Thompson, 2003).

Finally, the service industry is the fastest-growing industry in the US economy, with a decline in manufacturing (Bureau of Labor Statistics, 2005). This is resulting in more jobs with a significant component of social interactions. Service-oriented work requires that employees regulate their emotions, especially in dealing with customers, and present themselves in a manner that enhances the impressions others have of the organization. Emotional regulation of this nature is associated with emotional exhaustion and employee energy depletion, particularly in jobs with a low degree of autonomy (Grandey *et al.*, 2005). Therefore, it is important for organizations to be aware of and manage these emotional labor demands on employees and adjust aspects of their jobs to enhance their control over their work.

Safety

There have been several recent trends with respect to occupational injuries and fatalities. We have seen the overall number of occupational injuries and days missed due to injuries decline between 1990 and 2005. Declines have been particularly notable in the occurrence of skin disease, poisoning, respiratory disease, and repeated trauma (Bureau of Labor Statistics, 2005). However, along with the expansion of service-producing businesses, we have seen an increase in the number of deaths in the retail and transportation industries. More specifically, from 1992 to 2004, the number of highway incidents (1,158 to 1,374) and falls from heights (600 to 815) that resulted in death increased considerably. There also has been an increase in the number of restricted work days, meaning that there are more employees coming to work unable to perform all work tasks due to an impairment of some sort. Hence, while improvements in employee safety have been made, workplace injuries remain a serious issue for HR management.

One area that has received recent attention in occupational safety research is safety climate. Safety climate refers to the shared perceptions of an organization's policies, practices, and procedures with respect to the priority placed on safety (Zohar, 1980). Employee safety can be accomplished through work design, such as by creating physical barriers between employees and known hazards, and through training and establishment of a climate that prioritizes safety and well-being. Organizations must be successful in managing the tension between safety and production, particularly when they have employees in hazardous occupations, to maintain their competitive advantage.

The trends discussed earlier relative to job stress and technology are also important for workplace safety. Factors that result in job stress also increase the chances of accident and injury (Barlow and Iverson, 2004). Advances in technology have created a training environment where employees are constantly being asked to learn to operate new machinery, and the use of computers can place individuals in physical positions that make them susceptible to musculoskeletal disorders (Coovert and Thompson, 2003). It is clear that while injuries are down overall since 1990, industry trends have created new challenges for organizations in maintaining the safety of employees.

Diversity and discrimination

The American workforce is more diverse than ever before. The percentage of the workforce comprised of women rose from 42.5 to 46.6 from 1980 to 2000, and is expected to increase to 47.9 by 2010 (NIOSH, 2004). There are also more non-whites, especially Hispanics, in the US workforce than in previous times. This creates the potential for discrimination or unequal treatment due to one's ascribed characteristics as opposed to qualifications for performance (Gutek et al., 1996). A national survey found that 6 percent of all respondents in the United States reported being fired, 13 percent reported not being given a promotion, and 16 percent reported not being hired for discriminatory reasons (Kessler et al., 1999). Discrimination is associated with negative mental health outcomes. Discrimination tied to an individual's group membership can have damaging effects on an individual's self-esteem. There also is some evidence that diversity can increase stress and make communication with co-workers more difficult. Hence, diversity brings forth issues related to health and well-being that managers need to address.

Sexual harassment, violence, and incivility

While workplace homicides have declined over the years, they still remain one of the leading causes of on-the-job fatalities. In general, it is safe to say that workplace violence, aggression, incivility, and harassment are serious issues for today's organizations. Interestingly, survey data suggest workers are more likely to report experiencing physical and non-physical aggression from members *outside* of the organization than they are from co-workers (LeBlanc and Kelloway, 2002). With the growth of service-related occupations, one would expect more interaction with customers in the coming years and in turn greater potential for aggression from outsiders. LeBlanc and Kelloway (2002) found that the experience of violence and aggression on the job and the perceived likelihood of future aggression were negatively related to psychosomatic well-being, and that aggression from co-workers and the likelihood of future violence were negatively related to emotional well-being.

Sexual harassment is also of concern to organizations. Sexual harassment can be broken down into three dimensions: gender harassment, unwanted sexual attention, and attempted sexual coercion. Organizational tolerance of harassing behaviors and the presence of women performing jobs that were traditionally held by men have been shown to predict the likelihood of harassment and warrant attention from managers. Research on sexual harassment has also shown it to be a proximal predictor of psychological distress and overall poor health (Fitzgerald *et al.*, 1997).

In summary, challenges exist for organizations in managing employee health and safety in a highly competitive and heavily service-based business environment. Furthermore, the workforce is as diverse as ever and problems with discrimination, harassment, and aggression still remain. These developments have led to several responses on the part of organizations in an attempt to enhance workforce health and safety.

HR responses

There are several current trends discussed above that are cause for concern with respect to the health and safety of employees, but there are a number of ways organizations can respond to these trends. In general, organizational health and safety interventions can be classified into two general categories: those that reduce and prevent strain and injury from occurring in the first place, and those that help to rehabilitate individuals who have already experienced strain and injury. The two main types of interventions that prevent strain are primary and secondary interventions. Primary interventions are those aimed at reducing or eliminating the *source* of strain and risk in the workplace and are targeted at everyone. Eliminating a workplace hazard or introducing more flexible working hours are examples of primary interventions. Secondary interventions target those individuals who are particularly at risk and help them to manage the causes of stress, strain, and injury. Finally, interventions that are aimed at rehabilitating those who have already experienced health decrements in order to mitigate the negative outcomes of those decrements are called tertiary interventions. Research supports the notion that primary prevention is the most effective to way manage workplace health (Cooper and Cartwright, 1997) and there are many ways that HR management can take a proactive and primary prevention approach to workforce well-being and safety. Here we discuss some specific examples of HR responses to health and safety trends.

Compensation

Underlying many analyses of hazardous occupations and jobs is the belief that differential compensation covers the increase in exposure to hazards. This economic perspective depends on the idea that organizations should compensate workers for the possible loss of their incomes at some future point in time because of work-related injuries and illnesses. While there is considerable evidence that suggests that hazardous duty pay at least partially compensates workers, there is very little evidence to suggest that hazardous duty pay actually increases safety (for a review see Sinclair and Tetrick, 2004). With that said, there is some evidence that financial incentives may promote safe behaviors as long as the incentive programs are aligned with other organizational systems and care is taken that such incentive programs are not having negative consequences such as underreporting of occupational illnesses and injuries.

Employee involvement and job enrichment

One way to promote employee well-being is to empower employees and involve them in organizational decisions. Jobs with a higher degree of autonomy, identity, and variety tend to result in more satisfied employees (Fried, 1991). Furthermore, employee participation in decisions has been shown to increase job satisfaction (Wagner, 1994). Organizations can involve their employees in the development and implementation of policies and practices related to occupational health and safety. It has been argued that giving employees more control over their situation can be helpful in reducing stress and anxiety. However, organizations must be cautious in targeting these "job enriching" factors so as not to overburden their workers. Responses that aim to redesign jobs must strike a balance to make work more interesting and meaningful while not creating excessive demands.

Diversity training

The growing diversity of the workforce has increased the need to train employees to work with others from a diverse set of backgrounds. Diversity training skyrocketed in the 1990s and includes training in areas such as sexual harassment and AIDS awareness. Diversity training can be integrated with other, more general training initiatives such as team building, mentoring programs, and management training. The goal of these programs is to change employee attitudes and behaviors and hopefully reduce discrimination, invalidation, workplace violence, incivility, and harassment. Evaluation of the various diversity programs in use is needed to insure they are having the intended results and to enhance our knowledge of the effects of the different components of such programs on various attitudes and behaviors. It is important for organizations to take into account the experience of the trainees and organizational goals when designing and implementing diversity training (Roberson *et al.*, 2001).

Work–life balance initiatives

In response to the growing number of dual-earning families and resulting non-work demands placed on many workers, organizations are engaging in practices that take into account the effect of employees' families on work and the effect of work on employees and their families. Policies that support work–life balance can be used to maintain and improve worker health and work–family balance. Flexible work hours and childcare assistance are examples of HR responses to the increasing number of dual-earning families in the workforce. Flexible leave options that go beyond the requirements of the FMLA are also used to promote a healthy balance between work and family. However, options such as these must be supported by management to be effective. A positive work–family culture characterized by managerial support and a lack of negative career consequences for utilizing work–family benefits increases the use of work–life balance initiatives (Thompson *et al.*, 1999).

Safety management

Injuries and fatalities on the job, while reduced in recent years, are still a concern for organizations, which means that interventions that target safety are of particular importance, especially to organizations with hazardous occupations. There are three general ways for organizations to target and prevent injuries. The first way is to eliminate hazards entirely by redesigning jobs such that exposure to hazards is no longer necessary. When possible, this is the most desirable option. Unfortunately, hazards are an inevitable part of many work environments, so the next option is to block access to hazards that the organization cannot eliminate. Barriers around hazards and machines that shut off automatically when contacted by humans are examples of this type of engineering control that organizations can use to protect their workers. The third and perhaps most common and important method for injury prevention involves training employees to recognize hazards and avoid them. An effective safety training program could involve a number of strategies. Traditionally on-the-job training has been a primary means for teaching knowledge and skills relative to safe workplace behavior. However, relatively brief classroom training sessions can be used to enhance employee knowledge about hazards. Classroom training can be especially effective if the main goal is to make sure employees have accurate information about risks and the organization's policies and practices with respect to those risks. Performance monitoring and feedback about safety performance are also important aspects of ongoing safety training; this feedback can be put into a meaningful context through the establishment of specific goals for safety to which employees can compare their performance. Finally, it is important for management to commit to and prioritize safety. Safety training programs are probably not going to be as effective in organizations that *in practice* penalize employees for the production costs that may result from safety compliance.

Employee assistance programs

While it is preferable to prevent injuries and health decrements, inevitably some workers are going to become injured or ill. Tertiary strategies are those used by organizations to help rehabilitate workers who have already experienced some degree of ill-health or injury. Employee assistance programs (EAPs) are one of the most common types of tertiary interventions. These programs are aimed at helping employees who are experiencing a range of personal concerns such as stress, family difficulties, substance abuse, financial troubles, and legal problems. They also are used to identify and fix productivity issues related to these experienced difficulties. Professional counseling on an individual and group level can be given to employees on-site or off-site and can be provided within or outside the organization. Research suggests that employees tend to be satisfied with these programs and that they can be successful in improving employee health and performance. However, the long-term benefits of EAPs may be limited, particularly when implemented without an accompanying primary prevention strategy, as discussed above.

Health promotion

Another way for HR to respond to increases in stress and job demands is to establish health promotion programs. Health promotion programs are aimed at increasing positive health behaviors such as exercise and relaxation techniques, while decreasing negative health behaviors such as smoking or unhealthy diets. Organizations can provide access to health and fitness facilities to further facilitate wellness. From a public health perspective, the workplace is a convenient location for providing information to adults about their health behavior and health promotion has been shown to potentially reduce the risk of chronic disease. From an organizational perspective, research on the effectiveness of health promotion activities has shown their potential to result in cost savings for companies (Bennett *et al.*, 2003).

Integration of health protection and health promotion

Most of the HR responses described above focus primarily on health protection by reducing exposure to unhealthy and unsafe work conditions or they focus primarily on health promotion including wellness programs. Health protection (safety) and health promotion (wellness) have developed through different literatures and have involved separate disciplines, for the most part. Health promotion activities such as smoking cessation and weight loss programs are typically voluntary and one of the challenges to these programs is getting those most at risk from these unhealthy behaviors to participate in the programs. One argument that is consistent with social exchange theory suggests that by incorporating health protection activities that include changes to the work environment, and employee advisory boards who signal to employees that the organization is committed to their health and safety, employees are more likely to reciprocate by participating in the health promotion activities (Sorensen *et al.*, 1996).

Guidelines

The above discussion has presented several internal and external factors that are affecting employees and organizations. These trends have significant implications for the health of employees, their families, and their employers. HR has responded in several ways as presented. Based on this review, we offer several guidelines (see Table 7.1 for a summary of these) for HR to maintain and enhance individual and organizational health.

Conduct health and safety audits

HR is ideally placed to conduct health and safety audits on a regular basis. These audits can involve reviewing absence information, health care insurance claims, workers' compensation claims, disability claims, incidences of accidents, and reports of job stress by units. Such monitoring makes it possible to identify areas within the organization that may be experiencing greater exposure to unhealthy or unsafe work conditions, allowing further investigation of possible factors that might be modified to reduce these exposures.

Incorporate health and safety into performance appraisals

Health and safety should be incorporated in formal performance appraisal systems of supervisors and managers, in recognition of the employer's responsibility to provide a safe and healthy work environment. Such a system needs to recognize the full spectrum of factors posing risks to safety and health as well as those factors that promote safety and health. Safety and health may be incorporated into workers' performance appraisals, but without safety and health being reinforced and rewarded at higher levels the results are not likely to be as desired.

Incorporate health and safety into compensation systems

In addition to formal performance appraisal systems, HR may consider providing incentives for safe behaviors and healthy behaviors. Such incentive programs must be

Table 7.1 Guidelines for health and safety through HR

1 Conduct health and safety audits.
2 Incorporate health and safety into performance appraisals.
3 Incorporate health and safety into compensation systems.
4 Integrate the health and safety functions within the organization.
5 Monitor the external environment for health and safety issues.
6 Promote the importance of health and safety.

designed and implemented in conjunction with other types of controls in the organization that affect safety and health.

Integrate the health and safety functions within the organization

The health and safety functions within the organization need to be integrated. This does not mean that HR has to incorporate all of these functions under the HR umbrella, but there need to be formal and informal linkages among the various units that are involved to insure that efforts by one unit are not offsetting activities in other units.

Monitor the external environment for health and safety issues

It is important for organizations to monitor the external environment to be aware of the identification of new risk factors and legal developments relative to employees' health and safety, and to be aware of new ways of promoting safe and healthy behaviors.

Promote the importance of health and safety

HR should continuously promote the importance of health and safety *in practice*, not just in policies. By following these guidelines, organizations will provide a healthier and safer workplace for their employees.

Conclusion

Numerous internal and external environmental factors have increased the importance of health and safety in the workplace. Organizations have responded by providing work–life balance initiatives, employee assistance programs, diversity training, and safety management, and by integrating health promotion with health protection. We have included some guidelines which can help organizations provide a healthier and safer workplace for their employees, which we believe will benefit the organization as well as the employees in the long term.

References

Allen, T.D., Herst, D.E.L., Bruck, C.S. and Sutton, M. (2000) Consequences associated with work-to-family conflict: A review and agenda for future research. *Journal of Occupational Health Psychology*, 5: 278–308.

Barlow, L. and Iverson, R.D. (2004) Workplace safety. In J. Barling, E.K. Kelloway and M.R. Frone (eds.), *Handbook of Work Stress* (pp. 247–265). Thousand Oaks, CA: Sage.

Bennett, J.B., Cook, R.F. and Pelletier, K.R. (2003) Toward an integrated framework for comprehensive organizational wellness: Concepts, practices, and research in workplace health promotion. In J.C. Quick and L.E. Tetrick (eds.), *Handbook of Occupational Health Psychology* (pp. 69–95). Washington, DC: American Psychological Association.

Bond, J.T., Galinsky, E. and Swanberg, J.E. (1998) *The 1997 National Study of the Changing Workforce*. New York: Families and Work Institute.

Buckley, J.E. and Van Giezen, R.W. (2004) Federal statistics on healthcare benefits and cost trends. *Monthly Labor Review*, 127(11): 43–56.

Bureau of Labor Statistics (2005) Available http://www.bls.gov/iif/oshcfoi1.htm#19922002 (accessed February 2, 2006).

Cooper, C.L. and Cartwright, S. (1997) An intervention strategy for workplace stress. *Journal of Psychosomatic Research*, 43: 7–16.

Coovert, M.D. and Thompson, L.F. (2003) Technology and workplace health. In J.C. Quick and L.E. Tetrick (eds.), *Handbook of Occupational Health Psychology* (pp. 221–241). Washington, DC: American Psychological Association.

Fitzgerald, L.F., Drasgow, F., Hulin, C.L., Gelfand, M.J. and Magley, V.J. (1997) Antecedents and consequences of sexual harassment in organizations: A test of an integrated model. *Journal of Applied Psychology*, 82: 578–589.

Fried, Y. (1991) A meta-analytic comparison of the Job Diagnostic Survey and Job Characteristics Inventory as correlates of work satisfaction and performance. *Journal of Applied Psychology*, 76: 690–697.

Grandey, A.A., Fisk, G.M. and Steiner, D.D. (2005) Must "service with a smile" be stressful? The moderating role of personal control for American and French employees. *Journal of Applied Psychology*, 90: 893–904.

Gutek, B.A., Cohen, A.G. and Tsui, A. (1996) Reactions to perceived sex discrimination. *Human Relations*, 49: 91–813.

Hofmann, D.A. and Tetrick, L.E. (2003) On the etiology of the concept of health: Implications for "organizing" individual and organizational health. In D.A. Hofmann and L.E. Tetrick (eds.), *Health and Safety in Organizations: A Multilevel Perspective*. Organizational Frontier Series, Society for Industrial and Organizational Psychology (pp. 1–26). San Francisco, CA: Jossey-Bass.

Kahn, R. (1980) Conflict, ambiguity, and overload: Three elements in job stress. In D. Katz, R. Kahn and J. Adams (eds.), *The Study of Organizations* (pp. 418–428). San Francisco, CA: Jossey-Bass.

Kessler, R.C., Mickelson, K.D. and Williams, D.R. (1999) The prevalence, distribution, and mental health correlates of perceived discrimination in the United States. *Journal of Health and Social Behavior*, 40: 208–230.

LeBlanc, M.M. and Kelloway, E.K. (2002) Predictors and outcomes of workplace violence and aggression. *Journal of Applied Psychology*, 87: 444–453.

National Institute for Occupational Safety and Health (NIOSH) (2004) *Worker Health Chartbook 2004*. Report number 2004–146. Washington, DC: NIOSH.

Roberson, L., Kulik, C.T. and Pepper, M.B. (2001) Designing effective diversity training: Influence of group composition and trainee experience. *Journal of Organizational Behavior*, 22: 871–885.

Sinclair, R.R. and Tetrick, L.E. (2004) Pay and benefits: The role of compensation systems in workplace safety. In J. Barling and M. Frone (eds.), *Psychology of Workplace Safety* (pp. 181–201). Washington, DC: American Psychological Association.

Sorensen, G., Stoddard, A. and Ockene, J.K. (1996) Worker participation in an integrated health promotion/health protection program: Results from the wellworks project. *Health Education Quarterly*, 23: 191–203.

Tetrick, L.E. and Toney, L. (2002) Job accommodations for mental health disabilities. In J.C. Thomas and M. Hersen (eds.), *Handbook of Mental Health in the Workplace* (pp. 519–534). Thousand Oaks, CA: Sage.

Thompson, C.A., Beauvais, L.L. and Lyness, K.S. (1999) When work–family benefits are not enough: The influence of work–family culture on benefit utilization, organizational attachment, and work–family conflict. *Journal of Vocational Behavior*, 54: 392–415.

Wagner, J.A. (1994) Participation's effects on performance and satisfaction: A reconsideration of research evidence. *Academy of Management Review*, 19: 312–330.

Waldfogel, J. (2001) Family and medical leave: Evidence from the 2000 surveys. *Monthly Labor Review*, 124(9): 17–23.

Yelin, E.H. and Trupin, L. (2003) Disability and the characteristics of employment. *Monthly Labor Review*, 126(5): 20–31.

Zohar, D. (1980) Safety climate in industrial organizations: Theoretical and applied implications. *Journal of Applied Psychology*, 85: 587–596.

THE HARD-HEADED WORKER

Norris Andersen is a foreman at a manufacturing plant in Alabama. He has noted on numerous occasions that one of his employees, Tex, does not wear his hard hat when working within the hard hat required zone of the plant. He has mentioned this to Tex on numerous occasions, but Tex still does not regularly wear his hard hat when in the zone. Tex says the hat impairs his vision and is uncomfortable. The hard hat zone is an Occupational Safety and Health Agency (OSHA) requirement, but OSHA has never found the company to be in violation of this requirement. Tex is an otherwise exemplary employee and Norris doesn't want to be too hard on him.

Related questions

1 What can Norris do to get Tex to wear his hard hat?
2 What policies and procedures could the company implement that would help enforce the safety standards?
3 What should the role of OSHA be in getting Tex to comply?

8 Competitive advantage through HRM

JASON D. SHAW

Researchers and practitioners in the field of human resource management are increasingly interested in how the management of people or work organizations relates to the ability of organizations to compete in the marketplace and, beyond this, to provide a sustainable competitive advantage. On the research side, this area of inquiry has come to be known as strategic HRM. The field of strategic HRM is relatively new – nearly all of the research has been conducted since the mid 1980s. Its origins can be traced to a few influential and innovative perspectives by authors such as Dyer (1984) and Schuler and Jackson (1987) and its progress can be tracked by the growing influence of empirical studies by authors such as Delery and Doty (1996), Huselid (1995), and MacDuffie (1995).

Although a number of judgment calls must be made in distinguishing between strategic HRM and other lines of HRM research, there are some clear differentiating features. First, research studies in the area of strategic HRM tend to be conducted at a higher level of analysis than the individual level, i.e., the business unit, facility, or organizational level. These studies are sometimes called "functionalist" HRM studies (e.g., Delery and Shaw, 2001). Second, strategic HRM studies typically involve an examination of the integration or fit among HRM practices (an internal alignment perspective) (e.g., Guthrie, 2000; Huselid, 1995) or an examination of the integration or fit between HRM practices and other features of the organization (an external alignment perspective). These organizational features include, but are not limited to, the business strategy of the organization (e.g., Delery and Doty, 1996) and organizational technologies (e.g., Shaw *et al.*, 2001). Third, although there are exceptions, most studies in the realm of strategic HRM focus on organizational performance – broadly defined – as the key dependent variable. Organizational performance has been conceptualized and operationalized as intermediate dimensions of workforce performance such as accident rates (Zacharatos *et al.*, 2005), voluntary and involuntary turnover (e.g., Guthrie, 2000; Shaw *et al.*, 1998), and productivity (e.g., Wright *et al.*, 2005), as well as measures of corporate financial performance (e.g., Delery and Doty, 1996; Huselid, 1995) and managerial perceptions of performance (Delaney and Huselid, 1996).

To be fair, there is strategic value to much of the functionalist or individual-level HRM research that appears in the literature. For example, Delery and Shaw (2001) noted that Taylor and Russell's (1939) pioneering work on valid selection techniques and organizational success, McGregor's (1960) research on participatory management, and Hackman and Oldham's (1980) work design models all have clear, although indirect, applicability in terms of competitive advantage. But strategic HRM research directly attempts to "demonstrate the importance of human resource management practices for organizational performance" (Delery and Doty, 1996: 802). Beyond this, one of the goals of the strategic HRM research movement has been to extend the realm of HRM beyond administrative services and regulatory requirements and to integrate it with other strategic and central aspects of organizational functioning. This approach was summarized by Lawler (2005):

> It is nearly unanimous that HR can and should add more value to corporations. The best way to do this is by being a business partner. In other words, it needs to move beyond performing the many administrative and legally mandated tasks that traditional personnel functions have performed to adding value through directly improving the performance of the business. There also is agreement that it can do this by effective talent management, helping with change management, influencing business strategy, and a host of other high-value-added activities that impact organizational effectiveness.
>
> (Lawler 2005: 166)

In this chapter, I will first briefly discuss some changes to the internal working environments of organizations as well as changes in the external environment of organizations that tend to increase the importance of the HR function and the organization's array of HRM practices. Second, I will discuss how the adoption of HRM practices that have strategic value can help organizations respond to these dynamics. Third, I will examine the existing empirical evidence regarding the relationship between strategic HRM systems and important organizational outcomes. Based on this evidence, I will offer some guidelines on how decision makers in organizations can create competitive advantage through HRM.

Environmental factors and the importance of strategic HRM

Several recent changes to the internal and external environments of organizations have important implications for HRM systems. There is a dramatically increasing percentage of white-collar as opposed to blue-collar jobs in the North American economy. The trend toward knowledge work in these economies and the increasing value that these types of occupations place on relationships and effective communication make it critical that organizations manage their people effectively. As an example, Shaw *et al.* (2005) found that losses in relationship value – or social capital – through staff turnover resulted in dramatic performance declines and that these losses were predictive of organizational performance above and beyond the losses the organization incurred from the ability of individuals to perform their jobs well.

Second, there are dramatic shifts occurring in terms of the management of technology both within and outside of organizational boundaries. The result is that organizations today must be much more flexible in terms of managing their internal processes and structures than they were in the past. In the late 1970s, Miles and Snow (1978) argued that some firms made strategic decisions to be innovative. These authors described such organizations as having an "aura of fluidity" (Miles and Snow, 1978: 56). But today "either by choice or by circumstance, firms increasingly find themselves operating in turbulent and highly unpredictable environments" (Dyer and Ericksen 2005: 183) and the aura of fluidity that once applied only to organizations that were doing so by design now often applies as a technological dictate.

As Greve and Taylor (2000: 55) note, changes in technologies often "change the incumbent skills, standard practices, technology, services, and products of the firm," cause coordination problems when changes in core technologies are required, and create an environment where "comparison of levels of efficiency over time becomes difficult and only partially meaningful" (Miles and Snow, 1978: 64). As organizations experiment with new technologies and organizational forms, many exciting HRM challenges and opportunities are created (Dyer and Ericksen, 2005).

Third, there is a growing debate in the labor economics literature concerning the future of the North American labor pool. Many have argued that the future will hold a labor supply shortage as the "baby boom" generation ages and the smaller cohort that follows it comes of age in the workforce. But more recently some authors have argued that the workforce may grow at a rate that meets or exceeds prior levels. For example, Cappelli (2005) noted that the workforce cohort one generation removed (the "echo" cohort) from the "baby boom" generation is larger and should supply new workers at a rate that mirrors past levels. In addition, he suggests that the key issue in terms of labor market growth is the fact that individuals will be working until an older age before retiring. Cappelli states that "those over age 65 account for roughly 13% of the population at present, a figure that will grow to 20% by 2050" (2005: 144). Thus, although many strategic HRM researchers and others have noted that organizations should use HRM practices as a way to maintain competitive advantage because of a coming labor shortage across industries, it may be that organizations that gear their HRM practices toward effectiveness with an aging workforce may fare better.

Fourth, there has been a dramatic shift since the mid 1980s in terms of how corporate decision makers manage the size of their workforces. As examples, Tsui and Wu (2005) reported that during a three-year stretch in the mid 1980s about half a million middle- to upper-level managers were laid off or "downsized" (e.g., see Bluestone and

Harrison, 1988). But the corresponding figure for the three years 2000–2003 was more than five times that number – about 2.7 million job reductions (Nussbaum, 2004). The marked shift in terms of the level of job stability for white-collar workers signals a dramatic change, not only in terms of how organizations manage their HRM practices and their workforces, but also in terms of how employees view their organizations.

One perhaps unintended consequence of the rapid flux or dynamism of today's workforce is that managing HRM in such environments involves a consideration that employees are much less committed to given organizations. The historical staple of a long-term career in a single organization has radically changed since the mid 1990s. Where once employers provided employees with a stable, fixed compensation and benefits package and some modicum of job stability and expected high levels of job performance and strong organizational commitment in return, today's contracts are often made without loyalty and commitment considerations (Tsui and Wu, 2005). The result is that organizations must find new ways of managing individuals in an environment without commitment. Cappelli (2000) argued that employers were primarily responsible for breaking the old system, but not for establishing the new one. As Cappelli states, "power is shifting toward employees, leading to new problems for employers and, in turn, fundamentally different ways of managing employees" (2000: 11).

Strategic HRM responses to environmental changes

Some recent research and empirical evidence provide several clues regarding how organizational decision makers can manage their HRM systems in order to respond effectively to environmental (internal and external) changes. In this section, I will give several examples of how HRM decision makers can use strategic HRM systems to respond to internal and external environment changes in order to provide competitive advantage for organizations. This section, and the research discussed in it, is designed not to be comprehensive, but rather to be suggestive of the possibilities with a particular focus on recent studies in this area.

First, although there is a clear downward trend in the North American labor markets in terms of employee commitment to their organizations, there is a growing body of evidence demonstrating that strategic HRM practices relate strongly – and positively – to retention rates (e.g., Guthrie, 2000; Shaw et al., 1998). This same group of commitment-enhancing practices (e.g., selective staffing, developmental appraisal, extensive training and development, above market pay rates, attractive benefits, procedural justice programs, job stability, etc.) are also shown in the literature to relate consistently to measures of workforce and organizational performance (e.g., for reviews see Delery and Shaw, 2001; Wright et al., 2001). The theoretical mechanisms are such that organizations that invest in these types of strategic HRM practices create an environment wherein employees give extra effort in order to accomplish organizational goals and identify with the organization. In addition, high levels of investments in commitment-enhancing practices tie individuals to the organization by reducing the attractiveness of other job alternatives in the marketplace.

Beyond these organizational-level effects, an ambitious study by Whitener (2001) demonstrated that HRM practices interacted with perceived organizational support in predicting organizational commitment levels. The nature of the relationship was such that organizational commitment was highest among individuals when commitment-enhancing HRM practices were used and employees had high levels of perceived organizational support. In the late 1990s, a consulting organization study examined these issues, looking at more than 7,500 US employees (Watson Wyatt, 1999). They found over a three-year window that returns to shareholders were 47 percent higher in organizations with high commitment levels and that employees reported that human resource practices were among the key factors in building commitment. Thus, the literature at the organizational level and cross-level research on individual attitudes and behaviors clearly demonstrate that strategic HRM practices can be used to enhance employee commitment and that commitment level is a key factor in terms of organizational performance.

With regard to the increasing importance of knowledge leveraging and exchange in the North American economies, several recent studies show how strategic HRM systems and the importance of social capital can help organizations achieve competitive advantage. First, two studies published in 2005 provide strong evidence that internal social structures play a role in turnover decisions at the individual level and, further, that losses of key people in knowledge-based networks can result in substantial performance losses at the organizational level. First, Mossholder *et al.* (2005) found that health care employees who were more embedded in the internal communication networks in their organizations were much less likely to quit over a five-year period, a finding especially relevant in a tight knowledge-based health care labor market. Importantly, the social capital effects were observed over and above the predictive power of known correlates of turnover (e.g., job satisfaction and tenure). These authors concluded that close identification with co-workers is "associated with perceived similarity and more frequent communication" and that these factors dampen "the effect of real or perceived shocks that may give rise to turnover" (Mossholder *et al.*, 2005: 613).

Similarly, Shaw *et al.* (2005) examined these issues, but from the perspective of organizations as opposed to individuals. They argued that in organizations where effective communication was a key factor for success, the losses of individuals who hold key places in the communication networks would be associated with performance decrements over and above the losses experienced from the actual performance levels of those leavers. Consistent with these expectations, they found the social capital losses related negatively to productivity measures over and above the in-role performance losses from the same leavers. Moreover, they found that these knowledge-transfer-based losses were most pronounced when the first holes were created in the communication networks. In terms of sales per employee, a low turnover organization produced approximately $17,653 per employee, but a slight increase in social capital losses through turnover resulted in a 26.3 percent drop in productivity.

What, then, is the connection to strategic HRM or, stated differently, how can strategic HRM decision makers respond to these issues? A study by Collins and Smith (2006) sheds additional light on this issue. Collins and Smith (2006) studied a group of 136 high-technology firms to explore how strategic HRM practices affected levels of knowledge exchange and knowledge combination. They argued that an index of commitment-oriented HRM practices (e.g., internal selection, group incentives, training, team building, etc.) would enhance the effectiveness of knowledge-centered organizations by improving their internal social climate. Specifically, in knowledge-based and high-technology organizations, the source of competitive advantage often shifts from physical or tangible resources to the ability of organizations to manage know-how and enhance knowledge transfer. These authors argued that commitment-oriented strategic HRM practices can enhance the level of trust and cooperation that is observed in a workforce and help create a shared or common language for accomplishing work. These dimensions – all aspects of the internal social climate of the organization – allow members of knowledge-based organizations to share and combine information more effectively and ultimately achieve competitive success.

The findings of Collins and Smith (2006) provide substantial support for this causal sequence. They demonstrated that organizations that invest in commitment-oriented HRM practices had high or more positive levels of internal social climate, exchanged and combined information more effectively, and in turn, outperformed their competitors on two dimensions of performance that are critical for high-technology organizations – revenue from new products and services and one-year sales growth. Specifically, they found in their sample that increasing investment in commitment-oriented HRM practices by one standard deviation results in a 17 percent differential in terms of sales from new products and almost a 19 percent increase in sales. They also found that more than three-quarters of these changes were explained by changes and improvements in social climate and knowledge sharing that accompanied the practices. Thus, these studies and others like them show clearly that organizational decision makers can respond to environmental changes in commitment and loyalty reductions by investing in practices designed and shown to enhance commitment (e.g., Guthrie, 2000; Shaw *et al.*, 1998). These investments not only improve retention rates, but also help preserve fragile communication networks that are crucial to the success of knowledge-based organizations.

An ambitious study by Zatzick and Iverson (2006) elegantly demonstrates how strategic HRM can help organizations respond to labor shortages, labor market demands, and dramatic changes in workforce size. The authors highlighted the recent trend toward downsizing and other forms of workforce reduction and argued that while these decisions were once reserved only for cost-cutting, they are now often part of a strategic decision-making process for changing workforce skill and competency levels and for enhancing the effectiveness of changes in business strategy. Managing these changes effectively is critical given that layoffs and downsizing are shown to reduce trust in management, increase work stress levels, and hamper productivity (e.g., Brockner, 1992). Interestingly, these authors showed that among a sample of several thousand organizations across Canada, negative reactions to layoffs were stronger in organizations that had high levels of investments in strategic HRM practices. That is, among organizations that invested heavily in HRM practices, productivity declined markedly when layoff rates were high. Among organizations with little investment in HRM practices, productivity levels were essentially the same in organizations with low and high layoff rates. These authors reasoned that in organizations that invest heavily in strategic practices, a strong mixed message is sent by this investment in conjunction with a layoff. Strategic HRM investments are made to strengthen employees' commitment to the organization, and as a result, layoffs in these situations create a severe violation of the psychological contract. When investments in strategic HRM practices are low, employee expectations regarding the psychological contract are much lower and layoffs have much less of a negative impact on productivity.

Extending these findings in a new and interesting way, Zatzick and Iverson (2006) argued further that strategic HRM practices were key in terms of helping manage downsizing situations over the course of time. They argued that continued or increased investments in strategic practices can help the organization accomplish several important goals during the transition period after layoffs. First, they suggested that continued investments in HRM can help reduce uncertainty, ambiguity, and conflict during the transition period after layoffs. Second, they suggested that continued or increased investments in HRM can buffer the negative effects of layoffs, once they have occurred. That is, from the viewpoint of layoff survivors, continued investments may not only improve morale, but also provide benefits that improve overall employee welfare. Finally, they noted that employees may respond positively to continued strategic HRM investments in part because they may receive benefits that ease fears about getting another job should they be laid off in the future (e.g., skill acquisition through training). In a subsequent analysis, they found strong support for these ideas. When layoff rates were high, but organizations continued investing in employees, their results suggested that organizations experienced a 4.7 percent productivity increase over the study period. In contrast, among organizations with high layoff rates and a lower level of strategic HRM investments over time, productivity declined by 22.5 percent over the period of study. Thus, although high-investment organizations may experience a severe negative reaction to workforce reductions initially, it is clear from these results that strategic HRM practices can help organizations achieve competitive advantage in the long run in an environment characterized by marked changes in workforce size.

The preceding discussion highlights several ways in which investments in strategic HRM practices can help organizations manage some of the dramatic changes occurring in the internal and external environments of organizations in the North American marketplace. First, although employee commitment levels are on the decline in many sectors of the workforce, the research evidence shows clearly that retention is lower, productivity is higher, and employees are more psychologically attached to organizations that invest heavily in strategic HRM systems. Second, as the nature of work in organizations changes from a reliance on physical resources and capital to the management of knowledge and other intangible resources, HRM practices can help organizations sustain competitive advantage by enhancing the efficiency of internal communication networks, building trust in management, improving the quality of social climates, and creating a shared and meaningful organizational language (Collins and Smith, 2006). Third, as layoffs and other forms of downsizing become a more common strategic tool, the results of Zatzick and Iverson (2006) elucidate that organizations can not only minimize but also reverse the negative effects of layoffs in terms of organizational productivity by continuing investments in strategic HRM systems.

Beyond responses to these current issues and concerns, there is general and consistent evidence that the use of strategic HRM systems relates to measures of workforce and organizational performance. Indeed, Delery and Shaw (2001) stated that there were two general conclusions that could be made about strategic HRM systems and competitive advantage. First, although researchers have taken a number of different approaches for examining these issues, most researchers agree that a system of HRM practices rather than an isolated or best-practice approach is necessary for sustained advantage. Although a given HRM practice may be more effective than another (e.g., structured interviews versus unstructured interviews), the evidence is clear that these practices must be integrated in a superior overall system (e.g., Uhl-Bien et al., 2000). Second, researchers generally agree that the effects of HRM systems on performance are partially indirect through their influence on the workforce and workforce outcomes such as turnover and productivity.

All else being equal, it is reasonable to take a view that organizations in general could realize substantial benefits from investing in these systems of practices. In addition to the studies and results noted in the preceding pages, a brief review of the literature reveals a consistent pattern of positive findings between HRM systems and performance-related outcomes in the North American context and beyond. Delery and Doty (1996) found that groups of HRM practices related positively to financial profitability in a sample of banks. MacDuffie (1995) found that groups of HRM practices related to product quality and workforce productivity in a sample of automobile assembly plants. Ichniowski and Shaw (1999) compared US and Japanese production lines and found that while Japanese plants were more productive in general, the productivity of US lines equaled that of Japanese lines when there was heavy investment in strategic HRM practices. The positive relationship may also extend to other types of practices not typically included in strategic or "high-performance" HRM indices. For example, Perry-Smith and Blum (2000) found that bundles of work–family HRM practices (e.g., daycare, elder care, parental leave, etc.) related to a perceptual measure of organizational performance, over and above a set of progressive HRM practices.

Guidelines

Drawing on the preceding discussion and the existing evidence regarding strategic HRM systems and competitive advantage, it is reasonable to offer several guidelines regarding decisions to invest in HRM and regarding the design of HRM systems. These should not be interpreted as rules that are "set in stone," but rather as general applications and logical extensions of the base of research in this area. See Table 8.1 for a complete list of the guidelines.

Guideline 1: Focus on sets of commitment-enhancing practices when work is knowledge based and when internal communication processes are critical for success

The existing research is unambiguous when it comes to the relationship between commitment-enhancing practices such as competitive pay and benefits, selective staffing, training, procedural justice systems and employee retention. High levels of investments in these types of practices serve a dual purpose for organizations as they attempt to maintain a competitive edge. First, they enhance retention, a factor that is especially important in knowledge-management situations where employees may be more committed to their profession than they are to their organization. Second, the evidence provided by Collins and Smith (2006) and others shows that investments in these types of practices facilitate the creation of environments where information can flow effectively within and between groups.

Table 8.1 Guidelines on how to achieve competitive advantage through HRM

1 Focus on sets of commitment-enhancing practices when work is knowledge based and when internal communication processes are critical for success.
2 Use the functional HRM literature as a guide in developing an effective system of HRM practices.
3 Combine practices across domains in logically and theoretically consistent ways.
4 Use HRM investment as a signal of future investment and an ambiguity reducer when workforce size fluctuates.
5 Focus on flexibility or agility in the HRM system and beyond.

Guideline 2: Use the functional HRM literature as a guide in developing an effective system of HRM practices

As Delery and Shaw (2001) noted, it is clear from the functional HRM literature that some HRM practices are better than others. Using a well-validated selection device such as a structured interview, for example, is likely to yield a higher-quality workforce than a reliance on walk-ins and the "gut feel" of an HRM decision maker. The functional HRM literature is replete with useful evidence regarding the validity of various types of practices, suggestions for effective implementation, evidence of situational applicability and inapplicability, and often information on incremental validity over other relevant practices. But as has been noted, a given HRM practice – regardless of its situational superiority – is unlikely to yield substantial benefits at the organizational level, unless it is combined with other effective practices.

Guideline 3: Combine practices across domains in logically and theoretically consistent ways

Much more is known in strategic HRM about the relationship between bundles of practices and outcomes than is known about the effective or ineffective combination of HRM practices and organizational outcomes. Research on the appropriate alignment of specific practices is a pressing need, but theory and some recent evidence suggest that it can be especially critical in terms of expected performance outcomes. Here the lessons learned at the individual level with regard to the effectiveness of a given practice must be combined with the lessons learned at the organizational level about internal synergies between various practices. As an example, Shaw *et al.* (2002) found that a wide variation in the pay structure across employees (i.e., highly dispersed pay) was associated with better performance only when combined with the use of performance-based pay. They also argued and found that highly dispersed pay was ineffective in terms of relating to better organizational performance when work was highly interdependent and the contributions of individuals were difficult to observe. The bottom line is that two practices may be well validated in a given situation, but may be competing or inconsistent when used concurrently.

Guideline 4: Use HRM investment as a signal of future investment and an ambiguity reducer when workforce size fluctuates

In trying times, individuals will often look for direct and indirect signals offered by the organization to ease their concerns or to determine their value. The results at the individual level in terms of open communication, justification, and feedback are clear (e.g., Brockner, 1992); direct and honest communication and open information sharing is an effective way of alleviating the negative effects of layoffs and downsizing among survivors. But the arguments and results of Zatzick and Iverson (2006) show that organizations can realize additional benefits by continuing their investments in strategic HRM practices after layoffs. Such investments provide additional and indirect signals that survivors are valued, may ease concerns about future layoffs by providing training and development that will be useful in future job searches, and may improve morale.

Guideline 5: Focus on flexibility or agility in the HRM system and beyond

Dyer and Ericksen (2005) argue that the future of HRM in terms of competitive advantage lies in its ability to adapt. As technology drives change in the structure underlying many organizations and as organizations in general are driven towards fluidity in their structures and processes, effective HRM systems must follow suit. It is likely that the guiding principles of strategic HRM systems will change markedly in the coming years and that the most successful organizations will have mastered HRM responses to many of the challenges outlined in this chapter. As Dyer and Ericksen (2005) state:

> Agile enterprises require guiding principles that encourage the inflow and outflow of talent in ways that facilitate and only minimally disrupt internal fluidity. These principles require balance. On the one hand, new entrants are needed to avoid the tendency toward groupthink and habituation that tend to imbue inbred social systems. Too much churn, on the other hand, undermines the mutual understanding and trust that allows for internal fluidity.
>
> (Dyer and Ericksen 2005: 187)

Conclusion

Dramatic changes in the nature of work, the evolution of technology, and unique labor market forces are creating many challenges for HRM decision makers today. In this chapter, I elaborated on these trends and focused on some recent findings that shed light on how strategic HRM systems can help organizations sustain competitive advantage in these times. These new ideas and findings are excellent complements to the existing literature showing consistent and positive relationships between the use of strategic HRM systems and organizational effectiveness. The guidelines that followed are offered as informed judgments about the future of HRM and competitive advantage as well as suggestive of future research needs on these topics.

References

Bluestone, B. and Harrison, B. (1988) The growth of low-wage employment: 1963–1986. *American Economic Review*, 78: 124–128.

Brockner, J. (1992) Managing the effects of layoffs on survivors. *California Management Review*, 34: 9–28.

Cappelli, P. (2000) Managing without commitment. *Organizational Dynamics*, 28(4): 11–24.

Cappelli, P. (2005) Will there really be a labor shortage? *Human Resource Management*, 44: 143–149.

Collins, C.J. and Smith, K.G. (2006) Knowledge exchange and combination: The role of human resource practices in the performance of high technology firms. *Academy of Management Journal*, 49: 544–560.

Delaney, J.T. and Huselid, M.A. (1996) The impact of human resource management practices on perceptions of organizational performance. *Academy of Management Journal*, 39: 949–969.

Delery, J.E. and Doty, D.H. (1996) Modes of theorizing in strategic human resource management: Tests of universalistic, contingency, and configurational performance predictions. *Academy of Management Journal*, 39: 802–835.

Delery, J.E. and Shaw, J.D. (2001) The strategic management of people in work organizations: Review, synthesis, and extension. *Research in Personnel and Human Resources Management*, 20: 165–197.

Dyer, L. (1984) Studying human resource strategy: An approach and an agenda. *Industrial Relations*, 23: 156–169.

Dyer, L. and Ericksen, J. (2005) In pursuit of marketplace agility: Applying precepts of self-organizing systems to optimize human resource scalability. *Human Resource Management*, 44: 183–188.

Greve, H.R. and Taylor, A. (2000) Innovations as catalysts for organizational change: Shifts in organizational cognition and search. *Administrative Science Quarterly*, 45: 54–80.

Guthrie, J.P. (2000) High involvement work practices, turnover and productivity: Evidence from New Zealand. *Academy of Management Journal*, 44: 180–190.

Hackman, J.R. and Oldham, G.R. (1980) *Work Redesign*. Reading, MA: Addison Wesley.

Huselid, M.A. (1995) The impact of human resource management practices on turnover, productivity, and corporate financial performance. *Academy of Management Journal*, 38: 635–672.

Ichniowski, C. and Shaw, K. (1999) The effects of human resource management systems on economic performance: An international comparison of U.S. and Japanese plants. *Management Science*, 45: 704–721.

Lawler, E.E., III (2005) From human resource management to organizational effectiveness. *Human Resource Management*, 44: 165–169.

MacDuffie, J.P. (1995) Human resource bundles and manufacturing performance: Organizational logic and flexible production systems in the world auto industry. *Industrial and Labor Relations Review*, 48: 197–221.

McGregor, D. (1960) *The Human Side of Enterprise*. New York: McGraw-Hill.

Miles, R.E. and Snow, C.C. (1978) *Organizational Strategy, Structure, and Process*. New York: McGraw-Hill.

Mossholder, K.W., Settoon, R.P. and Henagan, S.C. (2005) A relational perspective on turnover: Examining structural, attitudinal, and behavioral predictors. *Academy of Management Journal*, 48: 607–618.

Nussbaum, B. (2004) Where are the jobs? *Business Week*, March 22: 36–37.

Perry-Smith, J.E. and Blum, T.C. (2000) Work–family human resource bundles and perceived organizational performance. *Academy of Management Journal*, 43: 1107–1117.

Schuler, R.S. and Jackson, S.E. (1987) Linking competitive strategies with human resource management practices. *Academy of Management Executive*, 1: 207–219.

Shaw, J.D., Gupta, N. and Delery, J.E. (2001) Congruence between technology and compensation systems: Implications for strategy implementation. *Strategic Management Journal*, 22: 379–386.

Shaw, J.D., Gupta, N. and Delery, J.E. (2002) Pay dispersion and workforce performance: Moderating effects of incentives and interdependence. *Strategic Management Journal*, 23: 491–512.

Shaw, J.D., Duffy, M.K., Johnson, J.J. and Lockhart, D. (2005) Turnover, social capital losses, and performance. *Academy of Management Journal*, 48: 594–606.

Shaw, J.D., Delery, J.E., Jenkins, G.D., Jr. and Gupta, N. (1998) An organizational-level analysis of voluntary and involuntary turnover. *Academy of Management Journal*, 41: 511–525.

Taylor, H.C. and Russell, J.T. (1939) The relationship of validity coefficients to the practical effectiveness of tests in selection. *Journal of Applied Psychology*, 23: 565–578.

Tsui, A.S. and Wu, J.B. (2005) The new employment relationship versus the mutual investment approach: Implications for human resource management. *Human Resource Management*, 44: 115–121.

Uhl-Bien, M., Graen, G.B. and Scandura, T.A. (2000) Implications of leader-member exchange (LMX) for strategic human resource management systems: Relationships as social capital for competitive advantage. *Research in Personnel and Human Resources Management*, 18: 137–185.

Watson Wyatt (1999) *WorkUSA 2000: Employee Commitment and the Bottom Line*. Bethesda, MD: Watson Wyatt.

Whitener, E.M. (2001) Do "high commitment" human resource practices affect employee commitment? A cross-level analysis using hierarchical linear modeling. *Journal of Management*, 27: 515–535.

Wright, P.M., Dunford, B. and Snell, S. (2001) Contributions of the resource based view of the firm to the field of strategic HRM: Convergence of two fields. *Journal of Management*, 27: 701–721.

Wright, P.M., Gardner, T.M., Moynihan, L.M. and Allen, M.R. (2005) The relationships between HR practices and firm performance: Examining causal order. *Personnel Psychology*, 58: 409–446.

Zacharatos, A., Barling, J. and Iverson, R. (2005) High-performance work systems and occupational safety. *Journal of Applied Psychology*, 90: 77–93.

Zatzick, C.D. and Iverson, R.D. (2006) High-involvement management and workforce reduction: Competitive advantage or disadvantage? *Academy of Management Journal*, 49: 999–1015.

THE DISJOINTED HR SYSTEM

Judith Russo is the VP of Human Resources at a large service firm, headquartered in Toronto, Canada. In trying to make the HR function more strategic, she asked each of her managers to come up with some policies that would help create competitive advantage for the firm through its human resources. The compensation and benefits manager, staffing manager, and training manager all came up with some policies that they thought would benefit the firm. Judith is now trying to decide which of these policies to implement.

Related questions

1 What are the disadvantages and advantages of having the managers come up with policies independently?
2 What is the problem with policies that "benefit the firm"?
3 What decision rules should Judith use when deciding which policies to implement?

9 Counterproductive leader behavior

HANNAH L. JACKSON AND DENIZ S. ONES

In recent years the media have reported numerous accounts of alleged and proven illegal and unethical behavior among leaders of organizations (e.g., Enron, WorldCom, Tyco, Arthur Andersen, to name but a few). The headlines that accompanied these stories signaled the end of a decade that had witnessed phenomenal wealth generation. Central to some of these successes, however, were ethical failures on the part of leaders; such behavior no longer seems to be rare, but is possibly widespread and very destructive. Since the mid 1990s scholars have realized that acts of counterproductive workplace behavior (CWB) are a prevalent aspect of organizational life which consequently merit scientific scrutiny (Sackett and DeVore, 2001; Vardi and Weitz, 2004). The study of CWB has advanced greatly beyond its origins, which mainly involved the examination of specific kinds or forms of rule-breaking, disobedience, misconduct, wrongdoing, and deviance in isolation from one another. Most forms of these behaviors can be subsumed under the general term CWB, and today it is increasingly common to find researchers drawing together previously distinct content areas and generating broad models and theories of CWB. Although various labels and definitions exist, this chapter refers to CWB as intentional/volitional behavior enacted by employees and viewed by the organization as contrary to its legitimate interests (Ones and Viswesvaran, 2003; Sackett and DeVore, 2001).

The burgeoning literature on CWB, however, has potentially overlooked at least one important domain of perpetrators of CWB and associated behaviors: leaders (e.g., managers and executives). We use the term "counterproductive leader behavior" to describe leader misconduct. Specifically, this term refers to intentional behavior enacted by leaders that involves misuse of position or authority for personal and/or organizational benefit. By "misuse" we mean a departure from accepted societal norms, which simultaneously allows for the fact that leader behavior may be viewed as counterproductive according to societal norms, while also acceptable within the context of a particular organization (see also Anand et al., 2004). Therefore, while an organization may appear to potentially benefit from some acts of counterproductive leader behavior, the behavior is ultimately viewed as contrary to its legitimate and long-term interests. This conceptualization in part reflects Kellerman's (2005) distinction between bad leadership as "ineffective" and bad leadership as "unethical."

To date, researchers have tended to treat leaders and their behaviors as essentially distinct from those considered in existing CWB theories and models. The fact they have not been incorporated into the literature on CWB is somewhat surprising given that many researchers acknowledge that CWB is not a phenomenon restricted to certain marginal members of organizations (Vardi and Weitz, 2004). Indeed it is often noted that CWB has been recorded for workers of all types of organizations and for employees at all levels within them, whether they be salaried professionals or non-professionals, managers or non-supervisory employees (Vardi and Weitz, 2004). Yet neither leaders as perpetrators nor their behaviors have traditionally been considered directly relevant to the literature on CWB. But leaders do have clear opportunities to steal, waste, or cost their organizations, in many damaging ways, millions or even billions of dollars. It can therefore be argued that opportunities for serious misconduct are at least as great among managers and executives, and that a handful of leaders engaging in CWB can do as much if not more damage than a large number of front-line workers. However, our knowledge of counterproductive leader behaviors lags behind what we know about conceptually similar behaviors elsewhere in the organization. This chapter calls for an expanded perspective on CWB such that the behaviors of leaders are integrated into the extant literature. In doing so, we explore the role of leader, current conceptualizations of CWB, how leader misconduct relates to the latter, and how HR can deal with it. This chapter concludes with some guidelines on how organizations can address counterproductive leader behavior.

The leader role: ethical considerations

Much of the research conducted on leader misconduct lies predominantly at the intersection of the business ethics and leadership literatures (Trevino *et al.*, 2003). A prevailing theme in the business ethics literature is that the role of leaders is replete with ethical content. This probably helps to explain why their misconduct has typically been characterized as unethical rather than counterproductive. Ethical issues are ever present for leaders, who must continually face conflict among stakeholders, interests, and values. In today's business climate, ethics are increasingly integral to the roles of leaders and their decision-making, a theme that is strongly reflected in the business ethics literature. Ultimately, because the decisions of leaders affect the lives and well-being of so many others, it is hardly surprising that their discretionary decision making is regarded as imbued in ethical choices. (See Chapter 6 for more on ethics and HRM.)

Scholars of leadership have made similar observations about the roles of leaders in today's organizations. Interestingly, their focus is not so much on negative behaviors that detract from job performance, but appears instead to be on *ethical* behaviors that enhance job performance. Survey research indicates that traits like credibility, integrity, honesty, and fair-mindedness are all associated with perceptions of effective leadership (Kouzes and Posner, 1993). A great deal of work has gone into understanding how such characteristics might be promoted among leaders. Yukl (2002) links ethical leadership with "exceptional" leadership categories. For example, the concept of transformational leadership involves leaders communicating a collective vision and inspiring their followers to look beyond self-interest and perform for the good of the group. In contrast, transactional leadership is regarded as a means of controlling followers' behaviors and handling problems by engaging in some transaction between the leader and subordinate.

Turner *et al.* (2002) characterize interest in the "moral potential of leadership" as reflecting a basic tension between altruism and egoism. In other words, they argue that some leaders choose to balance the development of themselves and their subordinates, which raises the aspirations of all involved in the process. Other leaders, by contrast, choose to use their power to selfishly satisfy personal needs and in doing so behave in socially unconstructive ways and/or forfeit the development of their subordinates. Not surprisingly, therefore, unethical leadership has been principally characterized as self-serving in nature. Kanungo and Mendonca (1996) specify that leaders are considered unethical if they frequently operate with egoistic intent, employ controlling versus empowering strategies to influence followers, and fail to abstain from vices.

While a great deal is made of the unethical behaviors of managers and executives, empirical attempts to define this domain, assess its dimensionality, and investigate causal antecedents are practically non-existent. This literature is instead more concerned with theoretically specifying the processes by which senior leaders engage in ethical decision making, a concern that largely exists in place of clearly specifying the key dependent variable itself. We feel that researchers should more closely examine critical behavioral incidents of counterproductive leader behavior and attempt to scale them. By tying leader behavior to an already established literature on CWB, it may subsequently be possible to better understand, predict, and develop interventions to address counterproductive leader behaviors.

Broad conceptualizations of CWB

The vast majority of CWB research to date has focused on behaviors occurring at lower levels in the organization, possibly at the expense of taking a broader perspective of the domain. There are several key reasons for studying broader conceptualizations of behavior rather than focusing on individual behaviors that happen to be counterproductive. According to Bennett and Robinson (2003), this approach allows researchers to generalize to unstudied but related behaviors. Understanding the pattern of interrelationships among varied forms of CWB may uncover their underlying dimensionality. Another benefit of this approach involves the antecedents of CWB. While it is possible that all different types of CWB have unique antecedents, it is more likely, consistent with our knowledge of other psychological constructs (e.g., withdrawal behaviors), that some or all are interrelated, with each being a behavioral manifestation of a latent construct that has common *individual differences* and/or *situational* antecedents (Ones and Viswesvaran, 2003; Sackett, 2002). Considerable progress has been made in recent years revealing insight into the interrelationships and dimensionality of CWB, which has implications for highlighting the common antecedents of the dimensions and developing HR interventions to address them.

Consolidating research on CWB

Several researchers have sought to identify conceptual frameworks for proposing relationships between forms of CWB. For example, Hollinger and Clark (1983) reported that behaviors could be grouped according to two broad categories, which they labeled "property deviance" and "production deviance." The former refers to the acquisition or damage of employer assets (e.g., theft, property damage, and misuse of discount privileges), while the latter involves the violation of norms specifying the quality and quantity of work to be accomplished (e.g., absence, tardiness, intentionally slow or sloppy work, and drug and alcohol use). Robinson and Bennett (1995) expanded upon this framework by noting that it and other previous research had failed to include interpersonal CWB, such as sexual harassment and verbal abuse. The basic dimensional distinction made by Robinson and Bennett (1995) between CWB directed toward individuals (i.e., interpersonal deviance) and those directed toward the organization (i.e., organizational deviance) has received considerable attention in the literature (Penney *et al.*, 2003).

Gruys and Sackett (2003) most recently turned to the literature and identified eighty-seven different forms of CWB. Using both rational sort and factor analytic techniques, they identified eleven categories of CWB: theft and related behavior, destruction of property, misuse of information, misuse of time and resources, unsafe behavior, poor attendance, poor quality of work, alcohol use, drug use, inappropriate verbal actions, and inappropriate physical actions. Gruys and Sackett (2003) also identified two dimensions of CWB. Like Robinson and Bennett (1995), they distinguished between behaviors targeted at the organization (e.g., theft, absence) and those targeted at organization members (e.g., verbal and physical acts toward others). Unlike Robinson and Bennett (1995), however, their second dimension differentiated between negative behaviors not directly related to job performance (e.g., theft) and acts that negatively impact job performance (e.g., absence, safety violations).

Interrelationships among CWB: evidence of an underlying construct

Research into the dimensionality of CWB has been of benefit to related research that examines whether an underlying construct can account for the interrelationships among specific forms of CWB. In meta-analyses of the CWB literature, Berry *et al.* (2007) reported that the true score correlation between interpersonal and organizational deviance is over 0.60. Individual forms of CWB correlate about 0.30 (Ones and Viswesvaran, 2003; Sackett, 2002). The domain of CWB can best be viewed as a broad construct, one that has many different behavioral manifestations across a smaller number of dimensions.

Therefore, the existing data appear to support the conclusion that seemingly different forms of CWB are aspects of an underlying construct. Interestingly, Sackett (2002) attributes this consistent finding to the *full range* of CWB. However, to date it is not clear whether research really has tapped more than just a portion of the entire domain of CWB and perpetrators. What is clear instead is that research has focused on behavioral manifestations that are typically demonstrated by front-line employees. Recall that Bennett and Robinson (2003) proposed that a key reason for broadly conceptualizing CWB is that it allows researchers to generalize to unstudied but related behaviors. We argue here that the misconduct of leaders falls into the category of seemingly related but unstudied CWB. No systematic empirical effort has yet examined the counterproductive behaviors that are enacted by leaders in organizations or the dimensions along which they vary. Given that the evidence for an underlying CWB construct is so compelling, it is difficult to imagine that the misconduct of leaders is entirely different from the domain of behaviors already studied at lower organizational levels and that they cannot be integrated, at least to some extent. If certain behaviors differ from or are unique to leaders, this should be viewed as an opportunity to expand the study of CWB so that it explores new ground. Moreover, these behaviors may vary along unique dimensions, reflecting the fact, for example, that leaders can misuse their position to potentially benefit themselves and/or the organization.

Antecedents of CWB

Examining the antecedents of CWB is another way to explore how counterproductive leader behavior fits into current conceptualizations. One promising explanation for the positive associations among different forms of CWB is the presence of common individual differences as antecedents. However, considering both personality *and* environmental antecedents will be essential for a complete understanding of CWB. Studying situations highlights the factors likely to affect mean levels of CWB, while studying individual differences highlights the factors likely to explain variance in CWB (Sackett and DeVore, 2001). As such, the different kinds of situations encountered by different levels of employees may help account for why mean levels of various behaviors differ across organizational levels. Similarly, it may be necessary to identify different antecedent variables to explain variance in CWB within organizational levels.

Major themes that prevail in research on the antecedents of CWB include such things as personality, social and interpersonal factors, job characteristics, work group characteristics, organizational culture, control systems, and injustice (see Penney *et al.*, 2003; Sackett and DeVore, 2001). Each of these categories may be more or less relevant to the study of counterproductive leader behavior, but it is likely that both situational and individual differences accounts of behavior are necessary for a comprehensive understanding of the domain, regardless of the organizational level of the perpetrator.

Variables examined as antecedents to CWB: what causes CWB?

A long list of individual differences variables have been examined as antecedents of CWB, including undependability, problems in socialization, attitudes regarding deviance and theft, problems with authority relationships, excitement seeking, work motivation, social influence, unstable upbringing, drug use, and unmet needs (Paajanen, 1988). A similarly long list of variables has been included in categories of situational influences on CWB, such as inflexible policies, organizational injustice, competitive environment, leadership style, rules and procedures, economic conditions, reward systems, adverse working conditions, task difficulty, home life, organizational culture, and prior outcomes (Martinko *et al.*, 2002; Penney *et al.*, 2003). The majority of these environmental influences on CWB have been identified in the context of lower-level employees, but several of them would appear relevant to individuals at all organizational levels.

Environmental factors

In thinking about the kinds of external influences that would be relevant to counterproductive leader behavior, it is worth considering that managers and executives themselves have a significant impact on some factors in the organizational environment. It is widely recognized that leaders play an important role in setting the "tone" at the top of an organization, which ultimately serves to shape its climate and culture (Trevino, 1990). Therefore, the kinds of rules, policies, procedures, reward systems, and working conditions present in a particular organization are in part a reflection of its leadership and associated goals and values. While such things as competitive pressures exist that are largely beyond the control of leaders, their position offers them some latitude to act as they see appropriate. As such, leaders have more discretion and autonomy regarding their behavior (compared to the typical front-line worker). In the presence of opportunity and in the absence of close monitoring, CWB represents more of a possibility and a temptation for those inclined to take advantage of such situations. Therefore, it is useful to consider the kinds of individual differences attributes that might help explain various counterproductive responses to and shaping of the organizational environment.

Individual differences

The broader literature on the prediction of CWB is clear; the construct of integrity is predictive of CWB. The criterion-related validity of integrity tests, which are paper-and-pencil instruments designed to identify individuals who are likely to engage in a range of CWB, has been most comprehensively established in the meta-analytic research of Ones *et al.* (1993). Cumulating 665 validity coefficients, they reported that integrity tests substantially predict CWB. In a discussion of potential reasons for why integrity tests predict CWB so well, Ones and Viswesvaran (2003) suggest that it is because the Big Five factors of conscientiousness, agreeableness, and emotional stability underlie these tests. Together, the three factors represent *factor alpha* (Digman, 1997), one of two higher order factors of the Big Five (the other being *factor beta*, which is comprised of extroversion and openness to experience). In other words, argue Ones and Viswesvaran (2003), integrity tests are essentially personality scales that assess the degree to which individuals will function well according to social rules.

Another line of work using personality variables to predict CWB suggests that individuals who score higher on agreeableness, conscientiousness, and emotional stability tend to refrain from CWB. Berry *et al.* (2007) meta-analytically showed that these three dimensions of the Big Five personality factors were most highly associated with self-reported CWB. However, interpersonal deviance was more highly correlated with agreeableness, followed by conscientiousness. The pattern was reversed for organizational deviance.

Are there other characteristics that differentiate senior leaders from front-line employees and which also potentially function as liabilities in terms of engaging in CWB? For example, individuals in leadership roles often exhibit high levels of traits like dominance, achievement orientation, independence, and narcissism, and low levels of traits like empathy, which under certain conditions may produce counterproductive behavior.

Rationalizing CWB: perpetrators' explanations for their CWB

Additional insight into CWB can be gained by examining the motives or rationalizations offered by white-collar criminals. A number of scholars over several decades have explored the use of motives or rationalizations to either pre-empt guilt or to allay misgivings about behavior. According to Murphy (1993) some motives might include: fear of failure, perceived norms, unsharable problems, outcome-focused altruism, careless expediency, and greed. In related research based in the sociological literature, Coleman (1987) offers a typology of rationalizations used by white-collar criminals. He found that the following rationalizations were commonly used as a means to sustain a positive self-image while engaging in workplace criminal behavior: denial of harm, unnecessary or unjust laws, achievement vital to economic goals or even survival, expectations and pressure from others, perception that everybody else is doing it, and being deserving of money. These six rationalizations represent those most commonly mentioned in both public statements and confidential replies to sociological investigators (Coleman, 1987).

More recently, Veiga *et al.* (2004) examined why managers bend company rules. Three distinct themes emerged: performance-based judgment calls (e.g., "necessary to get the job done," "performance contingencies demand otherwise"), faulty rules (e.g., "ambiguous rules," "emergency situations supersede some rules"), and socially embedded norms ("everyone else does it," "pressure from others"). Lastly, Anand *et al.* (2004) highlight six rationalizing tactics they believe are used most often in organizations, including: denial of responsibility (i.e., no other choice), denial of injury (i.e., no one is harmed), denial of victim (i.e., the violated party is deserving), social weighting (i.e., condemn the condemner and selective social comparison), appeal to higher authorities (i.e., attempt to realize a higher-order value), and metaphor of the ledger (i.e., entitlement to engage in CWB). Evident across each of these discussions of rationalizing behavior is a striking amount of overlap as scholars seek to account for why otherwise respectable and able leaders engage in CWB, illegal or otherwise.

Guidelines for HR

The victims and costs of counterproductive leader behavior are likely to be wide ranging. Statistical data on the victims of white-collar crime are surprisingly scarce, but an increasing number of scholars in this area estimate that the costs associated with such behavior are more than those of common crimes such as robbery (Ivancevich *et al.*, 2003). It is also widely noted that leaders, especially the most senior, create the "tone" at the top of an organization (Trevino, 1990). Misconduct at this level can therefore impact behavior across an entire organization. A 1990 national survey illustrates these implications (Patterson and Kim, 1991). The survey found that 60 percent of the workers surveyed believed that the unethical behavior of executives is the primary cause of a decline in business standards, productivity, and success. Furthermore, the survey suggested that because of the perceived low ethical standards of executives, workers feel justified in responding in kind (e.g., with absenteeism, petty theft, malingering, and alcohol or drug use). As such, the "standards equation" of the US workplace is straightforward: American workers are as ethical/dutiful in doing their jobs as their bosses and companies are perceived to be ethical/dutiful in leading and directing them (Patterson and Kim, 1991). In other words, counterproductive leader behavior may foster more of the same among lower levels of employees. Perpetuation of behavior in this way can be especially risky when it involves rationalizations of the kind described above. For example, if rationalizations become what Anand *et al.* (2004) describe as a "shared resource" in an organization's culture, they may promulgate CWB as normal business practice. The key question, therefore, is can HR address counterproductive leader behavior by employing such things as selection, ethics-based rewards and discipline, and cultural norms, and by tying ethics to career advancement?

There are no easy or quick solutions to dealing with leader misconduct. However, a review of the literature reveals a number of guidelines that HR can follow. (See Table 9.1 for a list of these guidelines.) For example, Anand *et al.* (2004) propose a set of actions that can address the challenges posed by rationalizing either before or after engaging in counterproductive leader behavior. First and foremost is the issue of prevention; once rationalization has become entrenched in an organization it is increasingly difficult to distinguish between ethical and unethical practices, and to detect the latter. The following factors were identified by Anand *et al.* (2004) as important for preventing corruption:

- Train employees to reflect upon a proposed action or decision from another perspective (e.g., customer, shareholder, or the public at large), sometimes known as the "headline test" – how would an action or decision be regarded if it were reported in the media?
- Consider some form of performance evaluation approach (as opposed to outcome-based) to enable others to focus on not only the numbers/financials produced by leaders, but also how they were met.
- Foster an ethical environment via mechanisms for reporting and discussing perceived ethical issues/problems without fear of retribution (e.g., ethics officer) and by the use of verification procedures for code-compliance during key activities; both of these strategies increase the likelihood of detection.
- Have top management be seen as ethical, and disseminate throughout the organization examples of when senior leaders resisted temptations and of conventional but questionable practices; by the same token, ethical lapses should be addressed promptly.

Other scholars of counterproductive leader behavior endorse similar prevention strategies. Veiga *et al.* (2004) suggest that organizations must teach leaders how to confront ethical dilemmas and, more widely, establish a culture that goes beyond strict adherence to rules and policies. In other words, leaders must take on some of the responsibility for identifying various considerations in determining what is right and fair. This is especially the case when the welfare of others is involved. Ivancevich *et al.* (2003) stress the importance of having a cadre of respected leaders who can project the style and behaviors that are expected from all managers when faced with difficult decisions. Such behaviors can be further reinforced by an ethics award program that recognizes exemplary cases of ethical behavior, ones which portray company values and standards. Similarly, ethical behavior criteria can also be incorporated within an organization's evaluation, promotion, and merit pay

Table 9.1 Guidelines on how HR can control counterproductive leader behaviors

1   Train employees and leaders to reflect upon a proposed action or decision from the perspective of how it would be regarded if it were reported in the media.
2   Consider some performance evaluation approaches that focus on not only outcomes, but also how they were met.
3   Foster an ethical environment via mechanisms for monitoring key activities and reporting and discussing perceived ethical issues/problems without fear of retribution.
4   Have top management be seen to be ethical by disseminating throughout the organization examples of when senior leaders resisted temptations and of conventional but questionable practices.
5   Introduce an ethics award program which recognizes exemplary cases of ethical behavior.
6   Include ethical behavior criteria in evaluation, promotion, and pay decisions.
7   Leaders should communicate how ethical consideration went into important organizational decisions.
8   Use external change agents to quickly take action when misconduct is discovered.
9   Use ethics as a criterion when selecting leaders.

decisions. This underscores the importance of ethical behavior as a part of the reward system (Ivancevich *et al.*, 2003). Training leaders to take even a little time to reflect upon an action or decision may provide them with insight into the values underlying their motives. Are they engaging in behavior to follow the letter or the spirit of the law? In a similar vein, articulating the underlying principles behind organizational codes of conduct is likely to guide interpretation beyond strict adherence (Veiga *et al.*, 2004).

To the extent possible, senior leaders should be encouraged to share information publicly about important organizational decisions, as well as the information about the principles and decision-making processes that went into them (Trevino *et al.*, 2003). Further, senior leaders should communicate with employees on a regular basis about ethical issues and use what Trevino *et al.* (2003) call "socially salient action" (e.g., punishments and rewards) to signal support for ethical values.

When counterproductive leader behavior has become entrenched, taking action to reverse deeply embedded tendencies is of paramount importance. Whether the misconduct is fraudulent or sexual in nature, Anand *et al.* (2004) suggest that acceptance of wrongdoing, coupled with quick action, is key to initiating a reversal away from counterproductive behavior supported by rationalizations. Moreover, external change agents are likely to be the most successful at reversing such behavior because not only do they signal a break with the past and an intention to change for the future, but also they bring with them a different perspective that promotes questions about long-held practices.

Finally, as Schneider (1987) so aptly and succinctly stated, "people make the place." This is even more so in the case of senior leaders in organizations. Therefore, all attempts to create an ethical work environment in which there is little place for counterproductive behaviors starts with good employee selection strategies. Selection of leaders has long focused on the display of job-relevant behaviors, as in the practice of assessment centers, at the expense of broader and perhaps more relevant traits such as integrity and honesty. If personality traits and dispositions are considered at all, the focus in managerial selection systems has been on extroversion facets of dominance, assertiveness, and energy, as well as conscientiousness facets of competence and achievement orientation. Yet, as we summarized in the section on antecedents of CWB, traits related to socialization/integrity/alpha are among the best predictors in this domain and await to be incorporated into managerial selection and promotion systems.

Conclusion

In this chapter, our main objective was to clarify the construct domain of counterproductive leader behaviors and call for an integration of the literature on CWB and ethical behavior in leadership roles. We provided a general theoretical background from these areas and briefly reviewed the empirical literature on the antecedents of CWB. A number of guidelines were also suggested to HR practitioners. We hope that this chapter marks the beginning of integration between the currently disparate literatures in industrial and organizational psychology and those from management.

References

Anand, V., Ashforth, B.E. and Joshi, M. (2004) Business as usual: The acceptance and perpetuation of corruption in organizations. *Academy of Management Executive*, 18: 39–53.

Bennett, R.J. and Robinson, S.L. (2003) The past, present, and future of workplace deviance research. In J. Greenberg (ed.), *Organizational Behavior: The State of the Science* (pp. 247–281). Mahwah, NJ: Lawrence Erlbaum.

Berry, C., Ones, D.S. and Sackett, P.R. (2007) Meta-analysis of interpersonal deviance, organizational deviance, and their common correlates. *Journal of Applied Psychology*.

Coleman, J.W. (1987) Toward an integrated theory of white-collar crime. *American Journal of Sociology*, 93: 406–439.

Digman, J.M. (1997) Higher-order factors of the Big Five. *Journal of Personality and Social Psychology*, 73: 1246–1256.

Gruys, M.L. and Sackett, P.R. (2003) Investigating the dimensionality of counterproductive work behavior. *International Journal of Selection and Assessment*, 11: 30–42.

Hollinger, R.C. and Clark, J.P. (1983) *Theft by Employees*. Lexington, MA: Lexington Books.

Ivancevich, J.M., Duening, T.N., Gilbert, J.A. and Konopaske, R. (2003) Deterring white-collar crime. *Academy of Management Executive*, 17: 114–127.

Kanungo, R.N. and Mendonca, M. (1996) *Ethical Dimensions of Leadership*. Thousand Oaks, CA: Sage.

Kellerman, B. (2005) How bad leadership happens. *Leader to Leader*, Winter: 41–46.

Kouzes, J.M. and Posner, B.Z. (1993) *Credibility*. San Francisco, CA: Jossey-Bass.

Martinko, M.J., Gundlach, M.J. and Douglas, S.C. (2002) Toward an integrative theory of counterproductive workplace behavior: A causal reasoning perspective. *International Journal of Selection and Assessment*, 10: 36–50.

Murphy, K.R. (1993) *Honesty in the Workplace*. Pacific Grove, CA: Brooks/Cole.

Ones, D.S. and Viswesvaran, C. (2003) The Big–5 personality and counterproductive work behaviors. In A. Sagie, S. Stashevsky and M. Koslowsky (eds.), *Misbehavior and Dysfunctional Attitudes in Organizations* (pp. 211–249). Basingstoke, UK: Palgrave/ Macmillan.

Ones, D.S., Viswesvaran, C. and Schmidt, F.L. (1993) Comprehensive meta-analysis of integrity test validities: Findings and implications for personnel selection and theories of job performance. *Journal of Applied Psychology*, 78: 679–703.

Paajanen, G.E. (1988) The prediction of counterproductive behavior by individual and organizational variables. Unpublished doctoral dissertation. University of Minnesota, Minneapolis, MN.

Patterson, J. and Kim, P. (1991) *The Day America Told the Truth*. Englewood Cliffs, NJ: Prentice-Hall.

Penney, L.M., Spector, P.F. and Fox, S. (2003) Stress, personality and counterproductive work behavior. In A. Sagie, S. Stashevsky and M. Koslowsky (eds.), *Misbehavior and Dysfunctional Attitudes in Organizations* (pp. 194–210). Basingstoke, UK: Palgrave/ Macmillan.

Robinson, S.L. and Bennett, R.J. (1995) A typology of deviant workplace behaviors: A multidimensional scaling study. *Academy of Management Journal*, 38: 555–572.

Sackett, P.R. (2002) The structure of counterproductive work behaviors: Dimensionality and relationships with facets of job performance. *International Journal of Selection and Assessment*, 10: 5–11.

Sackett, P.R. and DeVore, C.J. (2001) Counterproductive behaviors at work. In N. Anderson and D.S. Ones (eds.), *Handbook of Industrial, Work and Organizational Psychology: Vol. 1. Personnel Psychology* (pp. 145–164). London: Sage.

Schneider, B. (1987) The people make the place. *Personnel Psychology*, 40: 437–453.

Trevino, L.K. (1990) A cultural perspective on changing and developing organizational ethics. *Research in Organizational Change and Development*, 4: 195–230.

Trevino, L.K., Brown, M. and Hartman, L.P. (2003) A qualitative investigation of perceived executive ethical leadership: Perceptions from inside and outside the executive suite. *Human Relations*, 56: 5–37.

Turner, N., Barling, J., Epitropaki, O., Butcher, V. and Milner, C. (2002) Transformational leadership and moral reasoning. *Journal of Applied Psychology*, 87: 304–311.

Vardi, Y. and Weitz, E. (2004) *Misbehavior in Organizations*. Mahwah, NJ: Lawrence Erlbaum.

Veiga, J.F., Golden, T.D. and Dechant, K. (2004) Why managers bend company rules. *Academy of Management Executive*, 18: 84–90.

Yukl, G. (2002) *Leadership in Organizations*, 5th edn. Upper Saddle River, NJ: Prentice Hall.

THE CANDY CONUNDRUM

Christopher Touchey is the Regional Manager (Northeast region) of a large chain of convenience stores. After visiting numerous stores, he noticed that many seemed to devote an inordinate amount of shelf space to Sweet-tooth candy products. When investigating the reason, Christopher learned that the Sweet-tooth representative was giving store managers $25 restaurant gift certificates every week in exchange for bigger candy orders. Christopher did not feel that devoting so much space to Sweet-tooth products was good for the company, since it was only a mediocre seller. Company policies forbid the accepting of any gifts greater than $50.

Related questions

1 What should Christopher do?
2 Are the store managers behaving unethically?
3 How can the company prevent such behaviors in the future?

Part III

Emerging trends and new issues

10 Outsourcing and HRM

BRIAN S. KLAAS

Estimates suggest that huge sums are now being spent by firms to outsource activities that a few decades ago were performed in-house by their own employees (Engardio, 2006). Indeed, the maturing of the outsourcing marketplace and the outsourcing of even critical work processes have transformed how we think about organizational design and organizational staffing (Quinn, 2000). Increasingly, organizations are being prompted to assess what jobs and functions should be integrated within the firm and what jobs and functions can be outsourced. Further, these changes have enormous implications for employment models and labor market policy within both developed and developing economies (Clott, 2004).

In this chapter, we will consider what factors have led to the increased use of outsourcing across a broad range of activities and functions. We also will address what firms should consider when determining whether to outsource organizational processes and how firms should manage the outsourcing process once the decision has been made. Finally, while many of the changes being observed in the use of outsourcing are being driven by developments that affect organizations throughout our economy, outsourcing decisions are also heavily influenced by institutional context and detail. We illustrate this point by closing with a discussion of outsourcing within the functional area of human resources. We discuss areas within HR where the trends discussed in this chapter have led to an increased use of outsourcing as well as areas where – because of institutional differences – very different approaches to outsourcing are being pursued.

Do environmental changes explain the growth in outsourcing?

Firms have always faced choices about whether activities should be performed in-house or whether services should be obtained via contractual relationships with a vendor or supplier. For much of the twentieth century, while managers made use of outsourcing, that use was often more selective. In many ways, the dominant organizational model was a vertically integrated firm with organizational control over most aspects of the production process (Lepak and Snell, 1999; Williamson, 1993). Now, quite clearly, we are moving away from that dominant model. But what explains the emergence of outsourcing and alternative models for organizational design?

What factors influence the outsourcing decision?

Extensive research has been done in transaction cost economics (TCE) to examine what factors influence the make or buy decision – the decision about whether to keep processes in-house or to outsource them (Shelanski and Klein, 1995). According to TCE, when outsourcing is used, firms are relying on a market-based form of governance (contractual relationships and market competition) to ensure they receive quality goods and services. When firms keep processes in-house, they are relying on organizational governance (hierarchical organizational structures). While outsourcing offers benefits that flow from increased economies of scale, the potential for high-powered incentives, and the ability to respond quickly to supply and demand shifts, it exposes firms to greater risks from opportunism by the vendor or supplier (Williamson, 1996).

Research within TCE has shown that characteristics of the task, the organization, and the institutional environment affect when an organization is likely to benefit from market governance (i.e., outsourcing) and when a firm is likely to benefit from organizational governance (Leiblein et al., 2002). For example, off-the-shelf products or services are generally viewed as more appropriate for outsourcing arrangements. Because limited customization is necessary, a firm is able to benefit from the economies of scale that result from using a vendor that provides that same product or service to other firms. Further, because the product is off-the-shelf, there are few switching costs (Williamson, 1996). Consequently, market competition is likely to serve as an effective tool by which to ensure high levels of performance by the vendor.

By contrast, when the product or service demands substantial customization, the firm must often make an asset-specific investment in order for the vendor to provide the necessary goods and services. Once having made such an investment, the firm is vulnerable to opportunistic behavior by the vendor, simply because the switching costs are so high. Thus, market competition may cease to be an adequate tool by which to ensure adequate vendor performance (Williamson, 1993). While contractual mechanisms might well serve as a substitute for market competition in managing vendor performance, incomplete contracting is thought to be inevitable within many buyer–vendor relationships. Where substantial uncertainty exists regarding what will be needed from the vendor (because of likely changes in the nature of the service or product over time), it is difficult to completely specify all relevant contingencies within the outsourcing contract. Consequently, as a firm's needs change, adjustments will be needed in the contract, which means the firm will once again be dependent on the vendor – and thus vulnerable to opportunism (Williamson, 1996).

Given that substantial evidence has been found to support the basic tenets of TCE (Shelanski and Klein, 1995), we must then consider whether the significant growth in outsourcing since the mid 1990s is because there is an increased demand for goods and services that are well suited to outsourcing and market governance mechanisms. While we are unaware of evidence suggesting an increased demand for off-the-shelf products and services, firms do now have a greater incentive to structure processes so that it is easier to identify components that can be treated as off-the-shelf. Further, firms may also have a greater incentive to accept the risk of opportunism associated with relying on outsourcing for customized tasks and services and/or to invest in mechanisms for more effectively managing that risk (Mol *et al.*, 2005; Quinn, 2000).

Globalization

What are the underlying factors that have altered the incentive structure facing firms? Globalization and what has been referred to as labor arbitrage is obviously an enormous driver of the trend toward outsourcing. (See Chapter 2 for more about globalization.) Within developing economies, investment in human capital and in production capacity has expanded dramatically. As a result, for a wide array of both skilled and unskilled labor, the wage differential between developed and developing economies is substantial (Engardio, 2006). Because of this wage differential, firms increasingly have an incentive to identify components within their service delivery or production process that can be compartmentalized and then outsourced to a vendor operating in a lower-wage economy. Indeed, it might be argued that the wage differential is now so great that firms may be willing to accept the risks associated with vendor opportunism when outsourcing activities that involve substantial amounts of customization and asset-specific investment (Clott, 2004).

Technology

Technology, particularly as it relates to the internet and improved communication, is thought to be another key driver of the increased trend toward outsourcing. Developments relating to technology allow for a broader range of tasks and activities to be candidates for outsourcing to suppliers located throughout the world. With developments in technology, a wide range of service activities, from call centers to software development to medical diagnostics, can be readily outsourced. This provides many additional opportunities for firms to benefit from the wage differential between different segments of the global economy (Conklin, 2005; Mol *et al.*, 2005).

Another reason why technology has led to an increased emphasis on outsourcing is that, when combined with vendors operating globally, it allows for increased speed in terms of product development. In many cases, the ability to contract out product development activities to locations throughout the world allows for work on key projects to occur 24/7, thus reducing the time required for a product to make it to market (Engardio, 2006).

It should also be noted that while the trend toward outsourcing was enabled by globalization and wage differentials and by developments relating to technology, the trend is now being accelerated as the outsourcing infrastructure has matured. Highly credible vendors have emerged for almost every sector of the outsourcing space. Further, the critical role being played by outsourcing within many successful business models has given outsourcing institutional credibility. Indeed, it has been suggested that because of this credibility, some managers feel pressure to move toward outsourcing simply to demonstrate that they are extracting all possible efficiencies within their functional area (Clott, 2004).

When should firms respond by outsourcing?

As noted above, the literature on transaction cost economics suggests that firms evaluating whether to outsource an activity or process should consider whether the task characteristics are compatible with an outsourcing model (Klaas *et al.*, 1999). While globalization and wage differentials and technological developments may have increased the expected utility of many outsourcing projects, clearly not all activities within a firm should be outsourced. What factors should managers consider when determining whether a particular task or activity should be outsourced?

Consistent with what might be suggested by TCE, those activities or processes that might be viewed as off-the-shelf are likely candidates for outsourcing (Lepak and Snell, 1999). Not only is market-based contracting likely to be effective for such activities, but also firms are more likely to benefit from economies of scale, simply because the cost of developing relevant infrastructure will be spread across multiple clients (Greer *et al.*, 1999). These activities would be likely candidates for outsourcing regardless of whether outsourcing allows the firm to take advantage of global wage differentials and regardless of enabling technological developments.

What about activities that involve some degree of asset-specificity – some degree of customization for the client? Conventionally, where asset-specificity is high, outsourcing is less likely to be recommended. To the extent that an asset-specific investment is required in order for a supplier to provide goods or services, the firm is likely to be vulnerable to opportunistic behavior by the supplier (Williamson, 1996). However, with the cost-saving opportunities presented by what has been referred to as labor arbitrage, might firms consider outsourcing even when there are significant levels of asset-specificity? Where opportunities for cost savings are substantial, there might well be instances where firms should consider accepting some risk by using outsourcing in a way that allows for global wage differentials to generate cost savings for the firm.

But at what point do outsourcing activities involving asset-specificity introduce too much risk? Research done on core competencies and the resource-based view of the firm would seem to offer some limits on the degree to which firms should outsource activities involving customization and asset-specific investments (Barney, 1991). As originally conceived by Prahalad and Hamel (1990) core competencies allow firms to gain competitive advantage and relate to a collective knowledge or understanding within an organization about how to perform a complex and interrelated set of activities. Further, this collective understanding is thought to allow the firm to produce value for customers across different markets or applications. Core competencies are thought to lead to competitive advantage because they involve knowledge that is often implicit, that resides within the collective, and that develops gradually over time.

For firms with well-established core competencies, the risks associated with outsourcing increase significantly as the connection between the activity being outsourced and the core competency increases (Connor and Prahalad, 1996). Further, because core competencies are rarely compartmentalized within specific parts of a firm, links to core competencies may sometimes be less than obvious. Thus, for firms with clear core competencies, the risks associated with outsourcing activities where customization or asset-specificity is high can potentially go well beyond the risks associated with vendor opportunism (Leiblein *et al.*, 2002). Clearly, not all activities that involve customization or asset-specificity are closely associated with a firm's core competencies. But where that link exists, outsourcing creates additional risk for the firm.

Conventionally, when a firm outsources activities that involve high levels of uncertainty or asset-specificity, the firm risks vendor opportunism due to incomplete contracting. For example, if a firm outsources activities relating to training and development, it is unlikely that the firm will be able to anticipate all needs likely to arise over time. Further, any vendor with which the firm contracts will likely have to customize many of its programs, requiring an asset-specific investment by the firm. Therefore, as the firm's needs change, the firm will likely need to modify the terms of the contract with the vendor. However, negotiations over changes to the contract would likely be affected by the asset-specific investment. The dependence created by this asset-specific investment may allow for vendor opportunism to affect negotiations over contract terms, resulting in increased costs for the services provided (Klaas *et al.*, 1999).

While such costs are important, the risks associated with outsourcing activities more closely linked to sources of competitive advantage will clearly be greater. For example, assume that the firm in question has well-established routines and norms regarding management development that have allowed it to develop a pipeline of highly effective leaders. Assume also that this pipeline of leadership talent has allowed the firm to build a culture that allows it to quickly evaluate and respond to market opportunities. By outsourcing training and development activities, the firm is assuming additional risk. It is outsourcing activities that depend on an appreciation of the collective and often implicit knowledge that underlies the firm's ability to develop leadership talent. The firm assumes some risk by giving control over an activity that supports a source of competitive advantage to an entity that may not fully share in the collective knowledge. Further, opportunism by the vendor may affect whether resources are devoted to providing services in a manner consistent with how the firm developed and maintained this potential source of competitive advantage (Gainey and Klaas, 2003).

Recent developments in outsourcing may well have changed how firms evaluate what activities they are willing to outsource. For some activities, wage differentials may now be such that firms are willing to outsource even activities where there is some level of task uncertainty or asset-specificity. Cost savings obtained in the near term may be leading decision makers to accept some opportunism risks over the longer term (Clott, 2004). Such an approach may at times be economically rational for activities that are far removed from potential sources of competitive advantage. However, firms which outsource activities that involve uncertainty and asset-specificity, as well as a link to sources of competitive advantage, may well be testing the limits of what is feasible with market-based governance mechanisms.

Manage the outsourcing relationship to improve outcomes

As noted above, the risks created by outsourcing will vary substantially with the type of activity being outsourced. In large part, this is because the effectiveness of market governance mechanisms will vary with the type of activity being outsourced. In consequence, the strategy for managing outsourcing relationships is likely to vary with the task being outsourced. Strategies that might be effective when dealing with activities that are well suited to outsourcing mechanisms might be problematic when the tasks being outsourced are ill suited to traditional market governance mechanisms (e.g., market competition) (Quinn, 2000).

When outsourcing off-the-shelf activities, appropriate use of the standard tools of market governance is thought to be sufficient to ensure effective performance by vendors (Greer et al., 1999). Careful specification within the contract of the tasks, performance metrics, and penalties for non-performance is generally thought to be essential. It should be acknowledged that even when tasks are well suited to outsourcing, incomplete contracts are still, at least to some extent, inevitable. Thus, firms are advised to make effective use of the discipline provided by market competition. As part of this, firms are advised to engage in regular benchmarking of the services available from alternative vendors and to ensure that contractual terms allow the firm to switch vendors without undue difficulty (Conklin, 2005). Similarly, firms are advised to carefully assess resources and skills possessed by a firm, relying on information available within the marketplace to assess vendor capabilities. Such behavior is, of course, appropriate and expected when the vendor is providing services through what might be viewed as an arm's-length relationship. The relationship between buyer and seller doesn't necessarily involve significant amounts of trust or information sharing (Klaas, 2003).

When firms opt to outsource activities that are less obviously suited to market governance, the task of managing the outsourcing relationship is more complex. For example, when the activities being outsourced involve high levels of task uncertainty and asset-specificity, contractual relationships and market competition are unlikely to be sufficient tools by which to manage the outsourcing relationship (Takeishi, 2001). Where such conditions exist, an investment must be made in order for the vendor to be able to deliver the desired goods and services. Making such an investment (particularly in light of uncertainty regarding what tasks will actually be needed over time) introduces a level of dependence that cannot typically be managed through a conventional arm's-length relationship. In some instances, firms compensate for the limitations of market-based governance through the development of strong personal ties. Not only do such ties allow for the free exchange of information about needs and constraints within the firm, but also such ties may serve to constrain opportunistic behavior by the vendor (Nooteboom *et al.*, 1997). By moving from an arm's-length relationship to one where trust is allowed to develop over time through a social exchange process, it becomes possible to limit the vendor's willingness to engage in opportunistic behavior. Further, where relationships are well established and visible within the general marketplace, the reputational cost of violating trust may be substantial.

Efforts to change the nature of contractual relationships may also be required. For example, some firms attempt to align the interests of the vendor and of the firm via gain-sharing mechanisms that allow both parties to benefit from improved performance and efficiency by the vendor. In other cases, vendor compensation is tied to broader measures of client performance, again based on the argument that opportunism is likely to be minimized where the interests of the vendor are tied to the interests of the client. Such features may well be combined with longer-term contracts that make the vendor responsible for the initial cost of any required asset-specific investments.

The moderating factors of outsourcing arrangements

The foregoing discussion highlighted major trends in outsourcing and addressed how these trends have affected decision making about whether firms should outsource and how outsourcing relationships should be managed. While firms are being affected by the broad trends identified here across a variety of settings, it is important to note that the institutional setting will likely play a critical role in determining how firms should respond to the broader trends being observed. The importance of institutional context can perhaps best be seen by examining how outsourcing decisions within one functional area (human resources) vary with both the activity and the organizational setting.

The nature of the outsourced activity

Consistent with many of the trends discussed above, business process outsourcing (BPO) is increasingly being used by significant global organizations to provide a wide range of largely transactional services (Conklin, 2005). Vendors such as Hewitt Associates, Accenture, IBM, and Convergys have all received substantial attention for significant BPO contracts from firms such as Procter and Gamble, Duke Energy, Whirlpool, and DuPont. For large global firms, managing transactional elements of the HR function requires a significant investment in IT infrastructure (Staff, 2006). Outsourcing to vendors such as those mentioned above allows for the cost of developing that infrastructure, in part, to be spread across multiple clients. Thus, economies of scale can generate substantial cost savings. Beyond this, vendors such as those mentioned above have the capacity to make ready use of skilled labor located throughout the world when developing and implementing human resources information systems (HRIS) applications, thus enabling them to extract cost savings from global wage differentials. Program administration also can be conducted in a way that allows vendors to extract benefits from global wage differentials (Conklin, 2005).

Moreover, through effective use of technology and business process expertise, these outsourcing arrangements are designed to help improve and standardize business processes as they relate to transactional HR issues. For example, in 2006 DuPont agreed to a thirteen-year $1.1 billion HR outsourcing contract, which is estimated to reduce costs by between 20 and 30 percent and, at the same time, improve the delivery of transactional services by improving and standardizing business processes (Staff, 2006).

For such BPO deals within the HR arena, the vendor is offering expertise in standardizing and improving business processes, cost savings that result from economies of scale, and cost savings that result from the ability to extract benefits from global wage differentials. Such contracts typically are dominated by activities and processes that might be referred to as the back-office part of HR. Transactional activities such as payroll administration, insurance enrollment, retirement program administration, and workforce event and salary administration tend to be core responsibilities within any such arrangement. While some level of customization is required, such activities seem far removed from what might be viewed as core competencies or critical resources within any firm (Klaas *et al.*, 1999). While providing effective services to employees and retirees may be viewed as a key ingredient to an organizational culture that revolves around a positive workplace environment, the nature of the services being provided may well allow firms to establish metrics that enable them to monitor and control the quality of services being provided.

Within large global firms, outsourcing within the HR function currently appears to be focused within the BPO arena (Conklin, 2005). BPO within the HR function allows firms to benefit from economies of scale, vendor expertise in standardizing processes, and the ability to compartmentalize tasks in a way that brings cost savings as a result of global wage differentials. Further, while the activities being outsourced are not entirely off-the-shelf, some level of standardization across clients is likely to be possible with activities such as payroll administration or insurance enrollment administration.

Interestingly, more complete outsourcing of the HR function appears to be less common. Leadership and organizational development, reward system design, employee relations and other less transactional activities are not typically included in these substantial BPO HR contracts. One reason for this might well relate to how outsourcing firms utilize global wage differentials to produce cost savings. A prerequisite for being able to generate such savings is the ability to compartmentalize tasks and to employ expertise in locations where wage levels are significantly lower. For many more strategic HR services, the service provider must acquire significant amounts of knowledge about issues unique to the firm. Much of the knowledge that must be acquired to determine appropriate solutions is tacit and obtained through close interaction with key stakeholders over time. Moreover, solutions often must be devised as new opportunities or problems arise, meaning it is difficult to specify in advance what is likely to be needed by the firm or how vendor performance should be measured. Because of these factors, if firms outsource activities from the more strategic side of HR, they are less likely to be able to take advantage of global wage differentials, to benefit from economies of scale, and to effectively utilize standard mechanisms for market governance.

But if this is true, how does one explain the outsourcing of processes such as executive search that clearly are more strategic in nature? Certainly, outsourcing search activities provides few opportunities for firms to take advantage of global wage differentials. But benefits do arise from the standpoint of economies of scale. While the needs of each firm might well differ and while there clearly is a need to invest in gaining information about the culture and needs of the firm, the cost of building a network of relationships within an industry or across industries can be spread across multiple clients when a search firm is used. Moreover, for retained executive search firms, market governance mechanisms might well be effective. First, while some level of asset-specific investment is needed in order for a retained search firm to conduct an effective search, this level of investment pales in comparison to the investment required to build the network of relationships that is used in conducting the search. Second, retained search firms are charged with the task of placing executives in highly senior and highly visible positions. Failure both in terms of identifying possible candidates and in terms of identifying the wrong candidate is therefore likely to be highly visible, both within the firm and beyond. And since the future earnings of a search executive are highly dependent upon his/her reputation, incomplete contracting is less likely to limit the effectiveness of market governance. Third, while there may be uncertainty as to what attributes will lead to effective performance in the executive roles being filled, there is little uncertainty regarding the outcomes that are expected from senior leadership. Because of this, quick and effective feedback regarding vendor performance is likely to emerge in this setting. Thus, while perhaps few activities have more strategic implications than the retained search for senior executive positions, both economies of scale and the impact of reputation on the operation of market governance make outsourcing a viable option (Greer *et al.*, 1999).

Firm size

In this section, it is being suggested that while very significant trends are affecting how firms do and should use outsourcing, the impact of those trends is likely to vary across different institutional settings. While we can offer broad generalizations regarding when firms should consider outsourcing, it is important to emphasize how institutional details might affect the validity of those generalizations in particular settings. As another example of this point within the HR function, consider the case of outsourcing of HR activities by small and medium enterprises (those with 500 or fewer employees). Compared to a diversified global firm, the complexities involved in providing any number of transactional HR services are less significant. However, these transactional tasks must still be performed and efficiencies might still be gained by outsourcing these activities to a third party vendor. With regard to more strategic HR services, it is important to note that while decisions must be made regarding such issues as staffing and rewards, access to professional expertise is likely to be more limited in smaller firms. Maintaining an HR professional on staff to address such matters is likely to be cost prohibitive for many smaller firms. Consequently, for many smaller organizations, gaining access to HR expertise when there is no internal HR staff member is likely to require some form of an outsourcing relationship. However, once again, questions might be raised about the utility of market-based governance mechanisms. Small business owners will be needing advice and services with regard to tasks involving high levels of uncertainty. Further, difficulties are likely to exist regarding how to effectively measure the quality of services and programs. Also, some knowledge regarding unique conditions within the firm is likely to be required, suggesting that some level of asset-specific investment will be required in order to provide effective service. To the extent that the firm pays for this investment, the firm then becomes vulnerable to opportunism. These factors would all suggest that use of market governance to obtain the benefit of professional expertise regarding more strategic HR issues may well be of limited utility for many small organizations (Klaas, 2003).

For many small firms, the choice is not between outsourcing and relying on internal staff members for HR services and programs. For many small firms, economies of scale prohibit making use of full-time HR staff members. As such, for many small organizations, their outsourcing decision is at least in part determined by the value associated with professional HR expertise (Klaas, 2003). Where that value is high, firms may be willing to accept some of the risks associated with outsourcing activities that may not be well suited to market-based governance. Interestingly, the relationship between using outsourcing to obtain HR services and the value assigned to HR expertise may actually be the reverse of what is observed within larger organizations, suggesting again the importance of the institutional context in determining how firms should and do manage outsourcing activities.

Related to this, small firms may face unique challenges in managing their relationship with their vendor. Typically, strategic HR services may not be well suited to market governance mechanisms, as noted above. How do small business owners manage the risks associated with outsourcing when such standard mechanisms are less effective? One strategy frequently observed relates to gradually building strong personal ties with service providers, thus minimizing the likelihood of opportunism. It should further be noted that within this unique context, opportunities to build such relationships may be more feasible than in other settings. For example, when working with professional employer organizations, small business leaders also work with service providers on a broad range of transactional matters – thus providing opportunities for trust to emerge over time (Klaas, 2003).

Guidelines and summary

This chapter examined some of the major reasons for growth in the use of outsourcing among organizations in our economy. Some of the most significant reasons for growth related to global wage differentials and enabling developments with regard to technology. This chapter also presented models that have traditionally been used to evaluate why firms outsource. We then addressed how some of the factors that have led to an increase in outsourcing are changing how firms assess outsourcing decisions and how they manage outsourcing relationships. Finally, we discussed outsourcing within one specific functional area, both to more concretely show how outsourcing decisions are being affected by the trends identified within this chapter and also to show the importance of the institutional context in determining how firms do and should utilize outsourcing. Table 10.1 lists some guidelines for firms based on these discussions. Following these guidelines should help firms improve their decision making on whether to outsource as well as improve their management of the outsourcing relationship.

Table 10.1 Guidelines for outsourcing

1 Outsourcing is more likely to be beneficial when the product or service is standardized.
2 Outsourcing is more likely to be beneficial when core competencies are not involved.
3 Outsourcing is more likely to be beneficial when the cost savings are high.
4 The risks involved with outsourcing uncertain tasks and core competencies may be worth taking if the cost savings are high enough.
5 When outsourcing standardized services or products use market information, careful specification of the tasks within the contract, performance metrics, and penalties for non-performance to manage the outsourcing relationship.
6 When outsourcing services that are uncertain, customized, or tied to core competencies, manage the outsourcing relationship with the development of strong personal ties and trust over time through a social exchange process.
7 For small firms, the risks involved with outsourcing uncertain tasks and core competencies may be worth taking to gain the vendor's expertise.

References

Barney, J. (1991) Firm resources and sustained competitive advantage. *Journal of Management*, 17: 99–120.
Clott, C.B. (2004) Perspectives on global outsourcing and the changing nature of work. *Business and Society Review*, 109: 153–170.
Conklin, D.W. (2005) Risks and rewards in HR business process outsourcing. *Long Range Planning*, 38: 579–598.
Connor, K.R. and Prahalad, C.K. (1996) A resource-based theory of the firm: Knowledge versus opportunism. *Organizational Science*, 7: 477–501.
Engardio, P. (2006) The future of outsourcing. *Business Week*, 30 January: 50–58.
Gainey, T. and Klaas, B.S. (2003) The outsourcing of training and development: Factors impacting client satisfaction. *Journal of Management*, 29: 207–229.
Greer, C.R., Youngblood, S.A. and Gray, D.A. (1999) Human resource outsourcing: The make or buy decision. *Academy of Management Executive*, 13: 85–96.
Klaas, B.S. (2003) Professional employer organizations and their role in small and medium enterprises: The impact of HR outsourcing. *Entrepreneurship Theory and Practice*, 25: 43–61.
Klaas, B.S., McClendon, J. and Gainey, T. (1999) HR outsourcing and its impact: The role of transaction costs. *Personnel Psychology*, 52: 113–136.
Leiblein, M.J., Reuer, J.J. and Dalsace, F. (2002) Do make or buy decisions matter? The influence of organizational governance on technological performance. *Strategic Management Journal*, 23: 817–828.
Lepak, D.P. and Snell, S.A. (1999) Virtual HR: Strategic human resources in the 21st century. *Human Resource Management Review*, 8: 215–234.
Mol, M.J., van Tulder, R.J.M. and Beije, P.R. (2005) Antecedents and performance consequences of international outsourcing. *International Business Review*, 14: 599–617.
Nooteboom, B., Berger, H. and Noorderhaven, N.G. (1997) Effects of trust and governance on relational risk. *Academy of Management Journal*, 40: 308–338.

Prahalad, C.K. and Hamel, G. (1990) The core competence of the corporation. *Harvard Business Review*, 68: 79–91.

Quinn, J.B. (2000) Outsourcing innovation: The new engine of growth. *MIT Sloan Management Review*, 41: 13–28.

Shelanski, H.A. and Klein, P.G. (1995) Empirical work in transaction cost economics. *Journal of Law, Economics, and Organization*, 11: 335–361.

Staff (2006) Top enterprise HRO deals. *HRO Today*. January–February: 21–23.

Takeishi, A. (2001) Bridging inter- and intra-firm boundaries: Management of supplier involvement in automobile product development. *Strategic Management Journal*, 22: 405–433.

Williamson, O.E. (1993) Transaction cost economics and organization theory. *Institutional and Corporate Change*, 2: 107–156.

Williamson, O.E. (1996) *The Mechanisms of Governance*. New York: Oxford University Press.

OUTSOURCING HR

Robert Kellar is the VP of Human Resources for a large firm located in Vancouver. He has been ordered to try to upgrade the HR function technologically and to reduce costs in the long term. The CEO has informed him that outsourcing some of the HR functions may be a way to reduce costs. Robert is considering outsourcing some of the following HR functions: Background Checks, Employee Assistance/Counseling, Healthcare Benefits Administration, Pension Benefits Administration, Temporary Staffing, Retirement Benefits Administration, Payroll and Software Services, Recruiting, Staffing and Search, Employee Relocation, Training and Development, Performance Management, Strategic Business Planning, Policy Development/ Implementation, and Employee Communication Plans.

Related questions

1 Which of the above HR functions would make the most sense to outsource?
2 Which of the above functions would make the least sense to outsource?
3 What factors could influence your answers to the previous two questions?

11 The costs of employee benefits

JOSEPH J. MARTOCCHIO

This chapter looks at the high costs of employee benefits and what firms are doing to control those costs. We begin with a brief introduction to the different types of employee benefits.

A brief introduction to employee benefits

Employee benefits refer to employee compensation other than hourly wage or salary. To organize the vast benefits information efficiently for the purposes of making an effective brief introduction, it is useful to think about two dimensions: the source of the benefit and the role the benefit serves recipients. First, the source of the benefit can be characterized as legally required or discretionary. Second, the role the benefit serves recipients can be characterized as protection, paid time off, or accommodation and enhancement. Table 11.1 lists employee benefits programs typically offered in Canadian and US companies, indicating the role and source of the benefits.

Legally required benefits

The US and Canadian governments require that most employers provide particular benefits to employees. We refer to these as legally required benefits. Legally required benefits are mandated by several laws, the most important of which are the Social Security Act of 1935, various state workers' compensation laws, and the Family and Medical Leave Act of 1993 in the United States. In Canada, noteworthy legislation includes the Canada Pension Plan, the Old Age Security Act, and the Canada Health Act. All provide protection programs to employees and their dependants.

For example, the Social Security Act of 1935 set up two programs: a federal system of income benefits for retired workers and a system of unemployment insurance administered by the federal and state governments. Amendments to the Social

Table 11.1 Typical employee benefits in Canadian and US companies

Legally required benefits
- Retirement income
- Health insurance
- Unemployment insurance
- Workers' compensation
- Family and medical leave

Discretionary benefits
Protection programs
- Medical insurance
- Dental insurance
- Vision insurance
- Life insurance
- Prescription drugs
- Mental health and substance abuse
- Maternity care
- Disability insurance
- Retirement plans

Paid time off
- Holidays
- Vacation
- Sick leave
- Personal leave
- Bereavement or funeral leave
- Military leave
- Non-production time (e.g., lunch periods)

Accommodation and enhancement programs

Employees' and family members' mental and physical well-being
- Employee assistance programs
- Wellness programs
- Family assistance programs

Educational benefits for employees
- Educational assistance programs
- Tuition reimbursement programs
- Scholarship programs

Security Act in 1965 established the disability insurance and Medicare programs. Medicare provides insurance coverage for hospitalization, convalescent care, major doctor bills, and, beginning in 2006, prescription drug coverage, to nearly all US citizens aged at least 65 and disabled Social Security beneficiaries.

Discretionary employee benefits

Companies can choose to offer employees a wide variety of benefits that are not legally required. Discretionary benefits fulfill three main roles. The first role is fulfilled through protection programs, which most closely parallel legally required benefits by offering protections to income and health. The second, paid time off, affords employees time off with pay for many purposes, including illness or to celebrate designated holidays. The third, accommodation and enhancements, offers a variety of benefits for improvements to employees and their families, and includes wellness and educational assistance programs.

Income protection programs

There are three types of income protection programs, namely, disability insurance, life insurance, and retirement plans. Disability insurance replaces income for employees who become unable to work on a regular basis because of an illness or injury beyond workers' compensation. Life insurance protects family members by paying a specified amount to an employee's beneficiaries upon the employee's death. Retirement plans provide income to individuals and beneficiaries throughout their retirement. Companies may establish their retirement plans as defined contribution plans or defined benefit plans. With defined benefit plans, retirees receive guaranteed payments for the duration of their lives based on years of employment, age, and final salary level before retirement. Defined contribution plans allow employees to set aside a portion of their salary for investment purposes. Sometimes employers will contribute a smaller amount (that is, a match contribution) on behalf of each employee. Defined contribution plans are much riskier for employees than defined benefit plans because the amount and duration of retirement income depend mainly on the performance of investments.

Health protection programs

These programs refer to a host of practices geared toward promoting sound health. Health insurance plans represent the largest portion of a company's health protection offerings. Health insurance covers the costs of a variety of services that promote sound physical and mental health. Companies can choose from four broad classes of health insurance programs including fee-for-service plans, managed care plans, point-of-service plans, and savings accounts based on the consumer-driven health care philosophy.

Fee-for-service plans, also known as indemnity plans, provide protection for three types of medical expenses: hospital expenses, surgical expenses, and physicians' charges. Generally, fee-for-service plans pay expenses according to a schedule of usual, customary, and reasonable charges. Under fee-for-service plans, policy-holders (employees) may generally select any licensed physician, surgeon, or medical facility for treatment, and the insurance plan reimburses (either wholly or partially) the policy-holders after medical services are rendered.

Health maintenance organizations (HMOs) and preferred provider organizations (PPOs) are the most common forms of managed care. HMOs and PPOs organize, deliver, and finance health care. Managed care plans became popular alternatives to fee-for-service plans mainly to help employers and insurance companies more effectively manage the costs of health care. By design, managed care plans impose substantial restrictions on an employee's ability to make choices about from whom they can receive medical treatment, on the gatekeeper role of primary care physicians, and on the level of benefits employees can receive based on designated in- and non-network providers.

A point-of-service plan combines features of fee-for-service systems and HMOs. Employees pay a nominal co-payment for each visit to a designated in-network physician. In this regard, point-of-service plans are similar to HMOs. Unlike HMOs, however, employees possess the option to receive care from health care providers outside the designated network of physicians, but they pay somewhat more for this choice. This choice feature is common to fee-for-service plans.

Consumer-driven health care refers to the objective of helping companies maintain control over costs while also enabling employees to make greater choices about health care. This approach may enable employers to lower the cost of insurance premiums by selecting plans with higher employee deductibles. The most popular consumer-driven approaches are flexible spending accounts and health reimbursement accounts.

Paid time off

The second type of discretionary benefit is paid time off. Paid time off policies compensate employees when they are not performing their primary work duties. Companies offer most paid time off as a matter of custom, particularly as paid holidays, vacations, and sick leave.

Accommodation and enhancement programs

These benefits promote opportunities for employees and family members. Four specific objectives of accommodation and enhancement benefits are: mental and physical well-being of employees and family members (e.g., stress management; smoking cessation); family assistance programs (e.g., childcare; elder care); flexible work schedules (e.g., telecommuting; flextime); and skills and knowledge acquisition through educational programs (e.g., tuition reimbursement for employees; college scholarships for employees' children).

Employer costs for compensation and benefits

The US Department of Labor's Bureau of Labor Statistics (BLS) regularly publishes current information about employer costs for compensation and benefits in the United States, and changes in these costs over time, on its website http://www.bls.gov. Benefits professionals may use these data to benchmark current benefits costs against reported averages, or as a starting point for budget planning. The following paragraphs are excerpted from a BLS news release, based on September 2005 data:

> Employer costs for employee compensation averaged $26.05 per hour worked. Wages and salaries, which averaged $18.28, accounted for 70.2 percent of these costs, while benefits, which averaged $7.77, accounted for the remaining 29.8 percent. Costs for legally required benefits, including Social Security, Medicare, unemployment insurance, and workers' compensation, averaged $2.13 per hour (8.2 percent of total compensation). Discretionary employer expenditures for life, health, and disability insurance benefits averaged $2.10 (8.0 percent); paid leave benefits (vacations, holidays, sick leave, and other leave) averaged $1.72 (6.6 percent); and retirement and savings benefits averaged $1.13 (4.3 percent) per hour worked.
>
> Private industry employer compensation costs averaged $24.34 per hour worked. Wages and salaries averaged $17.23 per hour (70.8 percent), while benefits averaged $7.11 (29.2 percent). Employer costs for paid leave averaged $1.55 per hour worked (6.4 percent), supplemental pay averaged 71 cents (2.9 percent), insurance benefits averaged $1.78 (7.3 percent), retirement and savings averaged 90 cents (3.7 percent), and legally required benefits $2.14 (8.8 percent) per hour worked.
>
> Employer costs in State and local governments averaged $36.16 per hour worked. Wages and salaries, which accounted for 67.8 percent of the total, averaged $24.52, while benefits, which accounted for the remaining 32.2 percent, averaged $11.64. Benefit costs increased from 31.4 percent of total compensation and $10.89 per hour for State and local government workers in September 2004.
>
> (US Bureau of Labor Statistics, 2005)

Overall, benefits accounted for approximately 30 percent of total compensation costs. Employers spend about $4,040 per employee per year just for insurance benefits. This is likely alarming to company management given the fact that health insurance premiums alone have been rising at an annual rate ranging between 10 and 15 percent for the past several years with no changes in sight.

The Canadian government's Statistics Canada (http://www.statcan.ca) published similar cost statistics until it discontinued this survey program in 2001. Nevertheless, a review of a multitude of articles that address employee benefits issues in Canada revealed that the amount of employers' expenditures on specific employee benefits as a percentage of total compensation is similar to expenditures by US employers.

How changes in environmental factors have raised the cost of benefits

Four significant changes in the environment which have contributed substantially to higher employee benefit costs are: industry prospects, economic conditions, and forecasts; government regulation of employee benefits; changing demographics of the labor force; and advances in health care.

Industry prospects with economic conditions and forecasts

The first factor, industry prospects along with current and anticipated economic conditions, can influence employee benefit costs. Industry prospects and economic forecasts set the backdrop for understanding a company's willingness to bear discretionary benefits costs because these factors are indicators of the future of companies. Forecasts indicating growth possibly call for strengthening discretionary benefits offerings and levels to help recruit and retain the most qualified employees. Pessimistic forecasts emphasize the need to save costs by shifting more of the responsibility onto employees. For example, more and more companies require that employees share a greater percentage of the cost of health insurance. Also, there has been a shift away from employer-sponsored defined benefit retirement plans to employer-sponsored defined contribution plans, which makes it easier for companies to predict its costs for retirement plan benefits. Further, negative outlooks may lead companies to expand outplacement services, an example of an accommodation and enhancement benefit, in anticipation of large-scale layoffs.

Employers will very likely continue to sponsor employee benefits despite economic conditions for two reasons. First, the Internal Revenue Code, the set of regulations pertaining to taxation in the United States, creates corporate income tax advantages for employee benefits plans that are offered on a non-discriminatory basis to employees. Employers may exclude limited contributions to these plans from taxable annual income, leading to reduced tax payments to the federal government. Second, generous benefits offerings facilitate a company's efforts to attract and retain the best-qualified employees. Although employer-sponsored benefits costs are significant at any point in time, well-qualified workforces presumably create lucrative advantages for companies as evidenced by high-quality customer service, competent business functions (such as innovative marketing), and research and development.

Government regulation of employee benefits

Three broad forces contribute to an employer's choice of discretionary benefits and its ability to fund them. The first two, adequacy of legally required benefits and employee expectations, directly influence an employer's choice. The third, the cost of legally required benefits, influences a company's ability to fund discretionary benefits. Naturally, money is a limited resource. Quite simply, the more money a company spends to meet its obligations under legally required benefits programs, the less money it has available to spend on discretionary employee benefits.

First, social plight during the industrialization of the US economy and the Great Depression promoted the rise of many legally required benefits such as retirement income and medical insurance under the Social Security Act and Canada Pension Plan. US federal and state governments, and provincial governments in Canada, mandated modest benefits which were never intended as the sole means of support. After all, the US and Canadian economies are based on free market principles, not on socialist principles more commonly found in many Eastern European countries and in large segments of the People's Republic of China. In addition, the cost of living has risen more quickly than government benefits. Finally, lawmakers could not anticipate the very high costs of health care due, in large part, to advances in medicine and health care technology. The entire structure of the health care industry is fundamentally different now than in prior years. These changes make the funding formulas inadequate to meet today's realities.

Second, the US government's imposition of wage freezes during World War II gave rise to many present-day discretionary benefits. Employers withdrew costly offerings after the government ended the wage freeze. The withdrawal of these benefits created discontent among employees; many viewed employer-sponsored benefits as entitlements. For instance, employees strongly reacted to the withdrawal of medical insurance. Legal battles followed, based on the claims of employees that health protection was a fundamental right. Health insurance benefits subsequently became a mandatory subject of collective bargaining in union settings.

Third, the US and Canadian governments require companies to support legally required benefits. A variety of laws require employer contributions with payroll taxes. For example, in the United States, the Federal Insurance Contributions Act requires support of the Social Security old-age, survivor, and disability insurance program. Unemployment insurance benefits are financed by federal taxes and sometimes state taxes levied on employers. A federal tax is levied on employers under the Federal Unemployment Tax Act. Of course, limited financial resources necessarily force employers to reduce the number and level of discretionary benefits. For example, legally required benefits in private industry typically equaled more than 30 percent of total benefits expenditures by US companies (i.e., $2.14/$7.11).

Changing demographics of the labor force

According to the US Bureau of Labor Statistics and Statistics Canada, labor force diversity will likely continue to increase based on gender, age, race, and ethnicity. (See Chapter 5 for more detail on the changing family.) An employer-sponsored benefits program is most effective when the workforce is relatively similar in terms of needs and preferences. For example, let's assume a company's workforce has 60 percent women and 40 percent men. Most of the women are of child-bearing age and most of the men range in age between their fifties and sixties. On the surface, one could say that this workforce is not very homogeneous in terms of needs and preferences for benefits because its composition varies considerably by gender and age. Below the surface, one could reasonably conclude that there will be substantial differences in the needs and preferences for benefits. Chances are most of the women may place a high value on daycare benefits while most of the men will not have a need for such benefits because their children are likely to be near or at adulthood.

The younger segment of the workforce may benefit from family assistance programs and educational assistance programs while the older segments of the workforce rely on generous health insurance benefits and pension plans that support progressive retirement income streams. Health insurance benefits may be redundant for some dual-income families. One spouse or partner will not elect health insurance benefits because he or she already receives coverage as a family member under the spouse's plan. As differences in employee need and desire for benefits becomes apparent to workforce members, some employees will likely protest benefits they believe disproportionately suit co-workers. Certainly, differences in employee preferences and needs based on life stage and life circumstances call for flexible benefits offerings.

Employees are more likely to endorse employer-sponsored benefits as long as these benefits fulfill their needs and preferences. Also, employees should believe that contributions for received benefits are determined fairly. As the prior paragraphs indicate, the workforce will continue to become increasingly diverse. This diversity will challenge a company's quest to establish benefits that satisfy the needs and preferences of workers.

Advances in health care

Health insurance premiums are likely to increase based on the trend in prices for medical services. For example, the price for medical care services overall has increased more than 300 percent since 1982 in the United States. Prices have risen virtually every year since then in both the United States and Canada. Four factors contribute to these increases. First, life expectancies have been increasing in North America. The life expectancy of 65-year-old individuals in the United States is more than seventeen years (US Social Security Administration, 2006). Second, the US baby boom era cohort are aging. As this large segment of the population ages, demands for health care are rising dramatically. Health insurance providers are raising health insurance premiums to offset the rising number of claims they must pay. Third, advances in medical research that add diagnostic tests and treatments, such as substantially more effective treatments to save low-birth-weight babies and for earlier detection of serious diseases that reduce mortality rates, likewise contribute to the higher health care costs. Fourth, there is a general tendency for the health profession and family members in both countries to treat death as unnatural rather than as a natural ending to life, leading to higher expenditures to prolong the lives of terminally ill people.

How firms are responding to the high cost of employee benefits

Competitive pressures in both US and Canadian companies require employers to institute cost control measures whenever possible. Employee benefits professionals have been called on by top management to stem the rising tide of benefits costs. In recent years, many companies have limited their expenditure on employee benefits by engaging one or more of the following initiatives:

- requiring employees to pay more for health care
- making greater investments in accommodation and enhancement benefits
- eliminating retiree health care insurance coverage.

Requiring employees to pay more for health care

Managed care plans became popular alternatives to fee-for-service plans mainly to help employers and insurance companies more effectively manage the costs of health care. By design, managed care plans impose substantial restrictions on an employee's ability to make choices about from whom they can receive medical treatment, on the gatekeeper role of primary care physicians, and on the level of benefits the employees can receive based on designated in- and non-network providers.

Despite the cost control objectives of managed care, health care costs have continued to rise dramatically over the years, fueling the consumer-driven health care objective of helping companies maintain control over costs while also enabling employees to make greater choices about health care. This approach may enable employers to lower the cost of insurance premiums by selecting plans with higher employee deductibles. The most popular consumer-driven approaches are flexible spending accounts (FSAs) and health reimbursement accounts (HRAs). These accounts provide employees with resources to pay for medical and related expenses not covered by higher deductible insurance plans at substantially lower costs to employers.

FSAs permit employees to pay for specified health care costs that are not covered by an employer's insurance plan. Prior to each plan year, employees elect the amount of pay they wish to allocate to this kind of plan. Employers then use these contributions to reimburse employees for expenses incurred during the plan year that qualify for repayment. Qualifying expenses include an individual's out-of-pocket costs for medical treatments, products, or services related to a mental or physical defect or disease, along with certain associated costs, such as health insurance deductibles or transportation to get medical care.

Alternatively, employers may establish HRAs. The purposes of HRAs and FSAs are similar but with two important differences. First, employers make the contributions to each employee's HRA whereas employees fund FSAs with pretax contributions deducted from their pay. Second, HRAs permit employees to carry over unused account balances from year to year whereas employees forfeit unused FSA account balances at the end of the year.

Most recently in the United States, the idea of consumer-driven health care has received substantially greater attention because of the George W. Bush administration and the Republican-led Congress; both favored greater employee involvement in medical care and reduction in cost burdens for companies, to help maintain competitiveness in the global market. The Medicare Prescription Drug, Improvement and Modernization Act of 2003 permits eligible individuals to establish HSAs to help employees pay for medical expenses. An employer, an employee, or both may contribute to these accounts subject to limits set by the federal government. Employers offer HSAs along with high deductible insurance policies to employees. High deductible health insurance plans require employees to pay substantially higher deductibles.

Making greater investments in accommodation and enhancement benefits

The decision to provide accommodation and enhancement benefits is based on three considerations. First, the cost of absenteeism and tardiness is usually much higher than the cost of offering accommodation and enhancement benefits which increase punctuality and attendance of employees at work. Programs that promote three particular objectives – the mental and physical well-being of employees and family members, family assistance, and flexible work schedules – contribute to this attendance imperative. After all, ill or dependent family members often rely on other family members (most of whom are also employed) to care for them, necessitating absence from work for both.

Second, many employees are not sufficiently productive for a variety of health-related reasons. For example, excessive smoking tends to limit physical capability because of impaired lung function. Too much alcohol consumption may inhibit an employee's ability to make sound decisions or it may impair physical coordination. Excess body weight may reduce an employee's stamina, leading to lower job performance. Employers may sponsor smoking cessation, alcohol treatment and weight control programs to promote better health for their employees.

Third, promoting educational opportunities for employees also yields benefits to both employers and employees. For example, scholarships and tuition reimbursement programs reduce the financial barriers to education, by sponsoring employees' pursuits of general equivalency diplomas, college courses, or college degrees. Employees benefit from acquiring greater credentials to compete for higher-level jobs in the company. Employers benefit from staffing flexibility because employees possess a wider range and depth of knowledge and skills. As technology changes the nature of work, skills and knowledge updates minimize the problem of employee obsolescence.

Eliminating retiree health care insurance coverage

Since the early 1990s, companies have encountered a strong financial disincentive to provide health insurance benefits to retired employees. The US Financial Accounting Standards Board (FASB), a non-profit organization responsible for improving standards of financial accounting and reporting in companies, implemented FASB 106. FASB 106 is a rule that changed the method of how companies recognize the costs of benefits offered to retired employees (e.g., health care insurance), on financial balance sheets. This rule effectively reduces the amount of a company's net profit as listed on the balance sheet.

The rapidly rising cost of retiree health care benefits has created a tremendous financial strain on companies that choose to offer them. Of course, the sharp economic slowdown between the years 2000 and 2003 in the United States has made it more difficult for companies to support full workforces, as evidenced by sluggish pay increases, reductions in benefits offerings, and layoffs. Thus, many companies have found it more difficult to meet their pension obligations to retirees. Nowadays, there is a sobering realization that the soaring costs of retiree health care benefits may be draining the coffers of some companies.

Some guidelines on how to curb benefits costs

Curbing benefits costs is essential because the already high costs continue to increase. In this section, guidelines that employee benefits professionals may consider adopting to help curb costs are discussed. Topics covered include employee contributions, waiting periods, utilization reviews, case management, and provider payment systems. See Table 11.2 for a summary of these guidelines.

Employee contributions help companies save money by requiring that employees pay a nominal portion of the benefit costs. Employees typically share the cost of benefits with either pretax or after-tax contributions. That is, various tax regulations permit employees to exclude contributions from annual income before calculating federal and state income tax obligations; these are called pretax contributions. Conversely, after-tax contributions do not reduce the amount of annual income subject to income tax. For instance, companies expect employees to share the cost of medical insurance coverage with pretax contributions, yet these companies base employee contributions on their total annual earnings.

Second, companies impose one or more waiting periods to limit participation in the benefits program. Waiting periods specify the minimum number of months or years

Table 11.2 Guidelines on how to control the high costs of benefits

1 Have employees pay a nominal amount of the costs paid by the employer to provide particular benefits.
2 Impose waiting periods on probationary employees to limit participation in the benefits program.
3 Educate employees about health care costs and the reasons for rising costs to promote cost containment.
4 Consider health insurers that use utilization reviews to evaluate the quality and appropriateness of specific health care services.
5 Consider health insurers that use the services of independent case management companies to ensure that participants with serious health problems receive essential medical attention on a cost-effective basis.
6 Consider health insurers that use provider payment systems (payment arrangements between managed care insurers and health care providers) which include percentage discounts, capped fee schedules, partial capitation, and full capitation to control the costs of health care.

an employee must remain employed before becoming eligible for one or more benefits. Waiting periods often correspond with the length of probationary periods. Companies impose probationary periods to judge a newcomer's job performance, and they explicitly reserve the right to dismiss employees who demonstrate low job performance. The use of waiting periods helps companies control costs.

Four additional cost-control methods – employee education, utilization reviews, case management, and provider payment systems – apply mainly to health insurance benefits. Employers and insurance companies set up cost-control programs to limit unnecessary costs while promoting the highest-quality health care. Without these methods, insurance companies would necessarily charge employers even higher premium amounts. Separate premiums usually apply to health, dental, and life insurance protection.

Educating employees about the cost of health care is essential to controlling the rising costs of health care insurance because past employer and insurance company practices of not educating employees about costs may have inadvertently led the employers to over utilize health insurance benefits for at least two reasons. First, since the 1940s and 1950s, most medium- and large-scale employers offered health insurance coverage to employees as a part of the benefits package. Offering health insurance coverage provided companies with lucrative tax breaks, and including health insurance in the benefits package helped companies to recruit and retain valued employees. Most employees viewed health care coverage, along with most other benefits such as paid time off, as an entitlement because it was included as a standard benefit and employees often did not pay to have employer-sponsored health insurance protection. Second, indemnity plans were quite common decades ago; by design, these plans provided individuals with substantial freedom to go directly to doctors of their choice, and oftentimes, employees went to very expensive medical specialists when situations did not require the expertise of a specialist.

Even as the costs of health care led insurance companies to raise health insurance premiums in the 1980s and 1990s, employers continued to offer generous insurance coverage while absorbing the cost for higher premiums. Since the US economy began weakening substantially in 2000 compared to the 1990s, and competitive pressures forced more companies to carefully audit their costs, employers began to shift health-related costs to employees by having them pay a greater share. Educating employees about health care costs and the reasons for rising costs should promote cost containment.

Utilization reviews serve various purposes. Health care providers conduct utilization reviews to evaluate the quality of specific health care services. Employers offering group health benefits and their insurers depend on utilization reviews to ensure that medical treatments received by participants were medically appropriate. Sponsors of these reviews hire medical doctors and registered nurses to carry out utilization reviews. These medical professionals rely on professional practice standards established by medical associations to judge the medical appropriateness of treatment and quality of patient care.

Three types of utilization reviews may be conducted. The first, prospective reviews or pre-certification reviews, evaluate the appropriateness of proposed medical treatment as a condition for authorizing payment. The second type, concurrent reviews, focus on current hospital patients. Insurers conduct concurrent reviews to judge whether additional inpatient hospitalization is medically necessary. Concurrent reviews take place approximately one day before a patient is scheduled to be discharged from the hospital if a physician is recommending extending hospitalization. Alternatively, insurers conduct utilization reviews shortly after admission to the hospital following emergency treatment. Physicians may appeal these decisions by providing further medical justification for treatment. The third type, retrospective reviews, take place prior to an insurance company's disbursement of benefits. Retrospective reviews have two main objectives, starting with a determination of whether the health insurance program covers the patient, the medical conditions, and the medical treatment, and then judging whether claims are not fraudulent by confirming that medical treatments were actually given and appropriate for the medical condition.

Many health insurance providers use the services of independent case management companies to ensure that participants with serious health problems receive essential medical attention on a cost-effective basis. Usually registered nurses or social workers who are employed as case managers collaborate with physicians to balance the medical needs of the patient and the cost-containment needs of the health insurer. Serious health problems arising from injuries or illnesses may be acute (short term) or chronic (ongoing).

Provider payment systems refer to payment arrangements between managed care insurers and health care providers. Managed care plans establish provider payment systems to control the costs of health care. Fee-for-service plans do not include this feature because health care providers seek reimbursement after rendering services. Therefore, provider payment systems begin with negotiations over amounts the system will pay participating physicians, health care facilities, and pharmacies for the duration of the managed care plan's contract with these providers, which is in effect for up to a few years. Agreements may include one or more cost-saving feature, including percentage discounts, capped fee schedules, partial capitation, and full capitation.

As the term implies, percentage discounts are fees that are discounted from the amounts health care providers would usually charge. Under this arrangement, health care providers agree to the percentage amount. Percentage discounts are not the most cost-effective method for two reasons. First, managed care plans do not enforce a limit on the number of services, making it difficult to anticipate total costs. Second, health care providers are free to increase their "regular" fees, adding to total costs.

Capped fee schedules set maximum dollar amounts for each service. Similar to percentage discount systems, capped fee schedules do not limit the volume of services, making it difficult to anticipate total costs. Managed care plans use usual, customary, and reasonable fees as a starting point for establishing capped fee schedules. From there, they set maximums by limiting payments to a percentage of usual, customary, and reasonable fees.

Conclusion

This chapter provided a brief overview of employee benefits practices in North America and some timely information about benefits costs to employers. Several forces are in play that will likely push costs even higher. The final section of this chapter reviewed methods which company management may consider as part of their efforts to control employee benefits costs.

References

US Bureau of Labor Statistics (BLS) (2005) *Employer Costs for Employee Compensation – September 2005 (USDL 05–2279)*. Washington, DC: BLS.
US Social Security Administration (2006) *Social Security Basic Facts*. Available http://www.ssa.gov/pressoffice/basicfact.htm (accessed March 20, 2006).

WHICH BENEFITS?

Suppose you've just accepted a new job and your new employer offers you the choice of a $75,000 annual salary plus a comprehensive fee-for-service health plan, or a $90,000 salary and no health plan. Which compensation package would you choose? Both options would probably have some takers. What if the choice was between a $75,000 salary plus the health plan, or a $100,000 salary and no health plan? Chances are that many people who would have opted for the health insurance in the first example would now choose the higher salary instead. Put differently, those who switched from the cash-only package to the health plan package value the health insurance at some amount between $15,000 and $25,000 per year.

What if the choice were between health insurance and putting the money in a retirement fund? Which would you choose?

Related questions

1 What factors do you think might cause people to take the $90,000 instead of the health insurance?
2 As an employer which would you rather have your employees choose?
3 What are the advantages and disadvantages of giving them that choice?

12 Executive compensation: something old, something new

MARIANNA MAKRI AND LUIS R. GOMEZ-MEJIA

Executive compensation has been a hot HR topic for a long time. Possibly because of its high visibility, its frequently perceived unfairness (particularly in North America), and its importance. A good corporate governance rating sends a signal to potential investors that the firm is a better investment because presumably the board of that firm is working for shareholders as opposed to cozying up to the CEO. Because such ratings are important indicators of corporate governance, executive pay should be a major concern for boards of directors. For instance, some analysts believe that when CEOs earn more than 20 percent above the mean at similar-sized firms this tends to decrease the firm's corporate-governance ratings (Useem, 2003). The executive compensation package can either be a motivational tool encouraging executives to pursue strategic decisions that are in the best interest of shareholders or it can be designed to reinforce the wrong strategic choices (e.g., rewarding short-term results at the expense of long-term performance). Simply put, because executives are particularly responsive to the incentive schemes designed for them, boards of directors need to be careful when designing such packages.

While every board's goal is to design a compensation package that rewards executives for outcomes important to shareholders, this is easier said than done. Structuring compensation schemes that shift the right amount of risk onto the CEOs and that use the right set of criteria to evaluate their performance is usually art more than it is science. In this chapter we discuss several issues for compensation committees related to the design of the executive compensation package. We revisit the same old questions like how much should CEOs make, whether their pay should be tied to firm performance, and the role of risk in their compensation package. In addressing these issues, we consider recent changes in legislation such as the Sarbanes–Oxley Act (SOX) of 2002, increased disclosure requirements by the Securities and Exchange Commission (SEC) as well as increased shareholder activism. We also introduce some new issues such as how executives of high-technology or family-owned firms should be compensated. We start by addressing the issue of extravagance in CEO pay.

The CEO pay package: how much is too much and who is to blame?

The level of executive compensation, although an old issue, is a pervasive one and the last few years have been characterized by big increases. For example, a 2004 Mercer Consulting study of 350 of the nation's largest public companies found that the total median CEO pay (cash plus long-term incentives such as options and restricted stock) increased by 17 percent in 2004, to $7 million. Bonuses increased by 20 percent, to $1.5 million, while salaries rose by almost 4 percent, to $975,000 (Countryman, 2005). Another 2004 study by *Business Week* yielded similar results and found that total CEO pay was up to an average of $9.6 million, a 15 percent increase from $8.3 million in 2003. That average was skewed by the outrageous pay package of the most highly compensated CEO, Yahoo! Inc.'s Terry Semel, who received a package worth $120 million made up almost entirely of stock options.

With nearly two out of three CEOs seeing their pay go up since 2003 (Lavelle, 2005), might they be worth the money? This is a sensitive subject and when asked, companies with the most highly paid executives say that their CEOs are worth every penny because they are great performers. For example, members of the compensation committee supporting Motorola Inc.'s Edward Zander's 2004 $38.8 million compensation package of cash, restricted stock and options said:

> Mr. Zander's compensation recognizes the exceptional performance of the company during 2004 under his leadership. The board unanimously believes that Mr. Zander's compensation is appropriate to help ensure that he is rewarded for effectively leading this company and is in line with other CEO packages.
>
> (Countryman, 2005)

But even if the CEO is a great performer, isn't the price tag for performance too high?

United Technologies is an example where the company's CEO helped produce impressive stock gains of three times the returns for the S&P 500. Was his $88.7 million paycheck justified when it was nineteen times the median CEO pay of $4.43 million at S&P 500 companies? Most would argue that it was not. And even if some CEOs' large pay packages were appropriate, research generally does not support the conventional belief that there is a strong relationship between CEO pay and firm performance. For example, Tosi *et al.* (2000) found that only a small percentage of the differences in pay among CEOs could be explained by differences in the performance of their firms. By contrast, 40 percent of the differences in CEO pay could be explained by differences in the size of their firms. In other words, the CEOs who were making more money were also running larger companies.

Who is to blame for these extravagant pay packages? The board of directors certainly plays a pivotal role in determining a CEO's pay which is often not based on how well the company is doing, but rather on how much the board of directors agrees to pay. The problem with many boards is that they can become closely allied with the CEOs and, in turn, not alert in monitoring their decisions. Personal interactions between

CEOs and board members often result in close relationships that can affect both the length of the compensation contracts by allowing the CEOs to stay on board beyond their useful contribution, as well as the value of the contracts by paying the executive premiums for their loyalty. Having charisma certainly adds to the CEO's influence on the board. Charismatic CEOs are particularly good at influencing board members to award them generous compensation packages even when there is no evidence that these CEOs perform better (Tosi *et al.*, 2004).

Even boards with independent directors are not shielded from the problems of close relationships with the CEO. Independent directors usually lack diverse skills (e.g. financial analysis skills) and in-depth information about the company, and they have to rely on the company executives or the CEO for that information. Thus, instead of challenging the CEO's decisions, these seemingly independent directors turn to CEOs for information and continue providing them with ever-increasing rewards, especially stock options. But what is the cost for firms for such lack of board vigilance besides the actual cost of the compensation package? Companies such as the Corporate Library that are in the business of rating firms' corporate governance based partially on CEO compensation, flag large pay packages as a sign of weak boards that are too cozy with management and not looking out for shareholders. Low ratings signal that the board is ineffective in monitoring the CEO which can in turn hurt the firm's stock price.

The role of risk in the executive compensation contract

In designing an executive compensation contract, the amount of risk shifted onto the executives needs to be carefully considered because it has a direct effect on their decisions regarding company growth. Three types of risk are most important. First, *employment risk* represents the possibility that the executive will be dismissed either due to unsatisfactory performance or due to change in control. Second, *compensation risk* represents the potential unpredictability in the executive's future pay constituted mainly by the proportion of stock options in the total pay package. Third, *business risk* reflects the uncertainty surrounding the firm's competitive environment. These three types of risk need to be carefully considered when putting together an executive compensation contract because they can affect the executive's propensity to take risks. In other words, boards in general and compensation committees in particular need to bear in mind how much risk is transferred to the executive via each pay component.

The executive compensation package consists of two main components: fixed pay (salary and benefits) and variable pay (bonuses and stock options), each carrying different risks or threats to wealth, and exerting varying influences on a CEO's risk taking. Fixed pay is generally taken for granted so it does not serve as a motivational tool. The fixed dimension is typically one of the smaller items among top executives because corporations can write off no more than $1 million in annual salaries. So most companies just top off salaries at about $1 million and supplement the executive's total pay with bonuses and stock options. These last two components, bonuses and stock options, draw the CEO's attention to performance results and can serve to align the goals of the company and its shareholders with the personal goals of the executive. In fact, stock options are the pay component that influences CEO decision making the most. Stock options have became one of the largest parts of CEO pay plans because up until recently, they didn't cost companies anything to issue, but they could be worth millions of dollars for CEOs.

Recent environmental changes affecting CEO risk

Some recent environmental changes that affect executive compensation warrant discussion. These include increased shareholder activism, the Sarbanes–Oxley Act, and new SEC disclosures.

Shareholder activism

In recent years there has been an increasing willingness on behalf of mutual funds and other institutional investors to vote against management. For example, in July 2005, Morgan Stanley was scrutinized when it awarded $113 million to departing CEO Phil Purcell despite the firm's disappointing performance. Central Laborers' Pension Fund, outraged by Morgan Stanley's award, began a suit in federal court against the firm's directors, former executives and lawyers, alleging breach of fiduciary duty. Another group, the Pennsylvania State Employees' Retirement System, also demanded immediate changes in governance and stronger ties between pay and performance.

Proxy resolutions sponsored by union and public pension funds, aimed at cutting CEO pay, are winning extraordinary victories. In fact, those entities accomplished more than two dozen majority votes on issues such as golden parachutes and expensing stock options in 2003, versus two in 2002 (Borrus, 2005). While shareholder resolutions are not binding since management can ignore them, if shareholder activism keeps spreading it will ignite a good amount of reform. For example, Bank of America and Norfolk Southern Corp., two companies that lost proxy battles over executive pay in 2003, eventually adopted the measures.

The Sarbanes–Oxley Act

SOX was signed into law on July 30, 2002, and introduced strict new rules in order "to protect investors by improving the accuracy and reliability of corporate disclosures made pursuant to the securities laws." The Act, named after its main architects, Senator Paul Sarbanes and Representative Michael Oxley, followed a series of high-profile scandals, such as Enron, and was intended to "deter and punish corporate and accounting fraud and corruption, ensure justice for wrongdoers, and protect the interests of workers and shareholders" (quote: US President George W. Bush). (See Chapters 4 and 6 for more details about SOX.)

SOX holds the new generation of CEOs personally accountable for their companies' financial statements. Under SOX, any reporting errors may be punishable by imprisonment. CEOs "are not being asked to guarantee their company's performance, but they are being pushed closer to that role," says University of Texas School of Law Securities Professor Henry T.C. Hu. "That's why they make the big bucks. If you are laying claim to the successes of your company, why not pick up the downside?" (France and Lavelle, 2004).

While some think that the Act increases corporate responsibility for financial reports, others argue that it is shifting a great amount of risk onto the executive. Sometimes CEOs rely upon the specialized expertise of tax lawyers, engineers, and other lower-level managers and may not be aware of any unlawful activity inside the firm. Some worry that SOX forces CEOs to place more focus on the internal control environment and the short term as opposed to focusing on the long term.

SEC disclosures

On January 17, 2006 the SEC voted on an expansion in disclosure requirements for executive pay. The SEC asks that each year, companies disclose the dollar value of every benefit that executives derived from their employment, including the annual increase in the value of pension plans as well as annual gains from a deferred benefit plan. Further, when executives sell options, companies should report the extent to which executives sell shares given to them as variable pay. Also, in terms of bonuses, companies should disclose not just the amounts paid but also the criteria based upon which those bonuses were awarded. Finally, because executives' incentives are influenced by their exit packages, companies should annually disclose the dollar value of the package that each executive will receive upon exit in the case of a change in control, dismissal, or retirement. These expanded disclosures will enable investors to better evaluate how companies are doing in terms of corporate governance and also highlight to boards any ineffectiveness in their firms' executive compensation system.

Managing executive risk

There are a number of responses to managing each of the three different kinds of risk. Here we look at stock options, change-in-control provisions, and pay for performance as risk management tools.

Stock options as a response to managing compensation risk

Stock options became most popular in the 1990s when high-technology companies low on cash started using them to attract talented employees. Other companies liked the idea and started using them as a motivational tool to encourage employees to work hard and raise the company's stock. Stock options do not cost any cash for companies to issue because a stock option is not an actual share of stock but rather the right to buy a share in the future at a predetermined price, also known as the strike price. The executive makes a profit from stock options if, when the option matures, he or she buys shares and then sells them at a market price higher than the strike price.

Since the mid 1990s, almost 80 percent of the increases in CEO pay came from stock options (Elson *et al.*, 2003) but now stock options are losing ground and are being replaced at least in part by restricted stock. Restricted stock is a right granted to the executive to purchase during a specified period, at the market price on the date of the option, a specified number of shares. A Mercer study revealed that the number of CEOs that received restricted shares from 2002 to 2004 increased by 60 percent. The reason for this change is the new accounting rules set by the Financial Accounting Standards Board which, starting in 2005, requires companies to determine the value of options when granted instead of when they are exercised. Up until recently, options, unlike salary or bonuses, did not show up as an expense on the income statement and the estimated cost of stock options was reported only in the footnotes of the annual report. This recent change in legislation will make companies count the cost of stock options against profits.

What does this mean for firms and compensation committees? On one hand, expensing options could discourage companies from granting outrageous amounts to CEOs, but on the other hand it can take away from small startup firms an important tool for attracting talented employees (Fowler, 2004). So far, as a response to these changes, many companies have shown preference for restricted stock. Time-vested restricted stock can be a good retention tool and an effective complement to traditional stock options. If the stock price falls, because restricted stock still has value, executives are motivated to work to push the shares higher. But while restricted stock options are an easy-to-implement alternative to stock options, the problem is that they are not as tightly linked to performance as stock options are. While stock options only have value if stock prices go up, time-vested restricted stock can have some value regardless of performance. If restricted stock is only time-vesting and not linked to some performance outcomes, is it anything other than "pay for pulse"?

Guidelines for compensation committees

As mentioned earlier, stock options are the dimension of pay that is variable because it is contingent upon stock price. This variability translates into more risk for the

CEO because it cannot be taken for granted. Boards of directors need to anticipate how the proportion of stock options in the CEO pay package would influence the CEO's attitude towards taking business risks. If a large percentage of CEOs' pay is uncertain, then CEOs may become risk averse in their decisions, always trying to protect the stock price.

The criteria on which stock options are granted can also affect CEOs' decisions. If the board uses growth in market share as a criterion for granting stocks, they may be tempted to pursue an aggressive merger and acquisition strategy even if this is not in the best interest of shareholders. If stock options are granted based on profitability ratios, executives may be tempted to reduce investments in research and development (R&D). Alternatively, if stock options are granted based on the number of patents granted to the firm, the quality of those patents may be overlooked.

Thus, for both traditional stock options and time-vested restricted stock, the challenge for boards lies in clearly defining the criteria for granting them. Companies can use combinations of different metrics such as shareholder returns, earnings per share, revenue growth and return on equity. A definite sign of improvement would be to tie CEO pay to broader metrics of performance that go well beyond financial measures, such as indicators of leadership and innovation.

With respect to SOX, it increases employment risk for CEOs, which in the presence of business risk may drive CEOs to seek to reduce the threat to future income by avoiding risk-enhancing strategies such as product diversification and investments in R&D. But avoiding these risk-enhancing strategies can create opportunity costs for shareholders. One way to encourage executives to take risks under the new legislative environment would be to link pay to performance very loosely and motivate them with restricted stock options.

Change-in-control provisions as a response to managing employment risk

Carly Fiorina's $42 million exit package from Hewlett-Packard and James Kilts' $100-million-plus goodbye kiss from Gillette show that we need to pay attention not only to CEO pay but also to the clauses in CEO pay contracts (Colvin, 2005). Having a contract as a CEO is a more recent HR practice and not necessarily a beneficial one for companies. Employment contracts make it almost impossible to fire a CEO because they include clauses that protect the executive from being fired without a "cause." While these contracts define "cause" in great detail ("cause" generally includes being convicted of a felony) the one thing "cause" never includes is doing a bad job. So firing a CEO for not performing well constitutes firing them without cause which can cost a company a lot of money. When a CEO gets fired without cause or quits "for good reason," or if there's a "change in control," the thousands of restricted stock options that CEO was awarded vest immediately. And when the restricted stock becomes unrestricted the CEO often receives a multimillion-dollar exit package. Again, take for instance the lavish exit package of Morgan Stanley's CEO Phil Purcell: in July 2005, Morgan Stanley awarded $113 million to departing CEO Phil Purcell despite the firm's sub-par performance.

Given the rising popularity of mergers and acquisitions, these exit packages, also known as golden parachutes, accompanied by change-in-control (CIC) protections, are receiving a lot of attention. A golden parachute is a payment in the form of cash, an acceleration of vesting or other benefit that occurs in connection with a change in the ownership or control of a company's stock or assets. A CIC protection is a guarantee of employment for CEOs if a change in control occurs. In other words, if a change in control arises, executives are protected from losing their job for a specified time while often receiving the following: a lump-sum payment equal to typically three times the base salary plus bonus; accelerated vesting of deferred compensation and supplemental executive retirement plan (SERP) benefits; additional age and service credit during the severance period (typically three years) for purposes of pension calculation; and accelerated vesting of equity awards. Some companies also continue perquisites during the severance period, and a very small number of companies provide for additional equity award grants during it (Mercer Human Resource Consulting, 2005).

Guidelines for compensation committees

While at first blush golden parachutes seem to be an unjustifiable and costly dimension to the CEO's pay package, they can be very beneficial for shareholders because they give CEOs an incentive to facilitate, or at least not to obstruct, a change in control transaction such as a merger or acquisition that may be valuable to shareholders. Also, designing a compensation contract with a golden parachute clause and a CIC provision may be needed in order to attract the best executives. With many companies already using them, a golden parachute along with a CIC makes an executive's compensation package more attractive and can help lure a CEO away from a rival firm.

When designing a CIC program, compensation committees need to carefully consider high severance multiples (three times benefits should be the upper limit) and whether the value of long-term incentive awards (stock options) is included in the severance multiple. Further, they need to ensure that CIC programs are able to meet their main objective which is to retain the management team through a period of uncertainty.

Linking pay to performance as a response to managing business risk

Prospect theory (Kahneman and Tversky, 1979) argues that the risk tendencies of individuals change depending on the context. Individuals in positive contexts can become risk averse while individuals in negative contexts can become risk seeking.

Applying this theory to CEOs suggests that those leading high-performing companies would become risk averse where those heading firms with below-average profitability would become risk seeking in hopes to improve firm performance. Now if the CEO's pay is closely linked to firm performance when the firm is performing poorly, the CEO may pursue detrimentally risky options because his or her personal wealth is in jeopardy. On the other hand, if the firm is performing well and the CEO's pay is tightly linked to performance then the CEO may become risk averse and avoid growth strategies such as diversification. So the key question is: what is the ideal level of risk that should be transferred to the executive and to what extent should pay be tied to performance?

Obviously the competitive environment in which the firm operates is a deciding factor. Firms operating in highly competitive, high-risk environments need to pay more to attract and retain high-quality executives than firms operating in low-risk environments. Also, in a high business risk scenario the amount of pay which is variable (e.g. stock options) should be kept to a minimum. Not doing so can lead to CEOs trying to reduce risk by engaging in activities that may be detrimental to shareholders, such as lowering R&D spending and avoiding high-risk/high-return projects such as international diversification (Miller *et al.*, 2002).

Guidelines for compensation committees

Even though researchers agree that linking some portion of a CEO's pay to firm performance is a good idea because it holds the CEO accountable to shareholders, unfortunately there is no straight answer as to what that percentage should be. Thus, compensation committees ought to be aware that if they decide to increase the portion of the CEO's pay that is variable, they also need to increase the total amount of pay if they want to prevent the CEO from becoming risk averse. In other words, increasing the proportion of variable pay needs to be balanced by the potential to earn more money. Also, the total pay should be highest in settings where risk is greatest for the CEO such as high-technology firms or family-controlled firms. These scenarios are discussed next.

Moderating factors

Firm industry and firm ownership are two moderating factors that affect how firms should respond to risk issues. Specifically, we will look at the differences in CEO pay in high-technology firms and in family-owned businesses.

CEO pay in high-technology firms

Most management researchers agree that innovation is critical for high-technology firms, but they lack consensus when it comes to the executive pay policies that are most appropriate for these types of firms. Some suggest that in high-technology firms CEO pay should be tightly linked to firm performance because it is difficult for the boards of those firms to monitor the CEO's behavior (e.g., Milkovich *et al.*, 1991). Others argue that doing so transfers too much risk to executives and can push them to avoid high-risk/high-return innovation projects that are important for the firm's long-term success (Eisenmann, 2002). A study by Makri *et al.* (2006) helped reconcile these views by suggesting that high-technology firms need to reward CEOs by using multiple performance criteria. Such criteria should include financial indicators as well as indicators of the CEO's emphasis on innovation. They find that high-technology firms would benefit by linking CEO bonuses and stock options to evidence of influential innovations as well as the degree to which the CEO supports basic research.

Guidelines for compensation committees

A CEO can influence a high-technology firm's knowledge creation environment through policies and resource allocation decisions. The CEO can encourage basic research by creating well-paid research fellow positions and by promoting partnerships with universities; alternatively the CEO may implement strategies that impair the productivity of scientists (for example by tying salary increases to the assumption of managerial responsibilities) (Stephan, 1996). For such firms innovation is crucial for success; thus, in addition to looking at financial indicators, the board of directors should evaluate the CEO by looking at the extent to which overall he or she promotes a culture of innovation. The board can collect such information from internal sources (e.g. subordinates, key scientists and engineers), external parties that have business ties with the firm, and outside experts (e.g. consultants, university faculty, and technical staff of private/public sector research centers).

CEO pay in family firms

In the United States families own approximately 80 percent of firms (Beehr *et al.*, 1997). Family-owned firms differ from non-family firms in two major ways, and these unique characteristics require that this category of firms and their issues relating to executive compensation are addressed separately. First, board members or executives who are members of the family exhibit a greater desire to retain control of the firm, stemming from a strong personal attachment, commitment, and identification with the firm. Second, their employment and compensation risk are highly concentrated in the firm (e.g., Schulze *et al.*, 2001).

In terms of compensation, CEOs of family firms who are not also members of the family tend to get paid more than CEOs who have family ties with the firm's owners. There are several reasons for this. First, family board members are more likely to make positive performance attributions to the CEO when there are emotional ties. Thus, family board members are more likely to ascribe negative results to the non-family CEO than to the family CEO. Also, while the board may give the benefit of the doubt to the family CEO, attributing disappointing results to bad luck or unfortunate circumstances, they may judge the outsider CEO as incompetent. So, in order to attract and retain a talented outsider, the family firm has to pay more because it offers lower employment security. On the other hand, because the family CEO enjoys greater employment security than a non-family CEO (Gomez-Mejia *et al.*, 2003) the family firm can get away with paying him or her less in exchange for this greater security.

Guidelines for compensation committees

In designing the executive compensation contract of a family CEO, directors may need to consider using more "transactional contracts." Transactional contracts are concrete, with specific timeframes, while at the other end of the spectrum, relational contracts are subjective, with loosely specified or open-ended time horizons. While most employment contracts have transactional and relational elements, boards of directors may consider operating a bit more at the transactional scale when it comes to family CEOs and a bit more at the relational end of the continuum for non-family CEOs. The presence of a stronger transactional contract for a family CEO reinforces the need for clear, less ambiguous performance criteria, and increases the likelihood that the evaluation of the CEO's performance will be done more objectively by family members. On the other hand, in the case of a non-family CEO, the presence of a stronger relational contract increases the likelihood that evaluation of the CEO's performance will be done informally by family members, giving the CEO the benefit of the doubt for negative results. In conclusion, while higher pay can compensate the non-family executive for being subjected to harsher judgments by the board of a family firm, adding a relational quality to the compensation contract can also be an effective strategy for family firms to attract non-family CEOs.

Conclusion

There are a wide variety of options when designing executive pay packages. While there are no clear-cut rules as to what makes an effective reward system, we have provided a number of guidelines throughout the chapter for compensation committees to consider. See Table 12.1 for a list of those guidelines. It is clear that compensation committees need to take into consideration the amount of risk they transfer onto the executive via the pay design. To be more specific, boards of

Table 12.1 Guidelines for executive compensation committees

1 Tie CEO pay to a broad range of financial performance metrics such as shareholder returns, earnings per share, revenue growth and return on equity, as well as indicators of leadership and innovation.
2 Link pay to performance very loosely and motivate executives with restricted stock options to encourage executives to take risks they might not take because of SOX.
3 When designing a change-in-control provision, consider limiting severance multiples, include stock options in the severance multiple, and make sure the provision is designed to retain the management team through a period of uncertainty.
4 When tying pay to performance, any increase in the proportion of variable pay needs to be balanced by the potential to earn more money.
5 When measuring CEO performance in high-technology firms, use internal sources, external parties that have business ties with the firm, and outside experts to evaluate the extent to which the CEO promotes a culture of innovation.
6 In family-owned firms, a family CEO's contract should be more concrete, with specific timeframes, while a non-family CEO's contract should be more subjective, with loosely specified or open-ended time horizons.

directors need to consider the firm's competitive environment (e.g. high technology), its external environment (e.g. Sarbanes–Oxley), and its internal environment (e.g. family firms). For instance, boards of high-technology firms should design pay packages that motivate executives to make resource allocation decisions that would assist the firm in sustaining its innovation capability. Further, boards of family firms may consider higher pay for the non-family executive as well as adding a relational quality to the compensation contract. Finally, all firms need to consider how the recent changes in legislation shift more risk onto the CEO. In conclusion, an effective compensation package is one that reflects the firm's unique characteristics.

References

Beehr, T.A., Drexler, J.A., Jr. and Faulkner, S. (1997) Working in small family businesses: Empirical comparisons to non-family businesses. *Journal of Organizational Behavior*, 18: 297–312.

Borrus, A. (2005) Learning to love Sarbanes–Oxley. *Business Week*, November 21 (3960): 126.

Colvin, G. (2005) Outraged over CEO exit packages? You're too late. *Fortune*, March 7, 151(5): 62–63.

Countryman, A. (2005) Options lose ground in race to reward CEOs. *Knight Ridder Tribune Business News*, May 16: 1.

Eisenmann, T.R. (2002) The effects of CEO equity ownership and firm diversification on risk taking. *Strategic Management Journal*, 23: 513–534.

Elson, C., Roiter, E., Clapman, P., Bachelder, J., England, J., Lau, G. *et al.* (2003) What's wrong with executive compensation? *Harvard Business Review*, 81(1): 5–12.

Fowler, T. (2004) Stock option excess may be costly to companies. *Knight Ridder Tribune Business News*, July 18: 1.

France, M. and Lavelle, L. (2004) The new accountability. *Business Week*, July 26 (3893): 30.

Gomez-Mejia, L.R., Larraza-Kintana, M. and Makri, M. (2003) The determinants of executive compensation in family-controlled public corporations. *Academy of Management Journal*, 46: 226–237.

Kahneman, D. and Tversky, A. (1979) Prospect theory: An analysis of decision under risk. *Econometrica*, 47: 263–291.

Lavelle, L. (2005) Fatter envelopes. *Business Week*, April 4 (3927): 13.

Makri, M., Lane, P.J. and Gomez-Mejia, L. (2006) CEO Incentives, Innovation, and Performance in Technology-intensive Firms. Working paper.

Mercer Human Resource Consulting (2005) M&A activity shifts governance spotlight to golden parachutes. *Mercer HR Alert*, May 16 (44).

Milkovich, G.T., Gerhart, B. and Hannon, J. (1991) The effects of research and development intensity on managerial compensation in large organizations. *Journal of High Technology Management Research*, 2(1): 133–145.

Miller, J.S., Wiseman, R.M. and Gomez-Mejia, L.R. (2002) The fit between CEO compensation design and firm risk. *Academy of Management Journal*, 45: 745–756.

Schulze, W., Lubatkin, M.H., Dino, R.N. and Buchholtz, A.K. (2001) Agency relationships in family firms. *Organization Science*, 12(2): 99–116.

Stephan, P. (1996) The economics of science. *Journal of Economic Literature*, 34: 1199–1235.

Tosi, H.L., Werner, S., Katz, J.P. and Gomez-Mejia, L.R. (2000) How much does performance matter? A meta-analysis of CEO pay studies. *Journal of Management*, 26(2): 301–338.

Tosi, H., Misangyi, V., Fanelli, A., Waldman, D. and Yammarino, F. (2004) CEO charisma, compensation, and firm performance. *Leadership Quarterly*, 15(3): 405–427.

Useem, J. (2003) Have they no shame? *Fortune*, April 28, 147(8): 56–64.

THE COMPENSATION COMMITTEE CHALLENGE

Naomi Renrew is the VP of Human Resources for a new, small, high-technology firm. She has been asked to join the compensation committee which determines the CEO's pay. The committee has been asked by the board to revise the CEO's pay package because it is not currently tied to firm performance. The board also suggested that the package should not inhibit the CEO's current risk-taking propensity.

Related questions

1 How can the pay package be structured to promote a culture of innovation?
2 What factors should affect the CEO's pay?
3 How can the committee make sure that factors outside of the CEO's control don't have a substantial impact on the CEO's pay?

HRM after 9/11 and Katrina

GERALD R. FERRIS, WAYNE A. HOCHWARTER AND
TIMOTHY A. MATHERLY

"Oh Lord, I can't believe this has happened to us."
Comment made by a police office in Florida following Hurricane Katrina

Traumatic events, including the 9/11 terrorist attacks in 2001 and Hurricane Katrina
in 2005, have dramatically altered the lives of all Americans. Most obvious is the
incredible loss of lives caused by these catastrophes as over 3,000 people were killed
as a result of the attacks on the World Trade Center, the Pentagon, and United
Airlines flight 93. Also, approximately 1,400 people perished after Hurricane
Katrina hit the Gulf Coast – a number expected to increase in the next several years
because of its long-term effects on health. Finally, a number of American firms had
business operations in Southeast Asia (e.g., KPMG), where approximately 220,000
lives were lost due to a tsunami in December 2004. Less direct consequences exist
as well.

In financial terms, it is impossible to accurately predict property and business losses
in the wake of these events, although the number is estimated to be in the tens of
trillions of dollars. Equally difficult to gauge are the effects of disasters on
individuals' long-term health and well-being. It is clear, however, that trauma has the
potential to affect one's quality of life across multiple domains (e.g., home, social,
church). It is also apparent that uncertainty and declining health, attributed to
trauma, impacts the workplace, which is our focal interest in this chapter.

Lazarus and Cohen (1977: 91) described trauma as "sudden, unique and powerful
single-life events requiring major adaptive responses from the groups sharing the
experience." Catastrophic events, as they relate to business organizations, have
typically fallen into four categories (Meichenbaum, 1995): natural phenomena (i.e.,
earthquakes, floods, tornadoes, hurricanes); technological events (computer-related,

industrial, toxic spills); terrorism/war; and internal catastrophes (e.g., violence and physical threats such as robbery). Throughout this chapter, we use the terms *disaster*, *trauma*, *crisis*, *tragedy*, and *catastrophe* interchangeably because of their commonalities. For example, each can be viewed in terms of speed of onset, scope, duration, predictability, strength, and threat of recurrence (Berren *et al.*, 1989), regardless of whether the event is weather induced, an assault on one's physical health, terrorism, or conflict related.

Our rationale for developing this chapter relates to the pervasiveness of the trauma experience. For example, it has been reported that up to 70 percent of the population will directly suffer a catastrophic event during their lifetime (O'Brien, 1998), while over 2 million Americans will experience nature-related (i.e., tornado, floods, brushfires) trauma in a given year (Rossi *et al.*, 1983). Other reports indicate that approximately 11 percent of individuals will develop disaster-provoked post-traumatic stress disorder (PTSD), making it one of the most frequently experienced psychological disorders (Green *et al.*, 1992).

Because of the magnitude of disasters such as 9/11 and Hurricane Katrina, secondary exposure can be equally distressing. For example, Mainiero and Gibson (2003) reported that over 20 percent of survey respondents living more than 500 miles away from the World Trade Center had difficulty sleeping (compared to 27.6 percent living within 150 miles) following the attacks. Also, the Greater San Antonio and Houston metropolitan areas experienced an arrival of more than 700,000 evacuees due to Katrina, taxing both infrastructure and health care resources. Finally, the tremendous number of media sources (e.g., television, radio, internet, print) have made it virtually impossible to distance oneself from the images of catastrophe, even if one lives several thousand miles away from the affected area.

In this chapter, we examine the influence of traumatic events from the perspective of a human resources manager. In doing so, we suggest that in addition to performing traditional functions (e.g., compensation, staffing, appraisal), HR managers will be increasingly required to actively plan for, and respond to, the many traumas capable of affecting their workplace organizations. We begin by discussing the role of disasters on firms' external and internal environments, with particular emphasis on the consequences of uncertainty generated by these events (Yates *et al.*, 1989). Because of the importance of employee health and well-being, we focus largely on the stress-related consequences of trauma. (See Chapter 7 for more on health and safety.) Following this, we provide guidelines for pre- and post-trauma activities that HR managers must undertake in order to protect the workforce and facilitate restoration. We close with suggestions for practicing HR managers related to modes of thinking necessary in this regard. Prior to each section, we provide actual quotes from managers that illustrate the magnitude of trauma and the need for active planning.

How 9/11 and Katrina have changed the environmental factors for business

> "I wonder if other companies got hit as bad as we did?"
> Comment made by an executive of a beer distribution company following
> Hurricane Charley (2003)

Changes in the external environmental factors

By definition, traumatic events are random, volatile, and erratic, and thus promote uncertainty. For example, Gulf Coast companies cannot predict the number of hurricanes they will experience, their exact locations, or their magnitudes despite forecasting improvements and the fact that they typically occur during a well-defined period (June 1 to November 30). Further, terrorist attacks typically provide no forewarning. Finally, companies usually do not know when a situation at work, like robbery or vandalism, will escalate to violence.

Extending this discussion, the inability to predict the onset of trauma has implications for organizations, largely as a function of the effects uncertainty has on the firm's external environment (see Figure 13.1). Of immediate interest is the capacity to remain a viable entity. Disasters often render organizations inoperable due to their effects on electricity, sanitation, and drinking water. Perhaps more

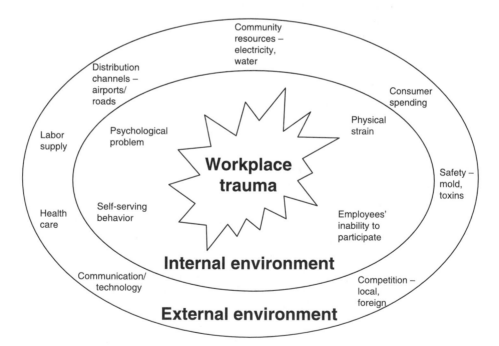

Figure 13.1 Trauma's implications for firms

dramatic are the images of businesses being totally destroyed. After Hurricane Katrina, thousands of businesses ceased to exist, many with little hope of returning. The World Trade Center housed approximately 50,000 employees prior to the 9/11 attacks, and firms such as Merrill-Lynch, Lehman Brothers, and TD Waterhouse.

Another matter relates to the firm's ability to acquire resources. Natural disasters often devastate distribution channels (i.e., roads, railroads, airports, shipping), causing the flow of goods and services to be delayed or completely unachievable. As an example, approximately 10 percent of crude oil used in the United States, and almost 50 percent of the gasoline produced, comes from refineries in states affected by Hurricane Katrina. Also, nearly one-quarter of the natural gas used in the United States is extracted or imported from this area.

Technology also has the potential to be affected following a catastrophe, causing considerable distress to those firms who are reliant upon it for its basic operations. Katrina and Rita destroyed over 90,000 square miles of electric and communications infrastructure in Louisiana and Mississippi. Also, because the 9/11 attacks caused extensive damage to a number of financial entities, the flow of funds needed to purchase emergency equipment and health care was significantly delayed for many organizations.

The competitive environment is also significantly altered by traumas. The number of companies contending for market space may change if a particular firm either suffers more distress than others or is inadequately prepared. This raises the possibility that other domestic firms will be able to increase their market penetration. Also, multinational organizations may find that a market has emerged for their products and services if domestic firms are unable to address the needs of their existing customer base.

Other external considerations exist. Management needs to ask, "Is health care available to those who remain?" Six months after Hurricane Katrina hit, only about one-third of the hospitals in the Greater New Orleans area were providing services. Similarly, "Is the work environment safe for those returning to the job?" The Environmental Protection Agency noted that sediment left over from Katrina's floodwaters contained metals, pesticides, and other chemicals. Contaminants can be detrimental to both short- and long-term health, their effects including nervous system damage and cancer. Also, these toxins continue to evaporate into the air that residents and employees breathe, increasing the onset of respiratory illnesses and other health-related difficulties that may not be fully realized for years.

Disasters almost always negatively impact consumer spending, initially as a result of the evacuation of both individual and industrial customer pools. For those who remain, most purchases will be of essential items (i.e., food, drinking water, medicine), at least until safety and security concerns are adequately met. In terms of industrial consequences, the 9/11 attacks caused the airline sector to shut down for four days, causing an estimated $2 billion in lost revenue (Goodrich, 2002). This lack of cash flow created a "ripple effect" on petroleum, tourism, and food-service companies, helping initiate lower revenues for firms in these sectors and related industries.

Equally important is the impact of the traumatic event on the external supply of labor. Catastrophes cause individuals to refocus priorities, replacing the energy directed toward the job to other life domains, including family and social activity. For example, Mainiero and Gibson (2003) reported that 71 percent of sampled individuals who experienced the attacks on the World Trade Center were more interested in spending time with friends and family after the event, than they had been prior to the event. This type of shift may cause many employees to quit work, especially if their organization fails to provide the flexibility needed to attend to non-work considerations. A consequence of increased turnover is the need to recruit, select, socialize, and train new employees from the external labor market, which is increasingly problematic in post-trauma settings.

What happens when there is no external labor market to recruit? Six months after Hurricane Katrina, only about one-third of the available workforce was actively participating in occupations-related activity. Of those who did not evacuate, nearly all continued to work for their pre-hurricane employer. Another consideration pertains to the competencies of those continuing to work. For example, employees who experienced the 9/11 attacks reported more disengagement from work (Kleinberg, 2005), shorter attention spans, and less commitment to the firm when they returned to work. We discuss the health-related aftermaths of traumas, as they affect the existing workforce, more fully in the next section.

As is often the case, challenges and opportunities exist in the external environment for those firms which prepare for them. In very few cases is this truer than in settings experiencing a trauma. Because organizations do not operate in a vacuum, attention to both the internal and external environment is essential before, during, and after the crisis.

Changes in the internal environmental factors

> "People walking around here look like a bunch of zombies."
> Comment made by a Gulf Coast supervisor of a refuse company

Employees who have experienced traumatic events are prone to suffer from a variety of physical and psychological maladies, all of which have the potential to impede the restoration effort. For example, trauma victims are hindered in their ability to think, learn tasks that promote reparation, and develop creative responses to challenging situations (Pennebaker, 1990). Moreover, when perceptions of safety are compromised, as is often the case following a catastrophe (Mainiero and Gibson, 2003), intellectual capacities are likewise compromised. In such cases, individuals are more concerned with self-preservation than with the work itself, leading to "downshifting" (Hart, 1983). Further, those experiencing post-traumatic anxiety typically experience immune system deficiencies, and as a result are less resilient to disease (Shalev, 1996), causing concurrent increases in absenteeism and benefit costs.

The composition of the internal workforce may be dramatically altered due to the pre-crisis commitments of many employees. For example, thousands of workers who were soldiers of the National Guard or reserve members of a military branch (e.g., Reserve Officers' Training Corps) in New Orleans/Mississippi and New York were called into duty following the 9/11 and Katrina disasters. Almost 60,000 National Guard personnel were activated from all fifty states, causing shortages in key occupations in affected areas as well as other locations. Because of the temporary nature of these deployments, organizations typically do not hire replacements, choosing instead to "make due" until its workforce is back to its pre-disaster level. In the short term, however, the firm's ability to serve its customers is likely reduced.

As expected, there is a long history linking experienced trauma to psychological destabilization. For example, survivors often become delusional, suffer from flashbacks, and become numb to external stimuli (Freedy *et al.*, 1994). These reactions, which may also include avoidance and frustration, can last for several years (O'Brien, 1998). Danieli (1998) described a post-trauma condition that he labeled "fixity," of feeling stuck in the catastrophic event. Other psychological reactions include increased negativity and feelings of despair. In response, many victims resort to self-destructive tactics, ranging from increased substance abuse to self-mutilation (van der Kolk, 1996).

Other aspects of the work setting are also affected by traumas. As discussed, some employees are unable to fully participate on the job because of non-work considerations. Others are simply physically or psychologically incapable. A reduction in both available and contributing employees creates a number of problems. First, individuals are required to "pick up the slack" for others, causing disproportionate levels of workload. Because the work is controlling the employee, instead of the employee controlling the work, a sense of powerlessness often develops. Helplessness, when added to an already unmanageable workload, intensifies job burnout, which promotes even more anxiety and disengagement.

Second, because employees perceive that they are being pulled in a number of different directions, interpersonal conflict, both at home and on the job, intensifies. Furthermore, conflict increases the potential for disputes between employees, prompting immediate concerns related to workplace aggression and violence. Also, because many employees become physically and mentally detached, lines of communication may be severed, leading to ambiguity. Finally, much of the workforce may be "on edge" due to a heightened level of arousal (Davidson and van der Kolk, 1996), causing comments perceived as innocuous prior to the trauma to be found anxiety-provoking afterwards.

Third, it is expected that conflict will escalate due to increased participation in self-serving behavior. Employees are more prone to disregard the needs of the organization, as well as those of co-workers, to focus on their own, when resources are scarce. Office space, technology, and personnel are commonly limited following a disaster. More relevant to most employees is scarcity as it relates to the job itself. It has been reported that more than 80,000 employees were layoff victims following the 9/11 attacks.

One form of self-serving activity, politicking, has been defined as egocentric behavior designed to secure outcomes not attainable through company-sanctioned means, such as developing valued skills or contributing to the firm's bottom line (see Ferris *et al.*, 2002). Less reputable examples of politicking include taking credit for others' work, sabotaging co-workers, and inappropriately inflating one's involvement in company successes. Because most employees would like to remain working following a disaster, if only for the salary and fringe benefits, it is expected that inventive ways of staying on the payroll will surface even if they are inconsistent with the long-term objectives of the firm. As such, conflict is inevitable in work environments fraught with politics, because the needs of one employee are pitted against those of others.

It is inconceivable that any organization would be unaffected by a trauma. Because the impact of crises pervades all life activities, considering a broader scope of internal operations that extend beyond task requirements is mandatory. Without doing so, companies may unintentionally promote anger, resentment, confusion, and turnover.

How firms are responding to these changes and preparing for catastrophes

"We didn't expect things to be this bad . . . we'll be more prepared next time."

Comment made by an HR manager of an insurance firm in Pensacola, Florida

In this section, we discuss HR's role as primary manager of traumatic events. First, we consider pre-crisis strategies as they relate to organizational and employee preparedness. Following this, we outline post-disaster steps aimed at minimizing the impact of trauma, focusing on stress-related repercussions on the remaining workforce. Table 13.1 summarizes these guidelines for HR-related pre- and post-trauma activities.

The role of HR prior to a disaster

Catastrophes can impact any organization, even those not typically susceptible to weather-related disasters. Because of this pervasiveness, preparation is critical. Even

Table 13.1 Guidelines for HR-related pre- and post-trauma activities

Pre-trauma activities	Post-trauma activities
1 Develop a disaster plan for all employees.	1 Allow employees to take control, increase accountability.
2 Decide communication/reporting channels.	2 Instill an environment of social support.
3 Train managers to identify signs of stress and appropriate sources of help.	3 Promote active coping (problem solving, etc.) rather than escapism, passive coping.
4 Develop conflict resolution skills.	
5 Review benefit offerings.	4 Put in place communication protocol.
6 Implement realistic job previews for new hires and existing staff.	5 Keep as many people on the payroll as possible.
7 Elicit the help of the employee assistance program (if applicable).	6 Allow employees access to pay benefits (early paychecks, loans, etc.).
8 Meet with community resource groups to see what is available away from work.	
9 Investigate and communicate government programs available to employees.	

if a disaster does not strike, a number of benefits to active planning will be realized. First, lines of communication are likely widened because of the need to discuss issues pertinent to the organization's survival. Second, increasing employee control will help workers deal with day-to-day stressors, such as job ambiguity and work–family conflict. Third, examining and communicating benefit offerings may serve to reduce turnover, as it is often the case that employees are simply not aware of what is in their package. Finally, realistic job previews can increase selection effectiveness, reinforce training and learning, and thus, promote retention.

The first objective of HR is to come up with a catastrophe plan, supported by top management, which can be communicated and understood by all employees. Guaranteeing that the program is understood is critical. Prior to the event, employees are typically concerned more with day-to-day tasks than preparing for something that may or may not occur. After the trauma, employees are inundated with information from both work and non-work sources, causing overload. Additionally, effectiveness is important because a cursory attempt to communicate the plan may have harmful consequences. First, it sends the message that employee health and safety are unimportant. Second, plans that are poorly understood will lead to a workforce that is ill prepared to respond, causing confusion, duplication of some tasks, and neglect of others.

Components of the plan will likely vary across industry and occupation. For example, first-line respondents, such as firefighters and health care providers, have plans that typically possess a different sequence of steps than do jobs not directly responsible for public health and safety. Commonalities, however, should exist across plans. First, all programs should have an implicit list of priorities, which include, but are not limited to, protecting life/minimizing injury, securing assets, and outlining steps for a return to normal operations. Second, all programs should have specific evacuation instructions, particularly for those with disabilities. Third, reporting channels should be clearly articulated to promote communication efficiency. As an example, emergency contact lists or phone trees can be used to ensure that pertinent information reaches all employees. Fourth, employees need to know where post-trauma information can be found. We contend that it is unacceptable to rely on only one resource (e.g., website, toll-free phone number), because the trauma may reduce or completely eliminate its delivery.

Another important step is to train managers to identify indicators of post-trauma stress. Physical and psychological signs of anxiety, which are often difficult to detect, include tiredness, inability to control emotions, a heightened sensitivity to loud sounds or commotion, loss of interest in activities once enjoyed, excessive weight gain/loss, feelings of blame/guilt, and a general sense of vulnerability (Yehuda, 1998). Behavioral consequences, which are typically more observable, include lower levels of performance, incapacity to prioritize tasks, increased agitation toward others, and absenteeism. Another consequence of trauma is theft, which is more likely if the commodity has value to one's family (e.g., drinking water, first-aid supplies, generators), or can be used by the victim to cope with post-trauma anxiety (e.g., alcohol, drugs).

Because post-trauma stress exists across multiple life domains, HR managers should be trained in identifying the aftereffects of disputes that occur away from the worksite, such as bruising and less emphasis on personal appearance. We do not encourage HR managers to assume the role of health care provider. Instead, HR managers should serve an advocacy role by identifying and communicating the sources of help available to those in need. Most often, this requires managers to familiarize themselves with the firm's employee assistance program (EAP), which can serve the dual role of assisting both employees and their families with coping after trauma (Wojcik, 2005). This step is important because many individuals suffering trauma (or suffering from the consequences of trauma, e.g., domestic disputes) do not immediately seek medical treatment (Bramsen and Van der Ploeg, 1999), promoting the escalation of other conditions, including depression (Kessler *et al.*, 1995).

HR managers may find it advantageous to review benefit plans. Some benefits likely go unutilized, and shifting resources to more desirable offerings may increase effectiveness. Examining the flexibility of time off benefits is a logical first step. For example, instead of carrying sick leave across time periods, companies may find that having these days available in the event of disaster better represents the needs of the workforce. Additionally, allowing employees to borrow against their retirement savings can ease the financial strain associated with trauma. Other options include offering short-term loans and temporarily suspending employee contributions to insurance and retirement plans.

As discussed, the post-trauma work environment is commonly laden with conflict. Developing resolution strategies that can be communicated from managers to subordinates is important. First, resolving conflict before it escalates can lessen the potential for violence. Second, conflict, when resolved effectively, can facilitate communication, address issues warranting such attention, build empathy, and increase ownership of important processes/outcomes. Finally, resolving conflict may assist coping by focusing on aspects of the job that promote anxiety. Developing such programs before a traumatic event is critical because rationality is often lessened and agitation amplified following a disaster.

Articulating an accurate representation of the post-trauma job expectations is essential for both new hires and existing employees. Although doing so is presumably more important for occupations that are immediate responders, we contend that all organizations will benefit by offering a "snapshot" of what work would be like after a disaster. Methods of illustrating changes in the post-disaster work environment include videos, role-playing, computer simulations, well-positioned posters, and narratives. An additional benefit to offering realistic previews is the ability to see whether the firm is able to address the many contingencies that typically follow a crisis.

A final objective of HR managers is to disseminate information to crisis victims gathered from sources outside of the organization. Both community (e.g., local Red Cross) and federal agencies (e.g., Federal Emergency Management Agency (FEMA), the Office of Personnel Management) provide information developed to assist individuals to cope and rebuild aspects of their lives. For example, the New Orleans Department of Health provided comprehensive health care services to hurricane victims. Also, the federal government has developed a number of programs assisting victims to secure low-interest loans for household repairs. Without a commitment to communication, however, most of these programs will go underutilized.

An understandable, albeit impractical, reason for an organization's failure to prepare for trauma is the admission of susceptibility. All companies would like to think that they could handle any event, whether it is an opportunity or a challenge, which comes its way. However, the reality is that they simply cannot without careful planning. Because predictions of fire, flood, terrorist attack, or earthquake are likely met with trepidation, decision makers may find short-term solace in opting for the "burying the head in the sand" approach. Unfortunately, doing so may lead to the demise of the company if, in fact, a crisis occurs.

The role of HR after a disaster

> "I feel like I'm overwhelmed . . . I just don't know how everything is going to get done."
>
> Comment made by a claims adjuster after Hurricane Rita

As noted, the first of objective of HR following a crisis is to ensure the health and welfare of its workforce. Following this, it is important to manage the trauma's short- and long-term consequences. Much of this strain can be neutralized if individuals are afforded the opportunity to manage personal and professional resources. Personal resources include energy, effort, expertise, as well as personality dimensions such as self-esteem and optimism, while company resources consist of equipment, funds, and personnel (Sumer *et al.*, 2005). Control is important because, in normal circumstances, resources are finite and typically expended more readily than replenished (Hobfoll, 1989). Given the severity of most crises, it is certain that resources are exhausted more quickly and restored more slowly in these settings, further substantiating the importance of resource management.

Managers have at their disposal a number of options to increase employee control. An initial recommendation is to have employees schedule the pace of work to match their peak times of effectiveness. Also, it may be constructive to put in place autonomous work teams that are responsible for the completion of a particular task (e.g., getting power restored to a certain geographic region, calling customers). Finally, employees should be able to choose the time for respite during their shift. Trauma introduces a great deal of emotionality to most work settings, and because its onset is often random, allowing time off only at well-defined times may fail to serve its purpose of revitalization.

Support from multiple sources, such as community, family, and church, can facilitate physical and psychological healing following a stressful experience (Norris and Kaniasty, 1996). Support at work may be equally important. First, individuals often spend considerable amounts of time at the job following the disaster, limiting the time available for participation in other support-gathering settings. Second, much of the support that individuals need post-trauma relates to specific aspects of the job. For example, the best person to help an engineer with a particular problem on the job is, in all probability, another engineer. Finally, other co-workers are better able to empathize because it is likely that they also are experiencing the same work-related stress as the afflicted employee.

To increase social support, both formal and informal programs should be initiated and encouraged. Formal programs may include scheduled roundtable discussions and presentations by health care professionals. Although formal programs are important, their role is largely symbolic. More effective in dealing with trauma is informal support, which consists of water-cooler discussions, lunches with colleagues, and after-work social events. By taking such initiatives, employees are more apt to receive support focusing on their particular concerns (e.g., work–family conflict, time management) rather than acquiring summary information that may or may not reflect the issues currently in need of attention.

Relatedly, management needs to support active, rather than passive, forms of coping. Passive forms of coping include avoidance, downward adjustment of performance expectations, disengagement from important life and work tasks, denial, and increased levels of substance abuse (Parkes, 1990). Conversely, active coping represents conduct designed to purposefully manage stressors (de Rijk et al., 1998). Examples of active coping include seeking novel ways to address situations deemed problematic, purposeful planning, and cognitively suppressing extraneous information. Not only is active coping important for organizational restoration/ effectiveness, but also its favorable effects can be seen on individual health and welfare. For example, active coping is predictive of favorable adjustment to stressors, lower levels of burnout, and fewer occurrences of sickness and disease (Carver et al., 1989). Passive coping is associated with incrementally more anxiety, a failure to engage, and an increased potential for mortality in some cases (Murberg and Bru, 2001).

Other post-trauma activities that will likely promote individual health and organization success include reestablishing the communication protocol, keeping as many workers on the payroll as possible, and allowing employees access to pay or other benefits prior to their scheduled distribution. The importance of communication has already been discussed, but cannot be overstated. Because communication facilitates control, and control reduces uncertainty, it is implausible that coping will occur without a basic understanding of post-trauma policies and procedures. Keeping employees on the payroll reflects an ethical perspective toward employees. (See Chapter 6 for more on ethics.) Also, it is the objective of HR to get the company where it was prior to the catastrophe, suggesting that the number of workers should not vary greatly. Downsizing takes effort and resources needed for the restoration, while hiring employees back when needed is taxing as well. Finally, HR managers should work closely with either their internal compensation/benefits department or external vendors to allow employees to collect pay before a catastrophe occurs, or soon thereafter, to ease their financial burden. If unavailable, employees will likely be forced to amass levels of debt (e.g., credit cards, loans from friends or family members) that may take years to pay off, increasing financial strain.

Conclusion

It appears that crises will remain an important part of organizational life. Various weather forecasting services predict that the next several years will be active with respect to hurricane activity. Also, the Department of State estimates that approximately 20 percent of all terror attacks are directed toward the United States (Pelton, 2003), and there is little reason to think that this number will decline in the immediate future. It is also expected that the prevalence of violence at work will continue at least at its present level.

In addition to the steps outlined in this chapter, we advocate that HR managers refocus their thinking. Managers in American companies have been accused of emphasizing short-term gains at the expense of long-term viability. Coupled with developing a more humanistic approach to employee relations, a shift in philosophy may assist managers to deal with the myriad of traumatic events capable of influencing contemporary work organizations.

References

Berren, M.R., Santiago, J.M., Beigel, A. and Timmons, S.A. (1989) A classification scheme for disasters. In R. Gist and B. Lubin (eds.), *Psychosocial Aspects of Disaster* (pp. 40–58). New York: Wiley.

Bramsen, I. and Van der Ploeg, H. (1999) Use of medical and mental health care by World War II survivors in the Netherlands. *Journal of Traumatic Stress*, 12: 243–261.

Carver, C., Scheier, M. and Weintraub, J. (1989) Assessing coping strategies: A theoretically based approach. *Journal of Personality and Social Psychology*, 56: 267–283.

Danieli, Y. (1998) *International Handbook of Multigenerational Legacies of Trauma*. New York: Kluwer Academic/Plenum.

Davidson, J. and van der Kolk, B. (1996) The psychopharmacological treatment of posttraumatic stress disorder. In B. van der Kolk, A. McFarlane and L. Weisaeth (eds.), *Traumatic Stress: The Effects of Overwhelming Experience on Mind, Body, and Society* (pp. 510–524). New York: Guilford.

de Rijk, A., Le Blanc, P., Schaufeli, W. and de Jonge, J. (1998) Active coping and need for control as moderators of the job demand-control model: Effects on burnout. *Journal of Occupational and Organizational Psychology*, 71: 1–19.

Ferris, G.R., Adams, G.A., Kolodinsky, R.W., Hochwarter, W.A. and Ammeter, A.P. (2002) Perceptions of organizational politics: Theory and research directions. In F.J. Yammarino and F. Dansereau (eds.), *Research in Multi-Level Issues, Volume 1: The Many Faces of Multi-Level Issues* (pp. 179–254). Oxford: Elsevier Science/JAI Press.

Freedy, J., Saladin, M., Kilpatrick, D., Resnick, H. and Saunders, B. (1994) Natural disasters and mental health: Theory, assessment, and intervention. *Journal of Social Behavior and Personality*, 8: 49–103.

Goodrich, J. (2002) September 11, 2001 attack on America: A record of the immediate impact and reaction in the USA travel and tourism industry. *Tourism Management*, 23: 573–580.

Green, B., Lindy, J., Grace, M. and Leonard, A. (1992) Chronic post-traumatic disorder and diagnostic comorbidity in a disaster sample. *Journal of Nervous and Mental Disease*, 180: 760–766.

Hart, L. (1983) *Human Brain, Human Learning*. New York: Longman.

Hobfoll, S.E. (1989) Conservation of resources: A new attempt at conceptualizing stress. *American Psychologist*, 44: 513–524.

Kessler, R., Sonnega, R., Bromet, E., Hughes, M. and Nelson, C. (1995) Post-traumatic stress disorder in the National Co-morbidity Survey. *Archives of General Psychiatry*, 52: 1048–1060.

Kleinberg, J. (2005) On the job after 9/11: Looking at worker's block through a group lens. *Group Analysis*, 38: 203–218.

Lazarus, R.S. and Cohen, J.P. (1977) Environmental stress. In I. Altman and J.F. Wohlwill (eds.),

Human Behavior and the Environment: Current Theory and Research (pp. 89–127). New York: Plenum.

Mainiero, L. and Gibson, D. (2003) Managing employee trauma: Dealing with the emotional fallout from 9/11. *Academy of Management Executive*, 17: 130–143.

Meichenbaum, D. (1995) *A Clinical Handbook/Practical Therapist Manual for Assessing and Treating Adults with Posttraumatic Stress Disorder*. Waterloo, Canada: Institute Press.

Murberg, T. and Bru, E. (2001) Coping and mortality among patients with congestive heart failure. *International Journal of Behavioral Medicine*, 8: 66–79.

Norris, F. and Kaniasty, K. (1996) Received and perceived support in times of stress: A test of social support deterioration deterrence models. *Journal of Personality and Social Psychology*, 71: 498–511.

O'Brien, L. (1998) *Traumatic Events and Mental Health*. Cambridge: Cambridge University Press.

Parkes, K. (1990) Coping, negative affectivity and the work environment: Additive and interactive predictors of mental health. *Journal of Applied Psychology*, 75: 399–409.

Pelton, R. (2003) *The World's Most Dangerous Places*, 5th edn. New York: Collins.

Pennebaker, J. (1990) *Opening Up: The Healing Power of Confiding in Others*. New York: Morrow.

Rossi, P., Wright, J., Weber-Burdin, E. and Perina, J. (1983) Victimization by natural disasters in the United States, 1970–1980: Survey estimates. *International Journal of Mass Emergencies and Disasters*, 1: 467–482.

Shalev, A. (1996) Stress versus traumatic stress: From acute homeostatic reactions to chronic pathology. In B. van der Kolk, A. McFarlane and L. Weisaeth (eds.), *Traumatic Stress: The Effects of Overwhelming Experience on Mind, Body, and Society* (pp. 77–101). New York: Guilford.

Sumer, N., Karanchi, A., Berument, S. and Gunes, H. (2005) Personal resources, coping self-efficacy, and quake exposure as predictors of psychological distress following the 1999 earthquakes in Turkey. *Journal of Traumatic Stress*, 18: 331–342.

van der Kolk, B. (1996) The complexity of adaptation to trauma: Self-regulation, stimulus discrimination, and characterological development. In B. van der Kolk, A. McFarlane and L. Weisaeth (eds.), *Traumatic Stress: The Effects of Overwhelming Experience on Mind, Body, and Society* (pp. 182–213). New York: Guilford.

Wojcik, J. (2005) EAPs extend role to help employers recover too. *Business Insurance*, 39: 51–53.

Yates, S., Axsom, D., Bickman, L. and Howe, G. (1989) Factors influencing help seeking for mental health problems after disasters. In R. Gust and B. Lubin (eds.), *Psychosocial Aspects of Disasters* (pp. 163–189). New York: Wiley.

Yehuda, R. (ed.) (1998) *Psychological Trauma*. Washington, DC: APA Press.

THE DISASTER PLAN

Jeffrey Luckey was put in charge of creating a disaster plan for his firm, a small service company with offices in San Francisco, Houston, and New York. The San Francisco office notified him, and encouraged him to focus on a plan for earthquakes. The Houston office was interested in having a plan for a hurricane, while the New York office wanted a plan for a possible terrorist attack. In a meeting with his boss, it was made clear that management really wanted only one plan that covered all offices.

Related questions

1 Should there be only one plan, or should each office have a different tailored one?
2 What are the similarities and the differences in planning for earthquakes, hurricanes and terrorist attacks?
3 What other disasters could affect the offices and how are those different?

14 Concluding thoughts

STEVE WERNER

The business environment is dynamic. An essential purpose of HRM is to insure that organizations can adapt to the changing environment (Snell *et al.*, 1996). The preceding chapters have discussed numerous recent environmental changes, how HRM departments in organizations have responded to the changes, the outcomes associated with those responses, some factors that can affect the effectiveness of the responses, and some guidelines on how organizations should respond to those changes. This chapter looks at some common themes and observations on the environmental changes, responses, outcomes, moderating factors, and guidelines across the previous chapters.

Summary of the major environmental changes

The first part of the book, "Major changes in environmental factors and HRM," looked at how changes in the global segment, the technological segment, the legal segment, and the demographic segment of the business environment have changed and affected HRM. Many of the other chapters also looked at the changes in the business environment and how they affected organizations and HRM. In looking across the chapters, a number of environmental changes can be identified that have dramatically affected the firm and its workforce. These include changes in the global segment, the technological segment, the legal segment, the demographic segment as well as the internal environment.

The global segment

The rapid evolution of the international economy is a critical environmental change for North American firms (see Chapter 2). This change has affected all aspects of doing business, from financing to location decisions, as well as HRM. As the chapters note, it has affected the staffing and development of the workforce, the importance of the technology of training, the cultural context of work, and outsourcing decisions. Of course, there are numerous other ways globalization has affected the HR functions of organizations (see Brewster *et al.*, 2005; Novicevic and Harvey, 2001).

The technological segment

Tremendous improvements in technology have also brought a critical environmental change to North American firms. It too affects all aspects of business, from production to marketing, as well as HRM. As noted in the chapters, the technological advancements affect employee communication, employee training, how organizations are structured, how work is organized, skills needed, outsourcing decisions, benefit costs, and post-catastrophe capabilities. Certainly, every function of HR has been affected by the advances in technology (Hempel, 2004).

The legal segment

Changes in US and Canadian laws are also important environmental changes for North American firms (see Chapter 4). Recent rulings that affect organizations and their HRM include rulings with respect to sexual harassment, age discrimination, and alternative dispute resolution. Recent laws affecting HRM include the Sarbanes–Oxley Act and changes in Securities and Exchange Commission disclosure requirements. Because these changes affect all conditions of employment for a firm's workers, they can substantially affect HR practices.

Demographic segment

Changes in the demographic segment are important external environment changes for North American firms (see Chapter 5). Demographic changes include more dual-career families, the changing shape of families, the aging workforce, increased diversity, and more women in the workforce. Because these changes affect the nature of the labor pool, the composition of the workforce, and the expectations of employees, they too can substantially affect HR practices (Schuler and Walker, 1990).

Internal environmental factors

Because of the changes in the external environment, the internal environment of North American firms is also changing. Important changes include altered employee expectations with respect to work–life balance, increased childcare and elder care responsibilities of employees, increased job stress, increased employee diversity, reduced employee commitment, and changes in employee benefit needs. Because these changes are related to the organization's internal labor market, they clearly can affect a firm's HRM.

Some common themes across responses

The environmental changes mentioned above have led to numerous firm responses. The firm responses mentioned in the chapters cover a wide range of HR topics. Nevertheless, some common themes in responses emerged across the chapters. These included modifying the company's culture, increasing training, using compensation and performance appraisals to support change, and introducing new programs and policies.

Modifying the company's culture

Modifying the company's culture was mentioned in numerous chapters as a common response to various environmental changes. The desired changes included cultures of diversity and tolerance, cultures of high ethics, safety-oriented cultures, cultures of employee empowerment, and cultures of social support. Thus, modifying the company culture appears to be an important mechanism in dealing with environmental changes. HR is a vital player in changing a company's culture. Things HR can do to help facilitate cultural changes include training, assessment and evaluation, communication of goals and good progress, adapting HR functions, and incorporating changes into policies, procedures, and programs (Burack, 1991; Sherriton and Stern, 1997).

New programs and policies

As stated above, new programs and policies can be part of an effort to change an organization's culture. However, because changing the culture is not necessarily the desired outcome of all new programs or policies, this response warrants separate discussion. New programs and policies can address any aspect of HR. Some examples include health awareness programs, safety programs, employee assistance programs, work–life programs, diversity programs, and commitment-enhancing programs.

Increased training

Another common response to environmental challenges mentioned in numerous chapters is to increase training. This training included diversity training, safety training, health awareness training, training for team building, and ethics training. Also suggested was training specific to supervisors regarding conflict resolution, post-traumatic stress behaviors, and employee assistance programs. With training becoming more cost-effective because of technological advances, it has emerged as a popular response to dealing with environmental changes.

Performance appraisal and compensation

Performance appraisal and compensation can be used in a number of ways to help organizations respond to environmental changes. First, they can be used to help foster cultural change, as mentioned above. For example, both can include safety, ethical, or training components to facilitate the desired cultural change. Second, compensation and benefits can be revised for cost savings as well as increased employee support. Finally, performance appraisal and compensation can be used as part of an employee commitment-enhancing program to improve strategic HR. Across the chapters, performance appraisal and compensation appear as two powerful tools HR has to facilitate organizational change through the workforce in dealing with environmental challenges.

Some observations about the outcomes

Naturally, HR responses are intended to achieve positive outcomes. These can be at the firm or at the employee level. Based on the chapters, the employee-level outcomes of the various HR responses include more ethical behaviors by employees and managers, better person–environment fit, increased employee productivity and performance, increased job satisfaction, improved employee attitudes, increased employee commitment to the organization, lower levels of turnover, fewer accidents, healthier employees, and increased trust and loyalty by employees. The positive firm-level outcomes include greater legal compliance and decreased vulnerability to lawsuits, more efficient and effective training, greater workforce flexibility, diversity, and tolerance, improved recruiting, increased profits, improved customer loyalty, and sustained competitive advantage.

Although the responses are intended to achieve positive outcomes, they may have associated costs, or in certain situations lead to negative outcomes. These negative outcomes tend to be the opposite of the positive outcomes just mentioned. The possible associated costs include reduced control, thereby allowing employees to make poor choices, reduced motivation, reduced social connectivity, greater administrative costs, under-reporting of accidents, and increased demands on employees. Frequently these negative outcomes result because of moderating factors that were not integrated properly into the responses. That is, the response tends to work in general, but under certain conditions may lead to a negative outcome. Some of the possible moderating factors are detailed below.

Some observations about the moderating factors

Most of the moderating factors mentioned in the chapters are consistent with the newer perspectives of strategic fit. The current strategic fit perspective suggests that a firm's strategies must complement the internal environment and external environment to produce desirable results (Burton *et al.*, 2004; Wright and Snell, 1998; Zajac *et al.*, 2000). The firm's internal environment includes not only its capabilities and resources, but also its size, nature of its ownership, current culture, and characteristics of its labor force. Many of the chapters mentioned how positive outcomes of the firm's responses depend on the firm's capabilities. Clearly, some responses are beyond the capabilities of some firms, which could lead to disastrous results if thoughtlessly implemented. Further, the effectiveness of some responses depends on the characteristics of the workforce itself, including the nature of the work performed (e.g., knowledge based, dependent on internal communication) and personal characteristics of the employees (e.g., cognitive ability, goal orientation). The point made in numerous chapters is that the appropriateness of the responses is likely to vary depending on the firm's internal environment. Very few responses are likely to have positive outcomes in all situations.

Some common themes across the guidelines

Up to now, much of our discussion could be interpreted as being about how firms react to environmental changes. Yet an important part of effective management involves proactive behaviors (Crant, 2000). What can firms do not only in response to environmental changes, but also to be prepared for and to benefit from anticipated environmental changes? This is the basis for many of the guidelines. They frequently are opinions on how to be proactive and ready for environmental changes that may occur. Most of the guidelines can be organized into three areas: monitor the external and internal environment; use HR functions to prepare and adapt to environmental changes; and educate and encourage employees.

Monitor the external and internal environment

The monitoring of the environment, also known as environmental scanning, allows firms to anticipate, detect, and adapt to environmental changes more quickly (Muralidharan, 2003). A number of the guidelines suggest that firms establish programs and mechanisms to anticipate and detect environmental changes. Of course, this would include monitoring changes in the legal environment, technological environment, demographic environment, and global environment. Specifically, monitoring should include any new guidelines issued by federal agencies, any new government programs that could assist employees in times of crisis, and any new health and safety issues. Monitoring should also include the measurement of the internal environment, including the progress of the organization in various areas.

Use HR functions to prepare and adapt to environmental change

Organizations should use the entire spectrum of HR functions at their disposal to prepare and adapt to environmental change. This includes training, performance appraisal, compensation, and staffing. Training can be used to increase employee skills, knowledge, and abilities to better adapt to changes. Performance appraisals can be used to provide feedback to employees regarding desired behaviors. Compensation can be used to reinforce and reward desired behaviors. Staffing can be used to attract, hire, and retain employees who better fit the new culture. Every new program and every new policy can be supported by HR functions.

Educate and encourage employees

HR can communicate important information to employees that will benefit the employees as well as the organization. HR can encourage employees to adapt to organizational changes, enroll in new programs, and follow new policies and procedures. HR can educate employees on how and why these changes will be beneficial. Some examples from the chapters include educating employees on stress reduction, creating support networks, training for safety awareness, and communicating about benefit cost containment.

Conclusion

A framework was presented in the introductory chapter of this book which provided a general model for looking at current issues in North American HR. Figure 14.1 shows this framework modified with specific examples taken from the chapters. The chapters in this book have pointed out numerous issues that are currently being tackled by HR departments in North American firms. The issues are largely due to changes in the business environment. The chapters covered many responses that firms are making to deal with these issues and the outcomes from these responses. Several chapters discussed how some internal environmental factors can affect these outcomes. Finally, guidelines were provided not only on how firms can successfully respond to the environmental changes, but also on how firms can proactively prepare for them. This book has shown that environmental changes have created complex and exciting challenges for firms in the area of HR. HR can strategically and adeptly facilitate every firm's ability to successfully prepare for and deal with each of the challenges, at both the employee and organizational levels.

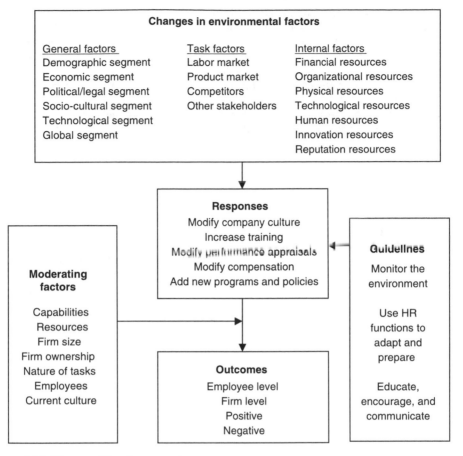

Figure 14.1 The resulting framework

References

Brewster, C., Sparrow, P. and Harris, H. (2005) Towards a new model of globalizing HRM. *International Journal of Human Resource Management*, 16(6): 949–970.

Burack, E.H. (1991) Changing the company culture – the role of human resource development. *Long Range Planning*, 24(1): 88–95.

Burton, R.M., Lauridsen, J. and Obel, B. (2004) The impact of organizational climate and strategic fit on firm performance. *Human Resource Management*, 43: 67–82.

Crant, J.M. (2000) Proactive behavior in organizations. *Journal of Management*, 26(3): 435–462.

Hempel, P.S. (2004) Preparing the HR profession for technology and information work. *Human Resource Management*, 43(2–3): 163–177.

Muralidharan, R. (2003) Environmental scanning and strategic decision in multinational corporations. *Multinational Business Review*, 11: 67–88.

Novicevic, M.M. and Harvey, M. (2001) The changing role of the corporate HR function in global organizations of the twenty-first century. *International Journal of Human Resource Management*, 12(8): 1251–1268.

Schuler, R. and Walker, J.W. (1990) Human resources stragegy: Focusing on issues and actions. *Organizational Dynamics*, 19(1): 4–19.

Sherriton, J. and Stern, J. (1997) HR's role in culture change. *HR Focus*, 74(4): 27.

Snell, S.A., Youndt, M.A. and Wright, P.M. (1996) Establishing a framework for research in strategic human resource management: Merging resource theory and organizational learning. In G.R. Ferris (ed.), *Research in Personnel and Human Resources Management* (vol. 14, pp. 61–90). Greenwich, CT: JAI Press.

Wright, P.M. and Snell, S.A. (1998) Toward a unifying framework for exploring fit and flexibility in strategic human resource management. *Academy of Management Review*, 23(4): 756–772.

Zajac, E.J., Kraatz, M.S. and Bresser, R.K.F. (2000) Modeling the dynamics of strategic fit: A normative approach to strategic change. *Strategic Management Journal*, 21(4): 429–454.

Index

Note: page numbers in *italic* denote references to figures/tables.